Women
to
Women

Companion Books by African-Americans

The Black Family: Past, Present, and Future (edited by Lee N. June, Ph.D.)

Men to Men: Perspectives of Sixteen African-American Christian Men (edited by Lee N. June, Ph.D., and Matthew Parker)

Women to Women: Perspectives of Fifteen African-American Christian Women (edited by Norvella Carter, Ph.D., and Matthew Parker)

Women to Women

*Perspectives of Fifteen
African-American Christian Women*

NORVELLA CARTER, Ph.D.
Editor

MATTHEW PARKER
Consulting Editor

ZondervanPublishingHouse
Grand Rapids, Michigan

A Division of HarperCollinsPublishers

Women to Women
Copyright © 1996 by the Institute for Black Family Development

Requests for information should be addressed to:

ZondervanPublishingHouse
Grand Rapids, Michigan 49530

Library of Congress Cataloging-in-Publication Data

Women to women: perspectives of fifteen African-American Christian women / Norvella Carter,
    editor ; Matthew Parker, consulting editor.
     p.   cm.
    Includes bibliographical references and index (p.   ).
    ISBN: 0-310-20145-4 (softcover)
    1. Afro-American women—Religious life.   2. Christian women—Religious life.
I. Carter, Norvella. II. Parker, Matthew, 1945– .
BR563.N4W59 1996
277.3'0089'96073—dc20
                                          95-47302
                                               CIP

Authors use various translations of the Bible in this book. The versions cited are identified in the
reference lists at the end of the chapters and in the text as needed. KJV stands for the *King James
Version.* LB stands for the *Living Bible.* NKJV stands for the *New King James Version.* NASB stands
for the *New American Standard Bible.* NIV® stands for the *Holy Bible: The New International
Version.*

Copy editing by Victoria L. Johnson
Interior design by Sherri L. Hoffman

Printed in the United States of America

---

98 99 00 01 02 /❖ DH/ 10 9

*Dedicated to Mrs. Barbara Walton, who has
invested her life in so many people.*

Contents

Preface

The best leaders I know accomplish goals without making people feel that they have been led. In 1968, I met Mrs. Barbara Walton at Cedine Bible Camp. There was a quality in her life that I liked. I recognized that because my mother died when I was three or four years old, and I needed a mother in my life. I asked Barbara Walton to become my spiritual mother. I gave her the right to be the final authority in my life. As I learned how to communicate with my spiritual mom, I began changing, because of this opportunity to converse intimately with a female. This led to a change in my attitude and behavior toward women, which has helped me have a healthy relationship with my wife, my daughters, and other women. Mrs. Barbara Walton did that for me.

This book is by fifteen African-American women who have shared their lives with others. The quality and character that they demonstrate will be an encouragement to all readers. As you read this book, it is my desire that you would begin to share these experiences with yourself and others.

Finally, I would like to thank Tracie Oberlton for her long hours of computer work and Tallulah Shinault for serving as a reader of this endeavor.

Matthew Parker, President
Institute for Black Family Development

Introduction

Polyphonic voices: Several voices occurring simultaneously, each one different, each one equally important, but all coming together to create a complex, melodic wonder.

This book exemplifies "polyphonic voices." The authors have a variety of backgrounds, experiences, and writing styles, but they all have come together in beautiful, melodic harmony to share with other women, in the name of the Lord, Jesus Christ. In addition to being women, they are Christians, African-American, dynamic, and spirit-filled. They are a stellar group of writers whose contributions are desperately needed to fill the void in a literary world that ignores African-American women.

The Christian African-American woman is part of the cornerstone of this nation. She is and continues to be a key player within the fabric of society, yet her voice and perspectives are not featured with the billboard proportions that other voices enjoy. Of course, if you want to read tragic horror stories that destroy the image of African-American women and suck the energy from our souls, you can find stacks of them in your neighborhood bookstore. This book is different and wonderfully so; it deals with reality, yet represents the positive hope that Christian women should have in their daily walk with Jesus Christ.

The book is divided into four parts. The first part looks at the African-American woman. Who is she? In a range of voices the authors express a glimpse of who she is and her significance in society. Shirley June opens the book with a look at the unmistakable presence of women of color in the Bible and church history. She grabs our attention immediately as she sets forth the truth about our heritage and the tremendous role Black women have played from the beginning, starting with Eve. If more African-Americans knew their history, we would not lose so many of our young adults to religious sects that claim the Bible is a "white man's book."

The legacy of the African-American woman falls into place naturally in the second chapter, because it builds on the history and provides insights into our heritage that have depth and meaning. Dr. Nancy Harrison beautifully highlights our foremothers and the prayers, traditions, and practices that have helped us to survive as a people. Her chapter reflects the beauty of the relationship between the Lord and the African-American woman. It is a relationship that must be emphasized and developed in our children. It is the strength of our legacy.

Dr. Carolyn Parks takes us into the present in chapter 3. She takes an exhilarating look at the modern-day African-American woman. As she skillfully takes us through the significant issues of our time, African-American women will be able to identify with every word and see themselves very clearly. A small part of her chapter dealing with Black male bashing (presently popular among television hosts and authors) is powerful and should be expanded into a more extensive work. You will read this chapter more than once and will refer it to friends.

The second section of the book deals with the African-American woman and relationships. Sheila Staley begins this section with a chapter on mentorship between older and younger women. Every African-American woman will recognize the relationships she writes about because they are connected to our extended families and Christian friends. She explains in detail the importance of being mentored and becoming a mentor. Every successful person has had someone to look to for guidance and direction. She also explains some of the pains that accompany mentor/protege interaction. This is an excellent chapter for anyone involved in the mentoring process.

One of the most important relationships for the African-American woman is the husband-wife relationship. Patricia Richardson's chapter deals with the crucial time in a woman's life before she marries. She identifies vital questions one must ask before making the decision to give up singleness. Her chapter is practical, down to earth, and urgently needed for women today.

Michelle Obleton has a special chapter that ministers to the pastor's wife and provides insights to those who need to understand this role. She speaks with candor about the complexities of being married to a man who has dedicated his life and livelihood to specific service for the Lord. She speaks with compassion to the woman who lives in a glass house and feels she cannot share her burdens with anyone in her church. Michelle Obleton's contribution is sure to meet the needs of many women.

The last chapter in the relationship portion of the book is a joy for those who have children. Dr. Deneese Jones writes magnificently on the faith it takes to raise children in today's society. She begins with her personal testimony and proceeds to take the reader from Africa to modern times, as she provides a beautiful legacy of motherhood for the African-American woman. In addition, she shares practical guidelines of faith building that will encourage and strengthen every mother.

The third part of the book deals with a variety of critical issues facing the African-American woman. Dr. Jacqueline Tilles begins this section with great power as she discusses the life of the single African-American woman. Her mastery of God's Word is apparent as she sets forth the problems women face being single, the false solutions they seek, and finally the great excitement and fulfillment that take place when one pursues "the way of Jesus." This masterful writer presents a chapter that provides the single woman with renewed appreciation for a life that can be wonderfully and beautifully fulfilling within the body of Christ.

The next chapter concerns the painful situation of an absent mate. Annie Roberson and I examine the emotional turmoil a married woman experiences when she must live without her husband. This critical issue faces many women today; it can be handled through seeking a closer relationship with the Lord and the support of Christians. Annie Roberson shares an excellent personal testimony that utilizes the principles set forth in the chapter. A similar work, yet different in scope, has been written by Dr. Jean Jackson-Swopes. She addresses the issue of wives living longer than their husbands and provides much comfort to the African-American widow. Dr. Jackson-Swopes identifies all the stages of mourning and helps the widow and other readers see how magnificently God takes care of his own, even in the midst of deepest sorrow. Her chapter will be read repeatedly by those who need comfort during times of loss.

The final section of the book deals with support and resources for the African-American woman. Millicent Lindo begins this section with a chapter that identifies issues and strategies for balancing a home and profession. She provides a historical perspective and lets the reader know that the working African-American mother is not new to our society. Very few books meet our needs directly by providing guidelines specifically for us.

Millicent Lindo's chapter provides guidance from a godly perspective and in superb fashion.

Next, Lisa Fort makes a major contribution to the book by addressing the need for successful money management by African-American women. Personal finances represent a crucial area that can make or break one's testimony as a good steward of God's resources. Lisa Fort's chapter is a joy to read and provides hilarious stories that may sound remarkably familiar. She lifts some of the weight of a heavy subject and enables the reader to seriously consider the adoption of her suggestions. After reading her chapter, we will surely vow "to do better."

Then Victoria Johnson, an excellent writer, discusses the passages in the Bible that may be difficult for women to understand and apply to their daily experience. She takes the reader step by step through each verse that needs clarification and insight. After reading Victoria Johnson's contribution, you will study God's Word with a renewed sense of joy, anticipation, and confidence as a godly woman.

Finally, the last chapter by Dr. Patricia Larke is a masterpiece. She takes on a topic of great magnitude as she deals with racism, sexism, and classism. She identifies issues and godly strategies for handling these "isms" that African-American women face in our society. Dr. Larke examines factors that have been talked about in secular society, but have not often been addressed from a Christian perspective. For example, she discusses a range of sensitive topics from skin color and hair texture to the myth of the "welfare queen." Her chapter is an excellent resource for women who find themselves struggling with racism, sexism, and classism on a regular basis.

This book is a timely contribution to the sparsely filled bookshelves about African-American women. As you read, you will see that we are several voices, occurring simultaneously, each one different, each one equally important, but all coming together to create a complex, melodic wonder in the service of our Lord and Savior, Jesus Christ.

Norvella Carter, Ph.D.
Editor

PART 1

KNOWING WHO I AM

Shirley Spencer June

Women of Color in the Bible and Church History

SHIRLEY SPENCER JUNE grew up in her birthplace, Thomasville, Georgia. She received a bachelor of science degree in biology from Knoxville College and master of science degree in zoology from the University of Illinois (Champaign-Urbana). She also did a year of post-baccalaureate study in biology at Knox College (1966–67). She is married to Lee N. June, and they are the parents of twin boys, Stephen and Brian. Currently, Shirley is a homemaker after working several years as a research assistant (electron microscopy) in a medical school. She is a member of New Mount Calvary Baptist Church in Lansing, Michigan, and has been a Sunday school teacher and superintendent and a youth worker.

Chapter 1

Shirley Spencer June

Women of Color in the Bible and Church History

In the veins of Hebrew-Israelite-Judahite-Jewish people flowed African blood. In numerous instances the biblical experience is an African experience. (Copher 1993)

This chapter seeks to examine the roles women of color have played in the Bible and church history. For the most part, the women discussed are (1) African women or women of color in Scripture, or (2) African-American women in church history, including African-American women as nurturers, in the preaching tradition, in missions, and in auxiliary ministries. To do this I give attention to scriptural roles, historical examples, and personal perspectives and encounters. This chapter represents the mere beginnings of my investigation into this massive subject.

WOMEN OF COLOR IN SCRIPTURE

Eden

The presence and role of women of color in Scripture are part of the overall picture of the African presence throughout the Bible. It has been proposed that the original Eden included mainland Africa to the Tigris/Euphrates valley (Copher 1993; Felder 1989; McKissic & Evans 1994) and that the location of the Garden of Eden was totally or partially situated in what has come to be known as Africa. Of the four rivers named in the biblical account of the Garden, two of these can be associated with regions in Africa (Genesis 2:13) where Hamitic people were significant early developers of both the Tigris and Euphrates civilizations. One of the rivers, Gihon, encircled the whole land of "Cush/Ethiopia."

Based on the biblical record of human origins geographically (in Africa) and an understanding of genetics, Adam and Eve must have been people of color (Hilliard 1992; McKissic & Evans 1994; Williams 1994). This position is foundational, because people of color seem to be the only human beings who possess all the genetic potential for the range of colors, traits, and variations seen among peoples and individuals in the world today.

Patriarchs

Africa has served as a temporary home to most of the famous patri-archs in the Bible, several of whom spent a considerable portion of their lives there. Abraham and his wife Sarah journeyed into Africa during the famine in Canaan. While in Africa they acquired Hagar, an Egyptian woman. Hagar later gave birth, by Abraham, to Ishmael the progenitor of twelve nations. Moses was born and grew up in Egypt. He was adopted by the Pharaoh's daughter and trained in "all the wisdom of the Egyptians" (Acts 7:22). Joseph was sold into slavery in Egypt and became an administrator and ruler in Egypt. He married an Egyptian wife, who gave birth to two sons, Ephraim and Manasseh. Thus, of the twelve tribes of Israel who later possessed the land of Canaan, two of them had partial African ancestry.

Not only the patriots, but the Lord Jesus Christ spent some of His early life in Egypt; Mary and Joseph took refuge there. They sought to escape the threat of death against Jesus by King Herod who governed Judea at that time.

Hamitic People

From the beginning of the biblical period there were interactions with Hamitic peoples. The table of nations in Genesis 10 identifies African nations of Cush/Ethiopia, Mizraim/Egypt, Put(Phut)/Libya, and Punt/Somaliland. The land God promised to Israel was at that time inhabited by Canaanites, descendants of Ham through his son Canaan. Many African-Americans have grown familiar with scriptural references or songs about the land of Canaan, but have not made the connection with Africa or its peoples. The Protestant canon includes African people and lands from Genesis to Revelation. These events and circumstances place Africa squarely in the center of biblical historical events.

Also, several portions of the Scripture were written in Africa and Africans were acquainted with and used Scriptures prior to the writing of the New Testament. The widespread use of the Bible throughout Africa in ancient and modern times is known (Copher 1993). Copher also concludes the following about the African presence in the Bible:

> It is present in the literature of many of the periods of biblical history, and in almost every type of literature. Africa figures as a home and a place of refuge from the time of Abraham through the time of Jesus. Africans, from slaves to rulers, appear as actors on the stage of history. Authors of much of the biblical content were native Africans in origin. And in the veins of Hebrew-Israelite-Judahite-Jewish people flowed African blood. In numerous instances the biblical experience is an African experience. (p. 148)

Walter McCray provides insights and tools to help readers discover for themselves the explicit presence of Black people in Scripture. He presents extensive coverage on the identities of Hamitic and other peoples in his two-volume work *The Black Presence in the Bible* (McCray 1991). He discusses the Black women named in the genealogy of the Lord Jesus Christ—Tamar, Rahab, and Bathsheba—people of Hamitic descent.

The study of the African presence in Scripture is needed because of the benign or purposed "bleaching" of biblical persons and nations with the result that people of color appear to be absent or unimportant in God's dealings with people and nations. All people and nations are the subject of the biblical record, because of their common origin. Scripture gives a clear statement of what God has done:

> *He created all the people of the world from one man, Adam, and scattered the nations across the face of the earth. He decided beforehand which should rise and fall, and when. He determined their boundaries. His purpose in all of this is that they should seek after God, and perhaps feel their way toward Him and find Him—though He is not far from any one of us. (Acts 17:26–27)*

Specific Women of Color in Scripture

Women referred to as "African" in Scripture are those of any racial group whose lineage could be traced to Ham or who had a birthplace in the land of Africa, a Hamitic territory (McKissic & Evans 1994). Using

Lockyer's (1995) work, a combined characterization of information from Scripture and definitions of what is meant by "African," the list includes a few women in their biblical and historical roles:

Adah One of Esau's Canaanite wives, and daughter of Elon the Hittite. Through Eliphaz (Esau's oldest son) and Esau's other sons and wives, she became ancestor of the Edomites (Genesis 26:34; 36:2–19).

Aholibamah Daughter of Anah, the daughter of Zibeon the Hivite, also a Canaanite wife of Esau (Genesis 36:2).

Bashemath Daughter of Abraham's son Ishmael, also a wife of Esau (Genesis 28:9; 36:3–4, 13).

Bathsheba Wife of Uriah the Hittite, who became wife of King David. Mother of Solomon, who succeeded his father David as king of Israel (2 Samuel 11:3–27).

Queen Candace Queen in Ethiopia during the time of the visit of the Ethiopian who was returning home from Jerusalem when he encountered Philip. Thus, the Ethiopian would have been returning to Queen Candace as a convert to Jesus Christ (Acts 8:27).

Delilah A Philistine who conspired against Samson with her people, who were descendants of Ham (Judges 16).

Eve "Mother of all flesh." Would likely have possessed the genetic potential to produce the full range of diverse skin types known today. The Garden of Eden description includes mention of Africa's land areas (Genesis 2–3).

Hagar Egyptian servant to Sarah, Abraham's wife. Given to Abraham to bear children because Sarah was barren. Gave birth to Ishmael, from whom the Ishmaelites descended (Genesis 25:12; 16).

Hammoleketh Granddaughter of Manasseh and mother of Ishdod and Abaser (Numbers 26:28–77; 1 Chronicles 7:17–18).

Bithiah Daughter of Pharaoh; wife of Mered (1 Chronicles 4:18).

Judith Wife of Esau and daughter of Beeri the Hittite (Genesis 26:3–4).

Keturah	Egyptian woman whom Abraham married after the death of his wife Sarah; the mother of Zimran, Jokshan, Medan, Midian, Iskbak, and Shuah and grandmother to Sheba and Dedan, Jokshan's sons (Genesis 25:1–6; 1 Chronicles 1:32–33).
Queen of Sheba	Also called "Queen of the South." Came to Jerusalem to visit and ask King Solomon questions after she "heard of the fame of Solomon concerning the name of the Lord." Brought abundant treasures of gold, spices, and precious gems as gifts for the king. Was granted all her requests of him. Jesus noted her quest (Matthew 12:42; 1 Kings 10:1).
Rahab	Canaanite woman of the city of Jericho. Protected the spies sent by Joshua. In return, requested and received protection for her household and family when the city of Jericho was destroyed. The scarlet cord used as a symbol of protection for Rahab and "all that were in her house" has been compared with the scarlet blood of the Lord Jesus as protection for all in the family of God through faith in Him. The Bible says that she "perished not with those who did not believe," and she is included in the Hebrews 11 account of men and women of faith (Joshua 2:1–21; 6:22–25).
Ruth	A Moabite woman, daughter-in-law of Naomi. Made a quality decision that "whither thou goest I will go; and where thou lodgest I will lodge; thy people shall be my people, and thy God my God" (Ruth 1:16). A woman whose story has been shared for years among African-Americans as an example of devotion, service, and faith. Grandmother of David and thus included in the genealogical record of Jesus Christ (Book of Ruth; Matthew 1:5).
Sherah	Daughter of Ephraim. Built three towns (1 Chronicles 7:22–28).
Wife of Moses	A Cushite, an Ethiopian woman. The object of complaints from Moses' sister Miriam and his brother Aaron, but vindicated in the Lord's response on Moses' behalf (Numbers 12:1).

The presence of women of color in the Bible is undeniable. For more in-depth treatment and a more inclusive basis for discovering Black people in Scripture, it is hoped that readers will consult authors and books listed at the end of this chapter.

AFRICAN-AMERICAN WOMEN IN CHURCH HISTORY

Before African-American women were involved as a distinct entity in the life and organization of the Black church, these women had an impact on the quality of the church's life and witness. They were nurturers in the roles of wives, mothers, and homemakers, and also intercessors for many who became leaders and spokesmen of their times. Those roles are still current.

I have fond memories and deep gratitude and appreciation for a mother who knew and trusted God, an aunt who prayed early mornings before daybreak, and a grandmother who lived a life that showed love toward others. They were examples that deeply affected my early childhood and my continual development and growth as a Christian. They fueled within me a desire to find and pursue God's purposes.

Many of us may have similar examples of African-American women who have deeply impacted our life's outlook and direction. They are a reminder of the debt of gratitude we owe to countless others whose stamina, acts of faith, and courage inspired us in the midst of discouraging odds: the woman, the mother, the grandmother, or the aunt who always knew from conviction and experience that "the Lord will make a way"; the teachers who wanted us to do our best and insisted on excellence; those in church who urged us to take on new challenges and opportunities to grow and serve; those who modeled before us a fulfilling life in Christ. These African-American women helped to fashion a girl, a woman, and a generation of African-American women with faith and convictions. Those women have been able to provide hope where voices of affirmation are all too few.

AFRICAN-AMERICAN WOMEN IN THE PREACHING TRADITION

According to historian Jualynne Dodson (1993), African-American women throughout the nineteenth century traveled this country by the hundreds, preaching the gospel of Christ. Most were successful in their ministries, but few were ordained. They were impelled by deep religious devotion and a desire to serve out the "call" to carry the gospel. These women, against many obstacles, became catalysts for change within their organizations, resulting in their parent bodies questioning the roles of women in ministry. With tremendous challenges and opposition from the outset, these women were persistent in their desire to live out the call to serve.

Jarena Lee was the first woman to formally petition for the sanction to preach in the African Methodist Episcopal Church (AME). She actually began preaching before the denomination was formally organized. When she first requested permission to preach in 1809, she was refused. She continued to preach anyway, and renewed her request several years later after the denomination was formally organized. The African Methodist Episcopal Church's first bishop, Richard Allen, then recognized and supported her efforts and gave her permission to hold Bible studies and "exhort" (Dodson 1993). As an itinerant minister, Mrs. Lee served throughout the northeastern region of the United States.

The ministry of early preaching women like Jarena Lee resulted in many people coming to a saving knowledge in the faith, and also increased membership and participation in the church. These successes in ministry continued amidst opposition and formal protests against the right of women to preach. Sophie Murray, Elizabeth Cole, Rachel Evans, Harriet Felson Taylor, Zilpha Elaw, and others were among the noted nineteenth-century AME women who were fruitful evangelists or preachers (Dodson 1993). Before formal sanctions against women as preachers, women contributed greatly to the support and expansion of the church. The African Methodist Episcopal Church added the categories of stewardess, evangelist, and deaconess in attempts to prescribe a female-specific role for church leadership.

Other denominations reflect a similar pattern of struggle to define the role of women in ministry. Lincoln and Mamiya (1990), in their book *The Black Church in the African-American Experience,* cite the existence of this historical pattern of struggle:

> Both historical and contemporary evidence underscore the fact that Black churches could scarcely have survived without the active support of Black women, but in spite of their importance in the life of the church, the offices of preacher and pastor of churches in the historic

Black churches remain a male preserve and are not generally available
to women. (p. 275)

These authors maintain that most women were forced to seek alternative, sublimated paths to ministry within their congregations. Jarena
Lee, Amanda Berry Smith, and many other female preachers paved the
way for hundreds of other women who were later preaching and pastoring
to storefront congregations. These roles and the biblical basis for them are
still matters of debate in some church bodies.

AFRICAN-AMERICAN WOMEN IN MISSIONS

African-American women supported mission efforts at home and
abroad long before they themselves were accepted as foreign missionaries.
Through prayer and by raising support for home and foreign mission
efforts they helped to support churches in their early beginnings in
America.

Within the African-American community, there has always been an
awareness of the implications of the gospel in the struggle for justice, freedom, and in helping to relieve the needs of the oppressed (Curry 1993;
June 1991). The need was felt to fight problems such as prejudice, which
were the same for African-American non-believers and believers alike.
Sojourner Truth and Harriett Tubman were effective abolitionists, as were
many others who felt the call to work for freedom and justice as an out-
ward work of an inner spiritual directive from God. This was reflected in
the nature and scope of their mission efforts. Home mission efforts targeted relief for the poor and needy. The women helped to provide clothing
and supplies for ministers and missionaries. In addition to assisting in
supplying material goods for those in Christian service, women's clubs and
organizations also gave much-needed financial support and organizational
and leadership skills. Women shared with men as co-laborers in this struggle. This was also the basis for cooperation with social and civic relief
organizations and movements that had the same justice and freedom
issues as their focus.

African-American women who wanted to go abroad as foreign missionaries faced additional challenges. There was the question of support,
which all missionaries face. But they also faced the reality of racism, in
society in general and with local mission boards in particular. Tensions
often resulted from differences in focus, intent, and motivation between

those involved in the Black missionary movement and non-Black boards. African-American women who succeeded in going on foreign missions served as teachers, medical workers, supervisors of schools, and founders of orphanages and hospitals.

AFRICAN-AMERICAN WOMEN IN AUXILIARY MINISTRIES

Many women who were blocked in efforts to preach or serve as missionaries chose to find different means of serving, such as teaching or helping to establish schools. For others, these auxiliary ministries were their primary choice of service opportunities. Darlene Clark Hine (1993) and other authors in the encyclopedia *Black Women in America* chronicle the achievements and struggles of hundreds of African-American women. Many women made their primary contributions through activities in their local churches. Following the formation of the National Baptist Convention, for example, it was noted that women read Bibles on home visitations, donated food and clothes to the needy, cared for the sick, trained other women in household responsibilities, established and supported orphanages and "old folks homes," crusaded for temperance, established daycare centers and kindergartens, published newspapers, instituted vocational training programs, and founded educational institutions.

CRUSADERS FOR FREEDOM—KEEPERS OF THE DREAM

Hine's encyclopedia (1993) includes biographical sketches and contributions of over 600 African-American women, some of whose lives were intricately involved in the early church history in this country. The women listed below are but a few of those women who were active in the establishment of African-American churches from the eighteenth to the twentieth century.

Sarah Allen	(1764–1849) Organized Daughters of the Conference in AME Church to help gather clothing for ministers.
Ida B. Wells Barnett	(1862–1931) Organized support for anti-lynching movement.
Jarena Lee	Published account of her call to preach the Gospel in 1869.

Mary McCleod Bethune	(1875–1955) Educator who had desired and trained to be foreign missionary. Helped establish Bethune College, which later became Bethune-Cookman College.
Nannie Helen Burroughs	(1879–1961) A member of the National Baptist Convention. Sought increased opportunities for women. Founded training school for women in Washington, D.C.
Julia A. Foote	(1823–1900) Began preaching after conversion experience. Later a missionary.
Eva Roberta C. Boone	(1880–1902) Went to Africa as missionary in 1902 with American Baptist Mission and Lott Carey Baptist Foreign Mission convention.
Virginia Broughton	Recording secretary to Women's Convention when National Baptist Convention formed in 1900. Organized Bible bands through which women studied Scripture.
Fanny Jackson Coppin	(1837–1913) Educator, administrator, later missionary to Africa.
Clara Howard	(1866–1935) Valedictorian of first graduating class of Spelman Seminary, now Spelman College.
Druscilla Houston	(1876–1941) Earliest cited African-American female to author a study on Ethiopia and ancient Black populations in Arabia, Persia, Babylonia, and India.
Victoria Earle Matthews	(1851–1907) Salvation Army field officer and missionary who established White Rose Mission.
Mary Smith Kelsey Peake	(1823–1862) Deeply committed in her Christian faith. Founded Daughters of Benevolence.
Maria Stewart	(1803–1879) Spoke out on issues regarding women's rights, religion, education.
Sojourner Truth	(1799–1881) Abolitionist and crusader for equal rights for women.

CONCLUSION

There is a prominent African presence in Scripture, as evidenced in numerous biblical references to African lands, nations, and people whose ancestral roots were African. Under this broad umbrella of the African presence in Scripture is, of course, the African female presence. Besides those named in this chapter, there are many unnamed women who also may have been in the ancestral lineage of Africans.

Women of color have been involved in the religious, political, and civic life of their communities as wives, mothers, teachers, rulers, and even military strategists. Church history reflects a critical involvement by women in the maintenance, nurture, and support of church missions and life. Women have been active in a wide variety of capacities in the organizational structure of churches. Increasingly, denominational norms have been changing to allow greater participation of women in preaching, pastoring missions, and church life. These roles are still subject to debate in some church bodies and congregations.

Considering women of color anew in Scripture and their contributions throughout history creates an appreciation for the diversity God designed in human beings. It can also correct a false assumption that is commonly accepted that Black history started with slavery in America. This kind of study of Black women can help African-American people recognize the redemptive work of God through Jesus Christ operating in the past and present individuals of our heritage. We owe it to our children to help them discover the truth.

ℛeferences

Carter, L. 1989. *Black heroes of the Bible.* Columbus, GA: Brentwood.

Copher, C. 1993. *Black biblical studies: An anthology of biblical and theological issues on the Black presence in the Bible.* Chicago: Black Light Fellowship.

Curry, B. 1993. The role of the Black church in the educational development of Black children. In *The family: Past, present, and future,* edited by L. N. June. Grand Rapids: Zondervan.

Dodson, J. 1993. Jarena Lee. In *Black women in America: An historical encyclopedia,* edited by D. C. Hine. Vol. 1. Brooklyn: Carlson.

Felder, C. 1989. *Troubling biblical waters.* Maryknoll, NY: Orbis.

Hickey, M. (speaker). 1944. *Finding the ark of the covenant.* Cassette recording no. 1171. Denver: Marilyn Hickey Ministries.

Hilliard, A. 1992. *The hidden light.* Houston: Hilliard.

Hine, D., ed. 1993. *Black women in America.* Brooklyn: Carlson.

June, L., ed. 1991. *The Black family: Past, present, and future.* Grand Rapids: Zondervan.

The King James version of the Bible.

1993. *The King James version of the Bible.* Original African Heritage edition. Nashville: Winston.

Lincoln, C., and L. Mamiya. 1990. *The Black church in the African-American experience.* Durham, NC: Duke University Press.

Lockyer, H. 1995. *All the women of the Bible.* Grand Rapids: Zondervan.

McCray, W. 1991. *The Black presence in the Bible.* Vol. 1: Discovering the Black and African identity of biblical persons and nations. Chicago: Black Light Fellowship.

_____. 1991. *The Black presence in the Bible and the table of nations.* Vol. 2: With emphasis on the Hamitic geneaological line from a Black perspective. Chicago: Black Light Fellowship.

McKissic, W., Sr., and T. Evans. 1994. *Beyond* Roots II: *If anyone ask you who I am.* Wenonah, NJ: Renaissance Productions.

Williams, A. 1994. *Black man come home.* Memphis: Williams.

Nancy Harrison

The Legacy
of the African-
American
Woman

NANCY HARRISON is an Associate Professor at Baylor University in Waco, Texas. She was born in Corsicana, Texas, and raised in Central and East Texas. She has a bachelor of science degree in elementary education and music, a master's degree in administration from Austin State University, and a Ph.D. in curriculum and instruction from Texas A&M University in College Station. She is married to George Harrison, and they have three children: David, George, and Martin. Nancy is a member of the First Baptist Church in Waco, where she serves as a Sunday school teacher and as pianist and organist for the adult choir.

Chapter 2

Nancy Harrison

The Legacy of the African-American Woman

For God is not unrighteous to forget your work and labor of love, which ye have shown toward his name, in that ye have ministered to the saints and do minister. And we desire that every one of you do show the same diligence to the full assurance of hope unto the end: That ye be not slothful, but followers of them who through faith and patience inherit the promises. (Hebrews 6:10–12)

During the past fifty years, a considerable amount of attention has focused on the African-American family in the United States. As a result, few researchers have written specifically about the African-American woman without placing her in the context of the family. The legacy of the African-American woman initially lies in the history of her people and her relationships with family members. To discover her past and present value in America we must examine testimonies, slave narratives, and current African-American family research.

Slave narratives and testimonies have been an increasingly popular source of information about slavery. These narratives provide an insight into a part of history which was once told only from the perspective of the plantation owner. Unfortunately, these accounts of slavery reveal little of the slaves' experiences in West Africa. Instead, the narratives tell of the slaves' experiences while in bondage and after their escapes. It is important to understand that most of the analyses of these narratives concerned with Black women are not historical nor do they attempt to place them in

the context of their African background. Additionally, Andrew Blassingame's (1977) compilations of slave testimonies revealed that only 12
percent of the narratives were written by women and only one testimony
reported the struggle of a slave to return to Africa after becoming free. The
narrative of one famous slave, Sojourner Truth, speaks to the importance
of Blacks in general and women in particular having the same rights as
Whites. In her speech commonly referred to as "Ain't I a Woman?" she
responds to a man's comment about women being the "weaker sex."

> "He says women need to be helped into carriages and lifted over ditches
> and to have the best everywhere. Nobody ever helps me into carriages,
> over mud puddles, or gets me any best places." And raising herself to
> her full six foot height, she asked, "Ain't I a woman?" She bared her
> right arm, which was muscular from hard work as a slave, and said she
> had ploughed, planted, and gathered into barns and that no man could
> head her. She asked again, "Ain't I a woman?" (McKissack & McKissack
> 1992, p. 112)

This chapter centers around the legacy of the African-American
woman, preserving her heritage, and passing the torch through the generations. These points will be addressed in regard to the African-American
family in general and the African-American woman in particular.

THE LEGACY

The Promises of God

The first component of the African-American woman's legacy is the
heritage that has been handed down to her from her ancestors. This legacy
is composed of belief in the promises of God, belief in building strong families, and belief in the importance of a moral value system. A belief in the
promises of God serves as an umbrella for the importance of strong families and the maintenance of a moral value system. During both the time
of slavery and today, the African-American woman faces various troubles:
the loss of loved ones to death or prison, bad relationships, unruly children, and injustices on the job, to name a few. For that reason she needs
the comfort brought only by God's promises in His Word. His promises for
times of suffering, discouragement, and depression, as well as His guidance and spirit of perseverance enabled the Black female to endure in days
of slavery as well as today.

For Times of Suffering

And the Lord *said: I have surely seen the oppression of My people who are in Egypt, and have heard their cry because of their taskmasters, for I know their sorrows. . . . These things I have spoken to you, that in Me you may have peace. In the world you will have tribulation; but be of good cheer, I have overcome the world. . . . Many are the afflictions of the righteous, but the Lord delivers him out of them all. (Exodus 3:7; John 16:33; Psalm 34:19)*

The hope of deliverance is a constant thread in the history of the Black female. From bondage in Egypt to the days of slavery to the days of the Civil Rights Movement, a time for being delivered has been keenly anticipated. The Black female knows that in many instances she must be her own deliverer. She thus receives her strength from the teachings she has received from her ancestors, which are based on God's promises.

For Times of Discouragement

And let us not grow weary while doing good, for in due season we shall reap if we do not lose heart. . . . We are hard pressed on every side, yet not crushed; we are perplexed, but not in despair; persecuted, but not forsaken; struck down, but not destroyed. . . . For the Lord *loves justice, and does not forsake His saints; they are preserved forever, but the descendants of the wicked shall be cut off. . . . Wait on the* Lord, *and keep His way, and He shall exalt you to inherit the land; when the wicked are cut off, you shall see it. (Galatians 6:9; 2 Corinthians 4:8–9; Psalm 37:28, 34)*

The African-American woman becomes discouraged when she knows she is carrying out God's instructions and things do not appear to be working. Whether the situation is a relationship with a loved one or a financial problem, discouragements will disappear when she decides to continue to believe in God's promises and chooses not to get down and stay down because of life's uncertainties.

For Times of Depression

He heals the broken-hearted and binds up their wounds. . . . And God will wipe away every tear from their eyes; there shall be no

more death, nor sorrow, nor crying; and there shall be no more
pain, for the former things have passed away. (Psalm 147:3;
Revelation 21:4)

These promises are important not only to adults, but also for children. When there are mental or physical wounds to bear, it helps to know that brighter times are ahead for God's children.

For Times of Guidance

For this is God, our God forever and ever; He will be our guide
even to death. . . . Then they cried out to the LORD in their trou-
ble, and He saved them out of their distresses. (Psalm 48:14;
107:19)

When the African-American woman is undecided about what to do, knowing that God is there to guide her brings a "peace in the midst of a storm." The legacy of depending on God when one is unsure of what to do still leads her in her quest to do God's will.

For Times of Perseverance

For God has not given us a spirit of fear, but of power and of love
and of a sound mind. For whatever is born of God overcomes the
world. . . . And this is the victory that has overcome the world—
our faith. Who is he who overcomes the world, but he who
believes that Jesus is the Son of God? (2 Timothy 1:7; 1 John
5:4–5)

Preserving the family was important to the slave mother, and often the mother suffered in her attempt to preserve her family. The African-American woman endures many hardships, from the pain of labor to the pain of a loved one's sufferings, but she continues to be a source of strength for her family because she depends on God. Her faith in His Word and His promises to "be there whenever she calls" is her hope and her mainstay. Many times, the African-American woman must struggle to hold on to her sanity. It is the Word of God that helps her make it through the day. Realizing that God's promises are true strengthens her to become an instrument for passing the legacy on to her children and their children.

A Strong Family

The second component of the African-American legacy is maintaining a strong family. The family has always been important to the African-American woman. The mother in the family inspired within her daughter the hope of freedom and provided an example of a woman who would not give in to despair. The African-American mother usually was the family member who reunited the family after slavery and war had scattered them. The mother at the turn of the century worked many jobs to take care of her home. (More will be said about the family later in the chapter.)

A Moral Value System

The final component of the legacy of the African-American woman is a moral value system. This value system in based on the knowledge that God, our all-seeing Father, is aware of all that we say and do. Knowing that He will keep His promises to us enables us to make the right choices when we face hard decisions. Striving to do what is right in spite of circumstances has been instilled in each African-American generation since the days of slavery. Whether committed in the dark or in the light, killing, stealing, cheating, lying, and all other "sins" are still forbidden by God. The African-American woman prepares the next generation to be able to function as Christians in an unchristian society. She must begin teaching God's principles on the first day of her child's life. The African-American woman is well aware that moral principles that are modeled are remembered much longer and probably followed by her children than those principles she only talks about and does not practice in her behavior.

Mary McLeod Bethune, in her "Last Will and Testament," beautifully writes about the legacy of African-American women:

> If I have a legacy to leave my people, it is my philosophy of living and serving.
>
> Here, then, is My Legacy.
>
> I leave you love. Love builds.
>
> It is positive and helpful.
>
> I leave you hope. Yesterday, our ancestors endured the degradation of slavery, yet they retained their dignity.
>
> I leave you the challenge of developing confidence in one another. This kind of confidence will aid the economic rise of the race by bringing

together the pennies and dollars of our people and ploughing them into useful channels.

I leave you thirst for education. Knowledge is the prime need of the hour.

I leave you a respect for the uses of power. Power, intelligently directed, can lead to more freedom.

I leave you faith. Faith in God is the greatest power, but great, too, is faith in oneself.

I leave you racial dignity. I want Negroes to retain their human dignity at all costs.

I leave you a desire to live harmoniously with your fellow man.

I leave you, finally, a responsibility to our young people.

The world around us really belongs to youth, for youth will take over its future management. (*Ebony*, 1992, p. 108)

PRESERVING THE HERITAGE

The African-American family in literature gives the world many opportunities to view Black history. Hank Allen asks, "Why is it important for Black families to recognize and preserve their heritage?" He gives three reasons in answer to this question.

Identity

First, the heritage of any ethnic group serves as the basis for its identity, social organization, productivity, planning, and responsibilities. The identity of the African-American family embodies the set of characteristics by which the family is definitively recognizable or known. This identity separates it from other groups and is highlighted by the accomplishments of its people, past and present. Famous inventors, educators, and leaders contributed to the rich heritage of the African-American. When the identity of a people is lost, the people as a group cease to exist. Without a transfer of knowledge of one's people, the heritage, within a few generations, forgets the accomplishments and struggles which were achieved and survived to get them to the present day.

Preserving the heritage of the African-American means that the African-American race will continue to be a viable entity in the world. It means that in the efforts to diversify our world, the possibility of our

African-American men and women assuming a more significant role in our government in larger numbers is a possibility. It means that our diverse work forces may have more diverse leaders. It means that people of other races can learn more about African-Americans because we have played a crucial role in the making of this nation.

As African-American women, preserving our heritage means that the promises taught of us through the generations will soon reach fruition. It also guarantees that the legacy of the African-American will continue through the generations to follow. African-American leaders continue to tell the story. From building our own schools and colleges to establishing Black churches, the heritage of the people has been told. The strong relationship between the family and the church in the history of the African-American has played an important part in building a foundation by which future generations will remember and relive some of the important events in history.

Needs

A second reason why it is important for African-American families to preserve their heritage is to gain a global perspective on the responsibilities and needs of African-American people. With today's technological advancements, people are no longer thought of as indigenous to one area of the globe. At one time, the thought of Black people in great need brought to mind only people living in Africa. This is not the case today. Black people who are struggling for survival can be found all over the world. Therefore, it is necessary for the "heritage" to be taught all over the world.

The legacy of the African-American female reaches from her home to the four corners of the world because that is the breadth of her influence. We are reminded as God's people to remember His words and to teach His words to our children (Deuteronomy 6:7). If we take the counsel of the Scripture seriously, we may witness less crime in our society and more families working together to do God's will. As African-American women it is imperative that we teach our children about their responsibility to God, self, family, society, and the world.

Hope

Lastly, it is important to anticipate and rejoice continually in God's goodness. The Psalmist tells us that the Lord is good, His mercy is everlasting, and His truth endures to all generations (Psalm 100:5). Generally, we get what we look for in life. Therefore, if we anticipate God's goodness we will we receive it. Scripture reminds us that goodness and mercy will follow us all the days of our life and that we will dwell in the house of the Lord for ever (Psalm 23:6). Sadly, there are many times when we miss God's blessings by taking for granted the many things that He does for us on a daily basis. As Christians, and especially as African-American women, it is crucial for the existence of our very souls to know that every good and perfect gift comes from God (James 1:17). The history of the treatment of women, from the days of being queens in Africa to becoming slaves in America, holds many events in which African-American women had only the words of God to hold on to within their hearts (Allen 1991, p. 21).

AFRICANISMS

In regard to preserving the heritage, it should be emphasized that the African-American woman does exhibit some cultural traits which are similar to those of her ancestors. This view, however, is still questionable for some people. On the one hand, E. Franklin Frazier (1948) asserts that as a result of the manner in which Blacks were enslaved, the African cultural heritage has had practically no effect on the evolution of the family in the United States. On the other hand, Henry H. Mitchell (1975) writes:

> I am now convinced that the slavecracy failed to erase African culture, but slowly succeeded in getting Blacks to be ashamed of it. The result was that even though we Blacks continued to use and adapt our own heritage, we eventually dropped many aspects of it. (p. 1)

Janice Hale-Benson (1982) provides the following list of aspects of Black culture that reflect Africanisms:

- Funerals
- Folklore (Uncle Remus stories are similar to the sacred myths of Africa)
- Dance
- Song
- Motor habits (walking, speaking, laughing, sitting, postures, burden carrying, dancing, singing, hoeing, and movements made in various agricultural and industrial activities)

- Ways of dressing hair (wrapping, braiding, cornrowing)
- Wearing of handkerchiefs and scarves (Women of the African Diaspora tend to wear hair coverings more than European women. In the United States, Black women wear scarves; in the Caribbean they wear bandannas; and in Africa they wear geles.)

In terms of whether there are distinct features which are similar to African and American families, Andrew Billingsley (1992) points out several distinctive features of the African family patterns which have survived the American experience.

Blood Ties

The first distinctive feature is the primacy given to blood ties over all other types of relationships. The African-American woman historically placed a strong emphasis on the importance of kinfolks in her life. Sisters, brothers, and cousins in need were relatives who were important to help even after the woman was married. The saying "blood is thicker than water" comes from this distinctive feature of the family. It was important for her not to forget "where she came from." Because of unforeseen situations, there were times when a woman had to return home to live with relatives and she always wanted to be welcomed back.

Extended Family

A second distinction is the primacy given to extended families versus nuclear families and the strong value placed on children. The African-American woman places a strong emphasis on the extended family versus the nuclear family. This was a survival mechanism and necessary in order to provide support for the family in Africa, during times of slavery, and now as we face the hardships of an oppressive society. Finding strength within the extended family is noted by Darlene B. Hannah (1991) who describes the multigenerational composition of African-American families as a major characteristic of extended families. From African times through slavery times until today, the extended family was comprised of a family with additional adult siblings or extra nieces or nephews. In today's society, the extended family may become necessary because of the addition of elderly parents or unmarried children with their offspring.

In reference to the strong value placed on children, African-American families generally disapproved of abortion (Hall & Ferree 1986). It was better to let the children arrive and have relatives help rear them or allow them to be adopted by another family (Billingsley 1992). Although African-Americans debate whether abortion was atypical of women enslaved in the United States, African women brought their beliefs about the value of children and motherhood with them. The African-American woman in Africa, during times of slavery, and today continued to value children. Helping one another rear children from birth to maturity has brought out the best in African-American women throughout history. The African-American woman was sometimes viewed as stern and strict with her children. She knew, however, that teaching children survival skills prepared them for making it in the world when they had to leave home. The African-American woman knew that the world would not be kind, so she taught her children techniques that would allow them to succeed in life.

Respect

A third distinctive feature of African-American family pattern is reverence and respect for the elderly and other family members. This feature is important because the African-American woman was taught that her elders were to be respected. Many African-American women of today were intimately involved with their grandparents and aunts. This relationship was significant for teaching the importance of respecting those in charge of your care. This respect was transferred to others within the home, as well as outside of the home—teachers, preachers, and other adults in authority. Many children who were reprimanded at school were also reprimanded at home for getting in trouble at school. Children were taught to be "on their best behavior" at all times. Children were reminded from passages in the Bible to honor their parents, listen to their fathers and their mothers, treat an elder as a father, and obey their parents (Ephesians 6:1–2; Exodus 20:12; 1 Timothy 5:2).

Sacrifice

Another distinctive feature of African family life is sacrifice. Sacrifice means that the rights of any person must always be balanced against the requirements of the family or the larger group and the rights of others. The African-American woman in Africa, during slavery, and in society today demonstrates her strength in this area. Many African-American women made physical sacrifices in order for their families to survive. Strong women worked outside the home, sometimes working two jobs so that the needs of the family were met. In many instances, older daughters stayed home from school to care for younger siblings while the mother was at work. Families today continue to have mothers who sacrifice their needs for the needs of their husbands and children. This practice is consistent with the legacy taught to African-American women throughout the generations.

The African-American woman of today is a product of Africa and many of the behaviors, traditions, and beliefs from her ancestors in Africa. Women as daughters, wives, mothers, and grandmothers were responsible for many tasks related to the family. They relied on family members and faith in God to achieve their goals and to continue the legacy begun many generations ago.

PASSING THE TORCH THROUGH THE GENERATIONS

African-American women of today are still an important spiritual part of the family. From singing lullabies to a crying baby in the early dawn hours to soothing the heartaches of grown children, the mother stands as a symbol of strength.

> This particular value is stressed more by the elder member of the family, who may often feel that younger family members do not depend on or believe in God as they ought. The elderly members are the transmitters of religious instruction; they are the ones most concerned about exposing the children to religious training. A respect for their position in the family serves to facilitate the transmission of religious belief to other family members. (Hannah 1991, pp. 41–42)

This list is expanded by the biblical writings of Solomon in Proverbs 31:10–31. He portrays the woman's spiritual character as being virtuous, trustworthy, a provider for her family, and loved and praised by her husband and children.

Strong

The term "virtuous" implies that the woman has strength. The African-American woman is strong in wisdom, grace, and the fear of God. This woman is a woman of spirit, who has the command of her own spirit and knows how to manage other people (Henry 1961). The African-American woman is resolved and firm in her principles. In today's society, the virtuous woman is modest and has good moral character. This characteristic is related to the legacy in the sense that it is a catalyst for transmitting strong value systems to the next generation. The African-American woman has to maintain this characteristic in order to be a good role model for her children and a good wife for her husband.

Respected

Because she is trustworthy, the African-American woman receives respect from her husband, her family, and the community. "The heart of her husband doth safely trust in her, so that he shall have no need of spoil" (Proverbs 31:11). Her character is such that her husband trusts her modest and discreet manner in public. The African-American woman has learned through many generations that being able to be trusted is the beginning of any relationship, whether in the family or the broader community.

Providing

The African-American woman is likewise a provider for her family. "She looketh well to the ways of her household, and eateth not the bread of idleness" (Proverbs 31:27). This verse speaks to the legacy of the woman in that she has always been a sustainer of the life of her family. She has been an integral part of the foundation of the family. A strong case has been made that West African women occupied influential roles in African family networks in spite of variation among societies. Since women were not dependent on men for economic support and provided certain key elements of their own and their children's economic support, mothers were central to the family structure. Continuing the lineage was essential in West African philosophies, during slavery times, and in society today. The ideology of Motherhood is present evidence of past teachings from our foremothers.

Praiseworthy

Lastly, the African-American woman is loved and praised by her husband and children. "Her children arise up, and call her blessed; her husband also, and he praiseth her" (Proverbs 31:28). Receiving honor from loved ones may be rare in some instances. The African-American woman, however, has always been considered a focal point in the family. She rears her children with firmness and is an advocate for their interests and training for later life. Her unselfish attitude in her family brings her praise from her loved ones. (Witness the athletes on television who constantly say hello to their mothers.) Her husband likewise gives her praise and is very thankful for her. African-American women who remember the legacy continue to receive praise from their children and husbands. It is her continuous labor, sacrifice, and love for her family that teaches children and future generations the importance of the African-American woman's legacy.

CONCLUSION

We have looked at the African-American woman's legacy, the importance of preserving her heritage, and passing the torch through the generations. The African-American woman shares some tasks and beliefs about herself and her abilities with her African ancestors.

In order for the legacy to continue, the African-American woman must value faith in Jesus Christ as Savior and the necessity of developing strong moral values in the family. These traits are essential in our society if the African-American race is to survive the obstacles set before us. If these components are missing, we will see further degradation of the family. We will see our children lost to drugs and prison. It is up to the African-American woman to teach, live, and transfer the cultural traits and philosophies from the biblical foundation of her ancestors to our descendants. This is our hope and prayer, so that future generations will put their faith in God alone.

References

Allen, H. 1991. The Black family: Its unique legacy, current challenges, and future prospects. In *The Black family: Past, present, and future*, edited by L. N. June. Grand Rapids: Zondervan.

Bethune, M. McL. 1992. My last will and testament.... *Ebony* 48: 108–12.

Billingsley, A. 1992. *Climbing Jacob's ladder: The legacy of African-American families*. New York: Simon & Schuster.

Blassingame, J. W., ed. 1977. *Slave testimony: Two centuries of letters, speeches, interviews, and autobiographies*. Baton Rouge: Louisiana State University Press.

Frazier, E. F. 1948. Ethnic family patterns: The Negro family in the United States. *American Journal of Sociology* 53 (61): 435–39.

Hale-Benson, J. 1982. *Black children: Their roots, culture and learning styles*. Rev. ed. Baltimore: Johns Hopkins University Press.

Hall, E., and M. Ferree. 1986. Race differences in abortion attitudes. *Public Opinion Quarterly* 50: 193–207.

Hannah, D. B. 1991. The Black extended family: Appraisal of its past, present, and future statuses. In *The Black family: Past, present, and future*, edited by L. N. June. Grand Rapids: Zondervan.

Henry, M. 1961. *Matthew Henry's commentary in one volume*. Edited by L. F. Church. Grand Rapids: Zondervan.

McKissack, P. C., and F. McKissack. 1992. *Sojourner Truth: Ain't I a woman?* New York: Scholastic, Inc.

Mitchell, H. H. 1975. *Black belief: Folk beliefs of Blacks in America and West Africa*. New York: Harper & Row.

1982. *The new King James version*. Nashville: Thomas Nelson.

1978. *The Ryrie study Bible*. King James version. Chicago: Moody Press.

1988. *Thompson chain-reference Bible*. 5th ed. Indianapolis: Kirkbride.

Carolyn Parks

Christian Women Today: Perspectives and Challenges

CAROLYN PARKS is Director of the Institute of Health Behavior and Health Education at the University of North Carolina–Chapel Hill in Raleigh. Born and raised in South Philadelphia, Pennsylvania, she has a bachelor of science degree in biology from Wheaton College in Wheaton, Illinois; a master's degree in health education from Western Illinois University; and a Ph.D. in health education from the University of Tennessee in Knoxville. She is a member of Macedonia United Church of Christ in Raleigh, North Carolina, where she is involved in the youth ministry, women's choir, Sunday school, and AIDS ministry.

Chapter 3

Carolyn Parks

Christian Women Today:
Perspectives and Challenges

I have known the women of many lands and nations. I have known, seen, and lived beside them, but none have I known more sweetly feminine, more unansweringly loyal, more desperately earnest, and more instinctively pure in body and in soul than the daughters of my African-American mothers. This, then—a little thing—to their memory and inspiration. (W. E. B. Du Bois 1920)

Being a Christian woman in this day and age ain't easy! Feminism and the women's movement, abortion rights issues, job and sex discrimination, and plain old daily living often make "walking the walk" and "talking the talk" very difficult. Being a Christian *African-American* woman today is even harder. The plight of many of our men (unemployment, drug abuse, imprisonment), problems of our children and youth (teen pregnancy, violence, substandard education), lack of "eligible" brothers for marrying, and the high number of single female-headed households often leave our hearts heavy and our minds burdened. Add to this list the issues of beauty, weight control, sexuality, self-perception and body-image, loneliness, tiredness, and simply "trying to make it" in a White male-dominated society, and you have a glimpse of some of the pressures faced by Christian women of African descent in America. Given these realities, it is no wonder that African-American women, in general, disproportionately suffer and die from many of our societal health ills, particularly the chronic diseases of high blood pressure, diabetes, stroke, obesity, and now AIDS (U.S. Department of Health and Human Services [USDHHS] 1991).

What is it like today being an African-American woman who professes Jesus Christ as Lord? What issues are unique to this experience of living out the gospel in Black female flesh?

What challenges do these times present to a growing number of educated, professional, and more affluent Christian African-American women?

The controversies are very real. Unanswered questions abound. But the opportunities are even greater. For as we stand and take our rightful place in the power and spirit of Christ, we will see God do great things through us—for our families, for our communities, for our churches, for our nation, and yes, even for ourselves. This chapter describes the contemporary Christian African-American woman and explores some of the major challenges we face as we prepare to enter the twenty-first century.

WHO IS SHE?

Very little has been written about Christian African-American women in general. Hence, any attempts at description are based largely on the cumulative knowledge, experiences, and testimonies of others and my personal interaction with African-American women. In preparation for this chapter, I asked many Christian women: "How would you describe the Christian African-American woman of today?" As you might expect, the responses were varied: "She's still the gatekeeper of the home, church, and community." "She is a beacon light amid the darkness of the world." "She is holy and sanctified." "She's a trip!" "She's starting to follow the world's standards and patterns." "She needs to be careful."

Attempting to define the modern-day Christian African-American woman is extremely difficult, for she represents a broad spectrum of women. She is a southern older woman of great wisdom and servanthood, who resides and works by choice in the very low socioeconomic public housing community where my office is housed. She is my own dear mother, who for the past forty years has worked diligently, tirelessly, and graciously with the youth, women, and families in our working-class community of South Philadelphia. They are my three precious sisters—powerful women of God—one a pastor, one an early childhood educator, and one a university secretary, who are terrific mothers (like their mom), and who also, like their mother, continue to live, work, and serve in our old neighborhood. She is my dearest and best friend, a college professor who holds three degrees in speech communication and rhetoric, who is a masterful elocutionist, and yet maintains a spirit of humility I have yet to see matched in other Christian women. She also serves faithfully by the side of her husband, who is a pastor. This wide scope of representation requires a general discussion of Christian African-American women today. Based on my discussions and observations, the modern-day Christian African-American woman can be characterized by three primary traits: (1) a powerful faith; (2) a strong commitment; and (3) an enduring love.

Powerful Faith

I have been blessed to travel throughout this nation. As a result, I have encountered Christian African-American women from all socioeconomic classes, from all walks of life, who possess various gifts and talents. In spite of their vast differences, the one binding factor between them all is their faith—an unshakable, no-nonsense kind of faith. These women, by faith, are moving mountains in their families, churches, and communities as they lead intercessory prayer meetings and local Bible studies. As a result, they are turning their corners of the world upside down for Christ much in the same way as did many of our foremothers, such as Harriet Tubman, Sojourner Truth, Mary McLeod Bethune, and Rosa Parks.

What does it take to be a woman of such faith? First, it takes an unrelenting love for God. African-American women of faith love God deeply. Thus, they long to please Him. "And without faith, it is impossible to please Him" (Hebrews 11:6). Secondly, they know God's Word. Women of faith study the Word of God, which empowers them to exercise their faith. Thirdly, women of faith obey God. Love and obedience are intertwined (John 14:23). These women are assured, like Job, "Though He slay me, yet I will hope in Him" (Job 13:15). They understand clearly that God's ways and thoughts are not like our own (Isaiah 55:8). Thus, they are willing to trust and obey God in all circumstances, through diverse trials and tribulations, of which they have seen many. How different our families, churches, and communities would be with more such women of powerful faith.

Strong Commitment

A second characteristic of these women, one intimately related to the first, is a firm commitment to the things of God. As I have traveled and worked with many different types of people, it has become fairly easy to identify when true Christian women are in the midst. Have you ever been in a setting, watching and listening to whatever is happening, and said to yourself: "Now that woman is a Christian?" Christian women of faith are committed to God. Their focus is not on the "blessings" that may be afforded from living the Christian life. They desire to know Christ and to serve Him. Such women are at the helm of many of our national and local Christian ministries today. Some of these are young women—under the age of forty—who have decided to follow Jesus relentlessly. And for them, there's no turning back!

Enduring Love

I have been the recipient of much love and care from African-American women, most of whom were Christian. I have made it through this portion of my life because of the great outpouring of genuine love from many sisters who called, prayed, wrote, gave money, counseled, sternly rebuked, gently reproved, listened long, and cried with me.

The ability of many African-American women to love deeply and unconditionally is a characteristic that people have attempted to capture in many ways—unfortunately, mostly negative ones. African-American women are often mythically portrayed as strong, domineering, smothering, or intentionally and excessively matriarchal (Staples 1979). These caricatures are in part the result of a misunderstanding of the depth and capacity of the African-American woman to love. For Christian African-American women, this love can run very deeply. Such women are extremely forgiving. They do not relish saying, "I told you so." Instead they listen patiently, then offer their wisdom as a gem to be cherished. They are nurturers, making sure you are fed, spiritually and physically. I distinctly remember the two older women at my church in Knoxville, Tennessee, who prayed, helped, and fed me through the initial three-and-a-half treacherous years of my doctoral program. They always made sure I had a good meal, gas in my car, and $5.00 in my pocket. They continually told me, "Baby, you're gonna make it 'cause the Lord is on your side. You keep on trusting Him." *Love!*—in action, through faith, and based on God's love for them.

These broad and largely observational characterizations in no way suggest that all Christian African-American women fit these descriptions. Nor do they suggest that these traits are exclusive to Christian women.

They do, however, provide insight into aspects of the character of African-American women of faith and propose areas for growth and development.

When I read about the virtuous woman in Proverbs 31, I think of African-American women—successful workers inside and outside of the home, strong family women, faithful and committed, wise, kind, and caring, women who are known in the "gates" of their world for their good deeds. The great challenge before us today is the transmission of these values and attributes to our young, and sometimes insolent, next generation of women.

CHALLENGES OF THE MODERN-DAY AFRICAN-AMERICAN CHRISTIAN WOMAN

In spite of the admirable and positive attributes just described, there are forces within society that are having a major impact on the thinking and actions of Christian women in general. These forces have a great potential to challenge our faith, diminish our commitment, and deaden our love. They pose some of the greatest challenges facing Christian and African-American women today.

Practicing Meekness

My best friend is one of the few people I know who consistently displays the Christian virtue of meekness. Most of us express meekness conditionally, that is, we are meek only when the Holy Spirit gives us a powerful "nudge" to be so. She, however, is consistently meek. As a result, she is often misperceived. Some people may think she does not know "what's happening," or is not "with it," or that they are "getting over" on her. This mistaken view of her character has often resulted in a strange sense of invisibility and loneliness, even when she is surrounded by many people.

We often confuse meekness with weakness, even in Christendom. According to Webster's dictionary, to be meek means to be characterized by patience and long-suffering. Biblically, it means to be humble or gentle. Paul lists it as one of the fruits (evidences) of the Spirit (Galatians 5:23). The Psalmist said God will "beautify the meek with salvation" (Psalms 149:4). Jesus said in the Beatitudes, "Blessed are the meek (the humble, gentle), for they shall inherit the earth" (Matthew 5:5). Thus, the expression of meekness is a major Christian attribute.

Being humble, gentle, or meek in today's society, however, is not a prized characteristic. Fight back, be strong, show what you're made of—these are the orders of the day, especially for women. Hence, to express meekness is to go against the tide of the human effort to be heard and to be equal. Further, it creates, especially for women, a level of invisibility or insignificance among their peers, their co-workers, and even their own family members. This, coupled with the "peculiar" nature of the Christian life, causes many Christian women to experience a painful loneliness and estrangement from society. Even more damaging, however, is the loneliness that emerges from such ostracism by other believers, who misconstrue meekness for weakness in a sister's character.

It can be especially lonely for Christian African-American women, who are by virtue of their physical appearance in society "different," but are also often viewed as "odd" for their modest dress, commitment to Christian values, and refusal to compromise personal standards. When these are accompanied by a true spirit of meekness, African-American women can become invisible in the eyes of others. This can take various forms: being overlooked for certain tasks or positions (even if qualified); not being spoken to or acknowledged in the presence of others; belittling comments; or rarely or never being asked out on a date.

Regarding the latter, many committed (versus carnal) Christian women in the African-American community are often not viewed as "marriage material." They may be considered either "too spiritual" or "asexual." If they are meek, then they may be viewed as pushovers. Some of us bring this on ourselves with our "holier-than-thou, I don't need no man, I've got Jesus and that's enough" attitudes. That aside, I have encountered literally hundreds of strong, attractive, committed, bright Christian African-American women who are unmarried. This, in turn, has created a very large population of lonely, and often, discontented Christian women.

This invisibility and loneliness may create the need in some women to "do" things to get noticed. Some women take pride in being known for "telling people off." Some flirt and tease men persistently. Others tend to be at the center of church and community conflicts. They may become malicious gossips and ardent backbiters. They may have a strong need to run things or be in control, and are usually in competition with other women. Humility and gentleness are nowhere to be found.

The expression of meekness today is an especially great challenge for African-American women of faith. As women of this era, we are in various high places in society, and are encouruaged to be aggressive, assertive, forthright, and sometimes downright demanding to get what we want. As a result, we have become arrogant and self-serving. Jesus said, "Happy [blessed] are the meek [the humble, gentle]" (Matthew 5:5). This may be one reason why so many of us are discontented and disillusioned. We have lost our meekness edge. We must pray and work to recover it!

How? Philippians 2:3–12 gives us wonderful guidance on how to develop and practice humility. It is expressed in several ways: not being selfish or conceited; putting others first; looking out for the interests of others in addition to your own; being like Christ, who lowered (humbled) Himself to human form in obedience to the Father in order to accomplish His will. For many of us, this will require a transformation of both the mind and heart.

Jesus promised that a life in Him could be lonely. "If any one wishes to come after Me, let him deny himself, and take up his cross, and follow me" (Matthew 16:24). Self-denial and cross-carrying require humility and can produce a life of suffering, separation, and loneliness. But, Jesus also promised us great peace in this life: "Peace I leave with you; My peace I give to you; not as the world gives, do I give to you. Let not your heart be troubled, nor let it be fearful" (John 14:27).

What a wonderful promise and consolation in a world that measures us according to the level of our prowess instead of according to our virtue and service. Stand firm, women of God, and having done everything, continue to stand (Galatians 6:13).

Rejecting Worldliness

A major challenge facing many Christian women today is a tendency toward worldliness. This tendency is so subtle, it can be missed. Its expression is varied, but with a significant focus on material possessions, specifically clothing, jewelry, and shoes.

The rationale often used goes something like this: "We are God's queens and princesses." "We are supposed to be the head and not the tail." "We should look like God's children." "There is nothing wrong with looking good for God. Besides, how else are you going to catch or keep a husband?"

This rhetoric has been detrimental to the women of God. While looking and feeling our best are very important aspects of a positive self-esteem, many of us have been consumed by that quest. Thus, we have begun to glory in our attire. We snub women whose dress is not quite "right." We have become more sensual and suggestive in our dress. It appears that whatever styles the world is wearing—whether in clothing, hair, or nails—it is not long before women of God join the crowd. I overheard one shocked, unsaved brother proclaim as he passed a local church in Philadelphia (which was not housed in a "traditional" church building) as the saints paraded out in their finery: "I didn't know that was a church. I thought it was a nightclub." Much of this self-directed grooming activity and physical glorification is directly related to the feelings of loneliness and insignificance mentioned earlier.

These tendencies have seeped into other areas of our lives as well. Our language and actions have become slipshod. Many of us think nothing of the "hand on the hip, snapping my finger in your face" gesture when someone angers us. We have begun to adopt negative attitudes about others, just as the world has. Some of us have become poor employees by not completing tasks appropriately or in a timely fashion, acting insubordinately, developing bad attitudes, and simply failing to render to "Caesar" a full eight-hour day. Even more disturbing are those sisters who use job time for Bible reading or job resources for church business without permission. Soap operas—day and nighttime—are a mainstay of our daily routine. For many of us, high credit card and other debt have resulted from our excessive spending and poor money management. The obvious result of this is limited resources to contribute to the work and ministry of the church.

Finally, and equally pervasive, is rampant sexual immorality among the people of God. I have talked with countless Christian men and women who view their sexual improprieties as simply a "part of life." "God understands, He knows I'm human." And, unfortunately, by observation, a respectable percentage of the teenage pregnancies and out-of-wedlock births to African-American women occur in the church. Also, with the shortage of eligible Christian men for dating and marriage, many sisters have resorted to becoming "unequally yoked" with unsaved men, with the expressed hope of winning them to Christ. This, of course, rarely happens.

These observations are not meant to be judgmental. They do, however, represent the thinking and actions of many Christian women today. We need to acknowledge and repent of this kind of mind-set and behavior, so that we can move on to higher levels of knowledge and growth in

Christ. Jesus proclaimed us to be salt and light for the world (Matthew 5:13–16). This means that our very lives and actions, more than our words, must provide the direction and guidance for those living in darkness. We are living in the presence of the world but the world is not supposed to live in us. Peter calls us a "chosen race, a royal priesthood, a holy nation, a peculiar people for God's own possession." Why? So that we can "proclaim the excellencies of Him who called us out of darkness into His marvelous light" (1 Peter 2:9). Thus, as women of God, we need to act, think, and be peculiar.

Hank Allen (1991) suggests that Christian African-American men and women must live morally and sexually pure lives as a mechanism for "modeling biblical femininity and masculinity for the next century." In addition, Peter's principle of the older women teaching the younger women is sorely needed. This need not be viewed purely from an age perspective. Certainly, godly female college students have much to offer our young teenage girls, especially those lacking appropriate role models. Seasoned married women can share a wealth of advice and counsel with engaged and newly married women, whatever their age. Those of us who are single and satisfied can be a tremendous support to fellow singles who are restless and struggling. All of this assumes that the "teacher" is spiritually mature and keenly aware of Paul's admonition to "bear the weaknesses of those without strength (Romans 15:1) and to restore "in the spirit of meekness" (Galatians 6:1).

> A generation ago, worldliness was smoking, dancing, drinking, lipstick, and playing cards. Today, worldliness is substituting for Christianity a pseudo-psychological, me-pampering, feelings-oriented religion that says, "If it feels good, do it." (Ortlund 1978)

Self-gratification, pleasure-seeking, and spirituality do not mix. Beware, precious sisters in Christ!

Appreciating Our Beauty

Intimately related to several of the concerns discussed above is the issue of the beauty of African-American women. From Moses to David to Solomon to Mark Antony and to our American slaveholders, the beauty and mystique of African and African-American women have intrigued men of all races, admitted or not. Our capture from Africa, the brutal rapes endured, the bearing of the master's children, and treatment as a "breeder and workhorse" have created silent, internal psychological damage in African-American women that has yet to be fully explored and described.

Great strides were made in the '60s and '70s regarding a more culturally acceptable definition of Black beauty. Many of the relevant issues, however, have re-emerged and are currently having a supreme impact on the way many African-American women feel about themselves. It appears we have taken a turn back to where we were thirty years ago. Unfortunately one of the most disturbing concepts that has reemerged is the emphasis on skin color—the dark versus light debate—especially among younger women. The old slogan is back: "If you're white, you're all right; if you're brown, stick around; if you're yellow, you're mellow; but if you're black, git back." I listened with much interest in a shopping mall to the conversation of three medium brown teenagers who discussed their friend's mother, who was nice but "*sooooo* Black."

Recently, a colleague related his disappointment after attending a Black History Month celebration sponsored by African-American students on a White college campus. The discussion apparently deteriorated into a gripe session by the largely darker sisters who accused the brothers of only dating either very fair sisters or White women. Despite gains made during the Black Power movement when the cry was "I'm Black and I'm proud," many African-American women still struggle with their beauty quotient in a society that prizes and celebrates women who are blonde, thin, and fair- or pale-skinned. Many of us struggle daily to sustain and nurture our personal identity as women of African descent. Sadly, some of the women with the lowest self-images that I know of are African-American Christians.

This struggle is manifested in many ways. We are preoccupied with our hair. It keeps us from exercising, swimming, and walking in the rain with the one we love. We have gone through a multitude of changes in hairstyles, most of which, due to the extreme use of chemicals, have damaged our hair and scalp. The latest trend is to make our hair as straight as possible so it can hang and flow freely. The ultimate measure of our self-degradation in relation to our hair is the names we've given it. We refer to our God-given, naturally woolly hair as "kinky," "nasty," or "naps." I get strange looks, and sometimes comments, from many sisters who view my preference for a natural hairstyle as outdated. Even one of my nieces, whose hair has been permed since she was a very young girl, innocently asked while she watched me towel dry my hair after a shampoo, "Auntie, how do you get your hair fluffy like that?" Another manifestation of our identity struggle is the very high level of dissatisfaction with the construction of our bodies as African women, especially our fuller hips and thighs, wider noses, and thicker lips.

We must take deeply into our spirits the words in Psalm 139:14: "I will give thanks to Thee, for I am fearfully and wonderfully made; wonderful are Thy works, and my soul knows it very well." We are fearfully (with great reverence) and wonderfully (distinctly, marvelously) made—dark or light skin, thick thighs, wide hips, big lips, woolly hair and all! This is not to negate the fact that many of us need to lose some weight, tone our muscles, freshen our faces, or update our wardrobes. But it does suggest that we need to re-examine and identify ourselves in light of what God has said about us.

We need to re-teach our daughters that Black is beautiful, not because it is ethnically appropriate, but because God made us! We need to shift our attention from a purely external focus to developing the inner person of the heart that Peter says is precious in God's sight. This will win over a disobedient husband, not the latest hairstyle, gold chains, and silk dresses (1 Peter 3:1–8). The virtuous woman of Proverbs was known in the gates not for her looks but for her *works* (although I imagine she looked pretty good draped in her fine linens and purple)! "Charm is deceitful and beauty is vain, but a woman who fears the Lord, she shall be praised" (Proverbs 31:30).

Improving Our Health

There is limited health research that is specific to African-American women, and even less on those who are also Christian. The available data suggest, however, that the health status of African-American women overall is critical, and therefore, represents an additional challenge for this era and beyond.

In spite of the sweeping gains made in health status and well-being for the general American population within the last two decades, African-Americans and other populations of color have not benefited significantly. According to the Black and Minority Health Report (USDHHS 1985), African-Americans experience more than 60,000 deaths per year largely from health conditions that are, in part, preventable. There is no doubt that a major crisis exists among our men. And yet, an almost "silent" burden is born by African-American women, who develop various health maladies at extreme rates. We are viewed as the "pillars" of our families, friends, and communities. We can carry the weight of the world on one shoulder and nurture ten babies on the other. We are strong. The evidence suggests, however, that African-American women experience a greater mortality and morbidity than their White counterparts. Thus, we may be fighting an "internal" battle for survival within our own bodies. We face many important health concerns, such as lupus, sickle cell anemia, certain forms of cancer, the effects of violence, teen pregnancy, and substance abuse, but I will discuss here those issues that have the greatest impact on African-American women.

Hypertension, also known as high blood pressure, is often the precipitating factor for heart disease, stroke, and diabetes. These represent the major health problems that kill African-American people. High blood pressure affects African-Americans greatly. It is a problem of the blood vessels, where too much pressure pushes against their walls as the blood flows through the arteries and veins. Despite popular opinion, it does not mean that someone has too much blood running through her body. Also, one cannot tell when her blood pressure is high based on how she feels. For this reason, hypertension is called the "silent killer" because it has few or no symptoms.

Of the sixty million Americans with hypertension, 28 percent are African-Americans (Hildreth & Saunders 1992). Among our women, 39 percent have high blood pressure and more than half of those over the age of fifty suffer from it. High blood pressure among African-Americans starts earlier, is more severe, and, when untreated, is more likely to lead to major complications—a stroke, kidney failure, heart disease, and diabetes or early death—than in the White population (Sherrod 1994). You can do several things to prevent high blood pressure. If it runs in your family, then you need to have your blood pressure checked once a month. If you have high blood pressure, you must take your medication as directed. In addition, a healthy diet, exercise, losing weight, lowering salt and alcohol intake, and quitting smoking can help to keep your blood pressure under control or even lower the amount of medication you have to take.

Diabetes and obesity are two conditions that are very closely linked and disproportionately impact African-American women. Diabetes is a problem of how the body uses food, due to a malfunction of the pancreas (which produces insulin). It does not come from eating too much sugar, as many African-Americans believe. It does seem to run in families and among people who are overweight. Eighty percent of people with type-II diabetes (also known as non-insulin-dependent diabetes) are overweight. This may partially explain why African-American women are almost 50 percent more likely to develop diabetes than White women (Williams 1994), because 44 percent of all African-American women over the age of twenty are overweight (USDHHS 1991). Like hypertension, diabetes can and must be controlled, or it can lead to kidney disease, heart disease, stroke, and blindness. A proper diet, weight control, and exercise are the three major keys for controlling diabetes. Also, the feet and legs must be given special care to avoid amputations, since injuries to these areas do not heal well in people who are diabetic (Williams 1994).

Stress is an underrated health concern whose impact is now gaining more attention. It is an especially important area of concern for African-American women, who are perceived as "strong" women. According to B. Y. Avery (1992), over half of African-American women between the ages of eighteen and twenty-five report that they live in a state of psychological distress. Stress may be the underlying factor for as much as 70 percent of the health problems for which we see a physician. For African-American women, it can pose tremendous problems.

> I don't know one Black woman, regardless of educational status, economic condition or social position, who is not faced with stress. Some people think stress is like the blues, but it's not. Blues is medicine because it's not meant to depress or pull one down—it has the opposite effect. The blues heals. . . . stress doesn't do that. Stress does not heal; it infects; it's only satisfied when you're dead. It's the venom that gets into all Black women's blood, causing our bodies to swell and explode, extinguishing our lives. (Adisa 1994)

This description depicts the potential negative impact that stress can have on the body. Thus, we must find ways to manage it, rather than pretending to be strong.

HIV/AIDS is our newest and most deadly malady. Despite its view by the general public (and African-Americans in particular) as a White gay male disease, it is increasing alarmingly in our community. Particularly affected in the '90s are African-American women and children, who now comprise most of the new cases of AIDS (52 percent of all female cases and 59 to 80 percent of all pediatric cases, respectively). Twenty-five percent of all people with AIDS are now African-American, and as of 1994, AIDS is the leading cause of death for African-American women who are twenty-four to thirty-six years of age (USDHHS 1994). This increased risk is believed to be the result of contact with men who have a history of either substance abuse and/or high risk sexual practices (Avery 1992; Richie 1994). Within the coming decade, there will be a tremendous need in the African-American community to care for the growing number of women affected by AIDS and the children they will leave behind as orphans. The AIDS issue represents, for the church and the women of God, one of the most powerful challenges to our faith in this century.

While these descriptions give a grim picture of the realities we face, there is actually much we can do about our health right now, with little or no help from the medical community. First, recognize that your body is the temple of the Holy Spirit. Thus, you must take care of it. That is not limited to just not smoking and drinking. It also includes what you eat and how much, your weight, your exercise patterns, how you control stress, and whether or not you control any diseases you may have. Many of us regularly violate both the natural and medical laws governing our bodies, and then pray for "healing." We must take charge of our health and be actively involved in the upkeep and strengthening of our bodies.

Use moderation in all things. Two chocolate cookies will not make you fat. A bag full on a daily basis will. Find ways to get rid of stress. Talk to a friend, pray, sing, mediate on God's Word, go for a walk, confess sin. Do something to release your tensions instead of pretending nothing is wrong. Finally, look for opportunities to minister to those who are sick, shut-in, and unhealthy. You will be surprised how helping others can assist in your personal pursuit of godly health and well-being.

Stop the Black Male Bashing

There is a popular and dangerous trend among females today, in the name of achieving "equality," to bash, belittle, and beleaguer men. This has taken the form of talk shows where the evils of the male species are exposed, countless magazine articles that admonish women to take what they can get from men, and television sitcoms that exploit the weaknesses and faults of men in the face of "female superiority." While issues of sexism are as poignant as those of racism and must be addressed, we, as women of Christ, must not jump on the bandwagon to proclaim the irreconcilable nature and character of men. Further, the plight of our men requires a deeper level of sensitivity and understanding from us.

The African-American female predicament is no doubt in crisis. Yet, the conditions facing African-American men are equally critical. Excessive rates of underemployment and unemployment, high crime, substance abuse, AIDS, and growing up poor or without a father have created an epidemic of death and destruction among our men (Edelman 1994; Richardson 1991). According to Juwauna Kunjufu (1985), it is an actual "conspiracy," which begins as early as third grade. Many churches have failed to adequately evangelize Black men (Richardson 1991). Thus, Christianity is viewed as a "woman thing," and many men are not being spiritually directed. These factors, and others, require a different approach to our men than the typical "men as the enemy" philosophy projected today.

These comments in no way suggest that the sexism often expressed by African-American men should be excused or endured. But, they do strongly imply that the African-American community cannot afford another "division." Besides, as women of Christ, we must view our brothers as fellow partners in the building of God's kingdom and fellow participants in the struggles of our community. Hence, we need to hang up our boxing gloves, roll up our sleeves, and get to work!

SPECIAL CHALLENGES

The final challenge is a special one to those of us who feel we have "made it" in this life. African-American women, in general, have been able to succeed professionally and educationally at a rate that exceeds African-American men. For example, between 1976 and 1984, more African-American females enrolled in American colleges than African-American men—5.2 percent versus 3.57 percent, respectively (Boamah-Wiafe 1990). While there are equal disparities in salaries between educated African-Americans and Whites along gender lines, the gap is wider for males than for females. Thus, for an African-American woman with a master's degree, her median annual income is about $3,000 less than that of a similarly educated White female. Conversely, the income differential between an African-American man with a master's degree and an equally prepared White man is almost $7,000. At the bachelor's degree level, the difference is close to $10,000 for men versus only $1,000 for women. The gap between men has not narrowed significantly since 1975 (Conrad 1995). In addition, there has been a dramatic increase in the numbers of African-

American males imprisoned in the last few decades (Edelman 1994). At the same time, success among African-American women has increased. Thus, an apparent natural "schism" has been created between African-American women and men.

Some have suggested this schism is due to the "woman of the '90s syndrome," whereby African-American women are choosing careers over marriage and relationships. This represents, however, a relatively small percentage of women. It is a myth that all African-American women are career-oriented and independent *by choice.* Most work because they have to, as they are either never-married singles, single heads of households, or married and supplementing their husband's salary. Regarding the first and second categories, the drastic reduction in marriage rates in the African-American community, coupled with the increased imprisonment rates over the last several years make it highly likely that many African-American women will have to continue to work out of necessity (Edelman 1994).

With the turning of these tides, however, there has crept into the psyche of some successful African-American women (and men, too!) a philosophy of superiority—a view that they have "made it" on their own; that the masses of women (and men) who remain in the community do so because they lack ambition and are simply lazy. We have left the old neighborhood in a "huff," grunting our need to get away from "these people." And now, those we have left behind must stand up, get up, and make it on their own, just like we did.

How ungodly! The audacity of any of us as people of color, African-Americans in particular, to think we have "pulled ourselves up by the bootstraps"! In my opinion, the bootstrap theory does not apply to us, because we started without boots! Instead, each of us is standing on the shoulders of others—our parents, our siblings, and extended families; the communities from which we have come; our foremothers and forefathers who paved the way for our footprints; and our African ancestors' royalty and greatness as the world's first human inhabitants. Most importantly, Jesus Christ has empowered us to be and to become His agents of good and hope in the world.

We, therefore, need a renewed vision of ourselves as servants of Christ and mankind. Like Esther, our education, success, degrees, social standing, finances, and material blessings are all for "such a time as this." We must always remember that but for the grace of God, we would be nothing.

May heaven help us, dear sisters, if we ever forget from whence we have come, or fail to reach back and offer our shoulders as support to the next generation of would-be women of faith. It is our time. It is our responsibility. Sankofa!

CONCLUSION

In the spirit of Sankofa,[1] I close with a tribute to my precious sisters in Christ, which in my view summarizes the ideas presented in this chapter. This is one of my favorite descriptions of the African-American female—heart, body, and soul—by the great intellect of the twentieth century, W. E. B. Du Bois (1920). He states:

> For this, their promise, and for their hard past, I honor the women of my race. Their beauty—their dark and mysterious beauty of midnight eyes, crumpled hair, and soft, full-featured faces—is perhaps more to me than to you, because I was born to its warm and subtle spell; but their worth is yours as well as mine. No other women on earth could have emerged from the hell of force and temptation that once engulfed and still surrounds Black women in America with half the modesty and womanliness that they retain. I have always felt like bowing myself before them in all abasement, searching to bring some tribute to these long-suffering victims, these burdened sisters of mine, whom the world, the wise, white world, loves to affront and ridicule and wantonly to insult. (p. 21)

This chapter outlined some of the major characteristics of the modern-day African-American woman along with the critical challenges she is facing in her walk of faith. But through the power of Christ and the unction of the Holy Spirit, she can and will do all things.

---

[1]*Sankofa* is a saying from Ghana that means "reach back into the past and fetch it."

References

Adisa, O. P. 1994. Rocking in the sunlight: Stress and Black women. In *The Black women's health book: Speaking for ourselves,* edited by E. C. White. Seattle: Seal Press.

Allen, H. L. 1991. The Black family: Its unique legacy, current challenges, and future prospects. In *The Black family: Past, present, and future,* edited by L. N. June. Grand Rapids: Zondervan.

Avery, B. Y. 1992. The health status of Black women. In *Health issues in the Black community,* edited by R. L. Braithwaite and S. Taylor. San Francisco: Jossey-Bass.

Boamah-Wiafe, D. 1990. *The Black experience in contemporary America.* Omaha: Wisdom Publishers.

Conrad, C. A. 1995. Race, earnings, and intelligence. *Black Enterprise* 25 (8): 26.

Du Bois, W. E. B. 1920. *The servant in the house.* New York: Schocken Books.

Edelman, M. W. 1994. The Black family in America. In *The Black women's health book: Speaking for ourselves,* edited by E. C. White. Seattle: Seal Press.

Hildreth, C. J., and E. Saunders. 1992. Heart disease, stroke, and hypertension in Blacks. In *Health issues in the Black community,* edited by R. L. Braithwaite and S. Taylor. San Francisco: Jossey-Bass.

Kunjufu, J. 1985. *The conspiracy to destroy Black boys.* Chicago: African-American Images.

1985. *The new American standard Bible.* Nashville: Holman.

Ortlund, A. 1978. *Disciplines of the beautiful woman.* Waco, TX: Word Books.

Richardson, W. 1991. Evangelizing Black males: Critical issues and how-to's. In *The Black family: Past, present, and future,* edited by L. N. June. Grand Rapids: Zondervan.

Richie, B. 1994. AIDS: In living color. In *The Black women's health book: Speaking for ourselves,* edited by E. C. White. Seattle: Seal Press.

Sherrod, P. 1994. Controlling hypertension. In *The Black women's health book: Speaking for ourselves,* edited by E. C. White. Seattle: Seal Press.

Staples, R. 1979. *The Black woman in America: Sex, marriage, and the family*. Chicago: Nelson Hall.

U.S. Department of Health and Human Services. 1994. *1993 chartbook*. Washington, DC: U.S. Government Printing Office.

U.S. Department of Health and Human Services. 1991. *Healthy people 2000: National health promotion and disease prevention objectives*. Washington, DC: U.S. Government Printing Office.

U.S. Department of Health and Human Services.1985. *The report of the secretary's task force on Black and minority health, executive summary*. Washington, DC: U.S. Government Printing Office.

Williams, K. M. 1994. The best foot forward: A Black woman deals with diabetes. In *The Black women's health book: Speaking for ourselves*, edited by E. C. White. Seattle: Seal Press.

PART 2

BUILDING RELATIONSHIPS

Sheila R. Staley

Bridging the Gap: Mentoring the Younger Woman

SHEILA R. STALEY is Executive Director of Resources for Better Families, Inc., in Philadelphia, Pennsylvania. She is also a staff lecturer for Christian Research & Development, Inc., in Philadelphia. Sheila has received training as a marriage and family counselor from Association of Marriage and Family Therapy (of which she is also a clinical member) and biblical counseling training from the Christian Research & Development Institute. She received a bachelor of arts degree in art history from Rosemont College and a master of education degree in secondary guidance and counseling from Antioch University. She attends Christian Stronghold Baptist Church in Philadelphia, where she formerly directed the single-parents ministry. Born in Philadelphia, she is married to Kenneth Staley, and they are the parents of three children: Tabbatha, Christina, and Harrison.

Chapter 4

Sheila R. Staley

Bridging the Gap:
Mentoring the Younger Woman

I was about eight years old and I opened the door one day and there was Mary McLeod Bethune. I remember sitting on the floor playing as my mother and she talked. Mrs. Bethune was saying that colored women need to stop playing bridge and start building bridges. (Leontine T. C. Kelly 1985)

Older African-American women have traditionally taught the younger women the skills necessary to sustain relationships and a marriage, establish a home, rear children, and create change in their community, as well as themselves, while enduring economic, social, and racial oppression.

Women of influence in many of our lives have initially been female relatives. This is a casual environment for mentoring within an informal framework of kinship ties.

MENTORS

Natural Mentors

My natural mentors—my mother, grandmother, great-grandmother, and aunts—taught me the requirements of God and the importance of spirituality, commitment, and insight. These attributes helped me to see beyond the present situation to greater possibilities for fulfillment, not just for me, but also for my community. My training and interaction with the women in my family enabled me to understand more fully my obligation to go beyond self-perpetuation. They enabled me to embrace God's command that I should be a channel of blessing to others.

The prophet Micah explained the simple truth of life's activities: "He has showed you, O [wo]man, what is good. And what does the LORD require of you? To act justly and to love mercy and to walk humbly with your God" (Micah 6:8). I learned these truths well from the significant females in my life during childhood and adolescence.

Chosen Mentors

As we begin to seek an identity separate from close female relatives, other women emerge as models and confidantes. I like to refer to them as "chosen" mentors to distinguish them from natural mentors. The chosen mentor is part of a more structured relationship; these women are usually outside of the kinship boundaries. To build the relationship, the mentor and the protege have to define the environment in which they will interact (environment meaning the present reality that shapes the values, goals, and decisions of an individual). Our chosen mentors can provide a different perspective regarding ourselves and the "awaiting world" with all its possibilities.

It was during the period of late adolescence and early adulthood (ages seventeen to thirty-five) that I acquired the desire to translate my knowledge, dreams, and experience into godly choices. I was led to seek counsel and interaction with women who were on the same path. We shared similar preferences, concerns, and burdens. Some of these women were eight to ten years older than I was at the time, and others were much older.

Despite shared similarities, many of my chosen mentors were quite different from me. But even in their diversity there were common threads that bound these women together in my eyes: love for the Lord, a commitment to be holy, an understanding of God's plan for their lives, and a willingness to share themselves with me. In their differences they provided an abundance of wisdom and counsel, which the Lord has used to refine my vision for my community, myself, and the world. In Jeremiah 29:11 the Lord declares, "I know the plans I have for you, plans to prosper you and not to harm you, plans to give you hope and a future."

Certain relationships with mentoring women have brought me greater understanding of God's plan for me. I learned to love the discipline of learning and the beauty of God's world from one of my professors. My mother-in-law, by her godly walk and candor, modeled the faith and grace needed to accept God's plan for marriage and family. From my pastor's wife I learned how to transfer a burden for people into a ministry plan that keeps God and family in proper focus.

Older Women

Visible groups of older women are desperately needed to influence the lives of younger women in the church today. The world provides many avenues for mentoring. These relationships often lead women into the thinking patterns, philosophies, and practices of the world. The core motivation is one of self-service rather than being God's servant. The conditions of our homes, communities, and world require women who understand God's principles for holy living and who live them out in a wicked society. It is time for the "older women" of the Lord to take on the charge of Paul:

> *Teach the older women to be reverent in the way they live, not to be slanderers or addicted to much wine, but to teach what is good. Then they can train the younger women to love their husbands and children, to be self-controlled and pure, to be busy at home, to be kind and to be subject to their husbands, so that no one will malign the Word of God. (Titus 2:3–5)*

If it means building bridges to span the gap created by age, values, or socioeconomic factions, then let's start constructing. A completed bridge provides the structure necessary to pass between two points that were separated by distance. God's command to love each other in the unity of the Spirit provides the structural foundation for the bridge (John 13:34; Ephesians 4:4–6). God's love and the unity of the Spirit will enable the older and younger women to reach beyond differences and fulfill the command in Titus 2:3–5. The Christian community, the larger community, and the world will greatly benefit from the legacy older, godly women can leave younger women. Now is the time to closely reexamine our chosen mentors. We need to create a generation of women who are equipped to be God's servants in the home and community.

I propose to examine the mentoring relationship, as well as the differences between mentorship and discipleship. Factors that have contributed to the breakdown in the mentorship tradition of seeing older women as the "wise advisors" of the African-American community will also be discussed. Finally, insight will be provided on how to rebuild the bridge between older and younger African-American women.

THE MENTORING RELATIONSHIP

The word "mentor" originated in Greek legend, where Mentor was the wise and trusted counselor to whom Odysseus entrusted the education of his son (Bushardt 1991). The mentor nurtures, supports, and provides wise counsel. She helps her protege set and realize goals. For the Christian woman, these goals are established and bathed in prayer. Growth emerges out of practical experiences, the mentor serving as a wise advisor.

Discipleship and Mentoring

There is a fine line between discipling and mentoring as we relate to one another in Christ. In the Great Commission, Jesus stated the emphasis of discipleship:

Therefore go and make disciples of all nations, baptizing them
in the name of the Father and of the Son and of the Holy Spirit,
and teaching them to obey everything I have commanded you.
And surely I am with you always, to the very end of the age.
(Matthew 28:19–20)

Discipleship emphasizes teaching the Word of God and the principles for Christian living. It requires a relationship based on mutual respect between the discipler and the disciple, but not necessarily a long-term dialoguing, supportive relationship. The discipleship relationship is usually short-term, ending once the teaching has been accomplished.

Phases of the Relationship

In secular society, the average duration of a mentoring relationship is three years; the maximum is ten years. The relationship often will take on a different form during various stages of the individual's development. Kathy Kram (1983) in the article "Phases of the Mentor Relationship" identifies four phases of a dynamic mentor/protege relationship: (1) initiation, (2) cultivation, (3) separation, and (4) redefinition.

The *initiation phase* is the period in which the relationship starts and begins to have importance to both individuals. The mentor helps the protege define her dreams as more concrete expectations. The mentor challenges and guides the protege in establishing goals. At the same time, the protege expresses her desire for the mentor's assistance.

During the *cultivation phase,* both the mentor and protege benefit from their relationship. The emotional bond deepens and intimacy is established, setting the stage for a freer exchange of ideas and concerns as well as the opportunity to challenge formed thinking patterns. This is a crucial stage for older Christian women mentoring younger Christian women. The relationship has developed to a level where the young woman is receptive to the older woman entering "her world." She is ready to share her most intimate thoughts and fears, and to allow the older woman to challenge her and provide practical biblical suggestions for change. The result is an environment in which the Word can readily transform the younger woman into a woman of God.

The *separation phase* marks a significant change in the structure of the relationship as well as its emotional dynamics. During this stage, the protege does not seek guidance, but looks for opportunities to demonstrate her independence. This is a natural progression. The protege has grown in confidence in her ability to carry out her responsibilities. At this point, the mentor must guard her heart against feelings of abandonment and resentment. It is easy for the older Christian woman to experience the "empty nest syndrome." Susan Hunt (1992) suggests that as spiritual mothers we often have feelings of abandonment as our children become independent.

To guard against these feelings, we need to remember that we are stewards of whatever God has entrusted to us, including our relationships with younger women. During the mentoring process we are to point proteges to Christ, so that they will rely on Him, not us, for guidance in everyday living. This goes back to the fine line between discipling and mentoring. The older woman teaches principles in godly living, but at the same time, she is concerned with helping the young woman integrate these principles into her "world" in a manner that is pleasing to God.

The final mentoring stage is the *redefinition phase.* During this phase, the mentor/protege relationship becomes more informal. Mutual support is evident. Even when the protege occasionally seeks counsel, and is sought for counsel, friendship is the operational relationship.

The relationships between Elizabeth and Mary (Luke 1:39–55) and between Naomi and Ruth (Book of Ruth) provide some understanding of how these phases are manifested in the lives of believers. Both Elizabeth and Naomi were older women, providing the younger women with nurture, support, and encouragement as well as the skills to carry out their God-given responsibilities. Mary and Ruth expressed their gratitude and appreciation for guidance by making wise use of the wealth of knowledge and experience of the older women. It is evident in the Word that the relationship between the two sets of women was defined by deep commitment to the Lord and a great love for one another. The end result of a mentoring relationship between an older and younger woman should be love and friendship. Wise counsel and encouragement from a friend can be trusted, for "a friend loves at all times" (Proverbs 17:17).

BREAKING DOWN THE CONTINUUM

Tarnished Paradigm

What happened to destroy the respect and love that young women once had for older women in our communities and churches? I believe that when younger African-American women look at us older women, they see us as a "tarnished paradigm." A paradigm is a model or an example. Younger women see us as dull models compared to our female ancestors who sacrificed and struggled with unyielding faith in God. Our foremothers struggled so that we could continue to move ahead as a people. Their goal was the preservation and success of the family and community; their tools were their God-given talents. Their anchor was their faith in a God of love, mercy, and justice. They were single-minded in their task. They were not ashamed of their position in the family or community. Wrinkles and gray hair were considered signs of wisdom and experience. They invested themselves in the next generation. They interacted with them, but their perspective of life stood apart from that of the younger generation.

Our female ancestors understood the cycle of life for a woman. One of these women might say:

> Now listen, you who say, "Today or tomorrow we will go to this or that city, spend a year there, carry on business and make money." Why, you do not even know what will happen tomorrow. What is your life? You are a mist that appears for a little while and then vanishes. Instead, you ought to say, "If it is the Lord's will, we will live and do this or that." As it is, you boast and brag. All such boasting is evil. Anyone, then, who knows the good he ought to do and doesn't do it, sins. (James 4:13–17)

How do older Christian women demonstrate to younger women that we understand that we are a mist that appears for a little while and then vanishes? How are we investing in the younger women? Are we enabling them to discover the deeper truths of God and His plan for their lives? Do we model holy living? Many older women, especially from my generation (the '60s), are busy taking advantage of the opportunities gained from the civil rights and women's movements. We have allowed the philosophies of this age to pollute our thinking and tarnish our example as holy women. Paul warns us regarding this danger: "See to it that no one takes you captive through hollow and deceptive philosophy, which depends on human tradition and the basic principles of this world rather than on Christ" (Colossians 2:8).

Paul states that the older woman should live a "reverent" life (Titus 2:3). The word "reverent," or "holy," refers to the Christian woman's position in Christ. She is seen as holy by God because of the redemptive work of Christ on the cross. Therefore, in her daily life she is to walk worthy of her calling as a joint heir of Jesus Christ (Ephesians 4:1; Colossians 1:10). She is a member of a holy priesthood (1 Peter 2:5). She is to conduct herself in her daily life as a priestess of the Lord, reconciling people to God through Jesus Christ by words and deeds.

We Christian women need to remember that we are holy, meaning that we are set aside by God for His purpose, not our own. We need to resume our role as the keeper of the home flame. We are the instruments God wishes to use to bring love back into relationships, families, and communities. God has given His women capacity to nurture the next generation of women in godly living. Our younger women need to know who they are in the Lord. They need to know His special love and care for women. They need to know their history as it relates to God's Word so that they can gain strength and direction. If younger African-American women do not learn about God's role in our struggle as a people, and as women, then they will continue to be prime targets for the destructive values and philosophies that presently have taken many of them captive.

REBUILDING THE BRIDGE

Certain changes must be made in our perspective of ourselves as women if we're to rebuild the bridge between older and younger women. Older women must be willing to adopt the biblical view of the older woman. She must be holy. She should be obedient to the Word of God, filled with the fruit of the Spirit, self-controlled, and ready to respond to God's revealed purpose for her life with a sincere love for the people of God (1 Peter 2:13–25). She should rejoice to be described as an older woman: "Gray hair is a crown of splendor, it is attained by a righteous life" (Proverbs 16:31).

The younger woman needs to develop a teachable spirit, forsaking the rebellious and independent spirit of this age. God in His wisdom uses interaction with older, more experienced women to unlock many doors to knowledge and wisdom. In order to obtain the maximum benefit from the relationship, a willingness to submit to the older woman's godly counsel is key. Submission implies a recognition of the older woman's authority in the area under counsel. Often pride blocks the younger woman from having a teachable spirit. "Pride goes before destruction, a haughty spirit before a fall" (Proverbs 16:18.) Older women and younger women have to gain from each other for personal growth. Change always occurs in the context of a relationship. The change will be either positive or negative, but a relationship is never stagnant.

Seek God's guidance before entering a mentoring relationship. Throughout the selection process as well as the development of the mentoring relationship, prayer and guidance from the Word of God is crucial in order to keep selfish, ungodly agendas from corrupting the relationship. Both older and younger women must be committed to principles of good communication (Ephesians 4:25, 29) and forgiveness (Ephesians 4:32; Matthew 18:15–17). The bridge will be complete if it is built on the foundation of God's divine love in action (1 Corinthians 13:1–13).

CONCLUSION

God has charged older women with the awesome responsibility of training younger women. This training is most effectively done in supportive, nurturing mentoring relationships. Our community is greatly in need of older women who will take the challenge of Titus 2:3–5 to heart and combine the tradition in our community of "other mothers" with God's Word in order to bring hope, deliverance, and revival to the lives of our younger women.

We will tell the next generation the praiseworthy deeds of the LORD, his power, and the wonders he has done . . . so the next generation would know them, even the children yet to be born, and they in turn would tell their children. Then they would put their trust in God and would not forget his deeds but would keep his commands. (Psalm 78:4, 6–7)

We are living through the first generation of young adults who have grown up in a society where our basic institutions have removed God and His Word. We are in danger of producing a generation of young women who neither know their legacy in God nor understand His requirements for holy living. We must pass on the legacy.

References

Bushardt, S. 1991. The mentor/protege relationship: A biological perspective. *Human Relations* 44 (July): 619–39.

1984. *The holy Bible: New international version.* Grand Rapids: Zondervan.

Hunt, S. 1992. *Spiritual mothering: The Titus 2 model for women mentoring women.* Franklin, TN: Legacy Communication.

Kram, K. 1983. Phases of the mentor relationship. *Academy of Management Journal* 25 (4): 608–25.

Lanker, B. 1989. Portrait of Leontine T. C. Kelly. Interview in *I dream a world: Portraits of Black women who changed America,* edited by B. Summer. New York: Stewart, Tabori & Chang.

Levinson, D., et al. 1978. *The seasons of a man's life.* New York: Ballantine.

Patricia Richardson

Seeking a Godly Mate: Questions Single Women Must Ask Themselves

PATRICIA RICHARDSON is Vice President of Christian Research & Development, Inc., in Philadelphia, Pennsylvania. Born in Seaford, Delaware, she grew up in Philadelphia, studied at Temple University there, and is a Certified Biblical Counselor. She leads the women's ministry at Christian Stronghold Baptist Church in Philadelphia and is also a national and international speaker at Christian conferences. Patricia and her husband, Willie, have four children: Gregory, Garin, Gwendolyn, and Gerald.

Chapter 5

Patricia Richardson

Seeking a Godly Mate: Questions Single Women Must Ask Themselves

No good thing will he withhold from those who walk uprightly.
(Psalm 84:11)

Our great and wonderful God, after creating the earth, the sky, the sea, the fish, and the animals, created man and woman in His image (Genesis 1:27). God created woman to be man's helper, partner, lover, and companion (2:18). Adam called her "woman" because she was made from his rib: "bone of his bone, flesh of his flesh" (Genesis 2:23). She was made to complete man. Adam and Eve were commanded to be fruitful and multiply, giving them the wonderful responsibility to reproduce children after their kind. Adam did not have to seek a mate; rather, God conveniently created his mate and brought her to him.

The mate selection process does not always go this easily for single women in today's society. Especially for African-American women who significantly outnumber African-American males. At times in her desperation to find a good man, marry, and settle down, she may be careless and hasty as she moves through her single years. To that end, this chapter will discuss several issues single African-American women should consider before choosing a mate and before getting married.

Usually, when a single woman wants to get married, she begins to think about what qualities she wants in a man. Very rarely does she start by evaluating her own character. Nor does she perceive her single years as a time the Lord has given her to work on areas in her personal life before she gets into a marriage relationship. Instead of praying "Lord, I want a Christian man, nice looking, with a good job, and all the rest," a single woman should be praying, "Lord, search my heart. See if there be any ways in me that do not please You, and help me to use my single years to work on those areas in my life." There are ten questions a single woman needs to ask herself.

1. DO I HAVE A GOOD RELATIONSHIP WITH THE LORD?

Your life needs to be in good spiritual order, so that when the right mate comes along, you will be prepared. To develop spiritually, you must

- Be born again, knowing Christ as Savior (Ephesians 2:8–10).
- Sanctify the Lord in your heart (1 Peter 3:15–17). You make this commitment to Christ by giving Him your life and your heart. You decide to turn from the broad road and pleasures of the world in order to live godly.
- Be a doer of the word (James 1:22–25). Do not just go to church and sing in the choir. You must study the Word daily and apply it to everyday living.
- Put off old habits (Ephesians 4:17–28). Avoid places that cause you to backslide. Seek associates who live to please the Lord.
- Learn to depend on the Lord (Proverbs 3:5–6). When you need Him, He's going to be there no matter what the case: sickness, unemployment, broken heart, trouble, or pain. God can and will heal and deliver you.
- Allow the Holy Spirit to control your life, day by day and moment by moment (Galatians 5).

2. AM I CONTENT WITH BEING SINGLE?

In the process of developing your spiritual life, it is also important for you to come to grips with your singleness. Being single is not a curse, and being celibate is a gift from the Lord. If you are enjoying the time of being a single, the following characteristics should apply to you:

- You are not terribly lonely when alone.

- You are at peace with God about your singleness and being alone.
- You do not have uncontrollable sexual desires that constantly nag you or consume your thought life.

A single woman who is comfortable without a mate and finds her fulfillment in the Lord is on the right track. After she marries she will seek the Lord to meet her needs and not expect her husband to try to satisfy her every desire. A single woman who spends most of her time longing for a man's strong arms to hold her close and a man's chest to lean on, and is constantly thinking about cooking her future husband's meals, cleaning their home, and bearing his children, is creating unrealistic expectations that may or may not be met in the marriage. A miserable single woman who is unhappy in her present state will probably be miserable in marriage.

Whether you are a widow, a woman abandoned, divorced, a single parent, or a never married single person without children, you must not be bitter and angry about your singleness. Jesus was single. Singleness is not second-rate. Everyone is single for a portion of their life, and Jesus wants you to be satisfied during that time. Singleness should not be a sad time of life. It can be an enriching time to enjoy the Lord and to grow in all that He has made you.

Although "the two shall become one" in marriage, each individual should be secure and satisfied in who they are individually before marriage. Singles experience a great time of freedom. It is a great time to serve the Lord and to help others anytime they call. You can schedule your own time; you can teach, motivate, train, and disciple others as much as you want. Use this time to get involved in church and community activities. You can take time for self-development, travel, and pleasures of all kinds. There should not be a rush or urgency to find a mate. The urgency should be to grow and develop to your greatest potential as a single. Time flies when you are occupied and busy doing work for the Lord.

3. WHY DO I WANT TO MARRY?

When seeking a godly mate, one of the most important questions to consider is your motive for marrying. One of the most tragic things a single person can do is get married for the wrong reasons. Evaluate yourself and your need for a mate. Some of the following factors reveal a number of popular reasons people use for getting married.

Desperation

"I am grabbing the first man that comes my way, regardless of his life situation—his past, personality, job, background. I don't care; I'd better grab him before someone else does. I want a man. I need a man." Water and oil don't mix, neither do saved and unsaved people. A godly choice isn't made in haste. You must take time to check his salvation, his commitment to the Lord and the church, whether he has a job, and whether he can provide a secure and stable home environment.

Tired of Being a Sister

"The last five men were happy to be my brother. They want a sister in the Lord's family. I want a husband." Call it chemistry or whatever you like, but accept it. Don't give up, don't get tired, and don't withdraw from all men.

Competition

Do you consider most women your enemies? Are you jealous of attractive women? Are you angry at well-dressed women? They are your sisters. Love them. Serve the Lord with them and worship and praise the Lord with them. Fellowship and socialize with them. The world will know us by our love for each other. We can also learn from them. A woman should never seek to acquire a mate in order to compete with other friends or associates who have mates. The grass is never greener on the other side of the fence. What others go through in order to obtain a mate may not apply to you. Also, what you see on the surface is not always reality.

Pregnancy

The number of pregnancies among singles is rising today. If you become pregnant before marriage, then according to Exodus 22:16, marriage is your first responsibility. Make a short-term plan for marriage in place of the long-term plan you had before the pregnancy. You can get married while you are pregnant. Do not wait nine months. Satan will very easily allow someone or something to hinder you from becoming a family.

If you want to please God, do not be deceived. Marriage means that two people are willing to be successful at living together according to God's purpose. Marriage is loving the Lord, loving each other, loving your child(ren), and bringing glory to the Lord.

4. AM I A GOOD FRIEND?

A godly single woman should be desirous of building solid friendships with the opposite sex, not just looking for romance and always wanting the relationship to culminate in marriage. Friendship is the foundation of all meaningful relationships. Developing a relationship where the two of you are able to talk, participate in activities together, and even do ministry together must be first on your agenda. A husband is someone with whom you are to spend the rest of your life. If you cannot appreciate the value and friendship of a prospective mate while he is single, how will you appreciate him when he is your husband?

5. HOW DO I FEEL ABOUT MYSELF?

Self-esteem, or how you feel about yourself, is extremely important. Often women look to men to fulfill the status or place in life that they desire for themselves. Is a man appealing to you because of how others will look at you if he is your mate? He should be appealing to you because you truly love him, regardless of what others think. Part of developing healthy self-esteem is focusing on the fruits of the spirit: "Love, joy, peace, patience, kindness, goodness, faithfulness, gentleness, and self-control" (Galatians 5:23). Other people (including men) will see Christ in you by the way you walk and talk. When you know you are all that you can be and find peace and contentment in your life, your self-esteem is okay.

6. AM I THE JEALOUS TYPE?

Marriage is a time of growing with one another as well as growing with others. Once a couple are married, they are not isolated from the world. Inevitably, others will be involved in your lives. While you are single is the time to address feelings of jealousy or an inability to trust. Marriage is built on trust and honesty. If you do not trust easily or quickly jump to conclusions concerning the motives and decisions of others, consider asking the Lord how to resolve this area of your life.

7. AM I WILLING TO BE HONEST AND TRUTHFUL?

Being private is fine if you are planning to stay single but acting aloof or trying to keep things from being overly personal will hinder a prospective mate from getting to know you and will hinder intimacy in marriage.

Being too private will not allow others to see the gifts and personality that God has given you.

When a relationship has passed friendship and is working its way toward intimacy and marriage, all of your deep, dark secrets should be revealed to your selected mate. "Kings take pleasure in honest lips; they value a man who speaks the truth" (Proverbs 16:13). We all have sinned and come short of God's glory. Regardless of your past, a good relationship can stand the truth. No one in the world should know anything about you that your mate does not know. A relationship begun on anything short of the truth is built on shaky ground. Ask the Lord to give you direction concerning who your mate may be and, when the time is right, to share certain issues. Telling the truth must be done, but timing must be considered as well.

8. HOW DO I PERCEIVE AND HANDLE FINANCIAL MATTERS?

You may like to eat fish, but on a date you order lobster because it is the most expensive. You like spending his money. You want the most expensive clothing and look down on sale items. You spend a great deal of money on your possessions and yourself. You look down on others who do not have the "best" clothing, the "best" car, or any of the other material things you value. If some of these examples describe you, it is imperative that you acknowledge and address this area.

These kinds of attitudes will probably not get you very many dates or a spouse. Most men will not be able to afford to date you, not to mention wanting to marry you and support your lifestyle. That is not to say that desiring the finer things in life is not good. It is to say that when material possessions dictate not only who we are, but whom we accept, a problem exists.

Arguing about finances is one of the major reasons couples divorce. It would be wise for you to learn what God's perspective is about finances and to start applying those principles before you marry.

9. AM I DOMINEERING AND OVERBEARING?

When he talks, you talk. If he does not talk, you talk. You talk over people, you talk too loudly, and you talk too long. Your opinion must be heard and accepted. There is not a correct or polite way to have a conversation with you. You should express your opinion in as few as five or six sentences at the most, and then stop speaking. If the hearer or hearers want more from you, they will ask you. If they do not, keep quiet. Do not insist on being right about everything and everybody. It isn't necessary to have an opinion on everything. Men often avoid loud, outspoken, opinionated, and persistent women because they do not want to be embarrassed. It is fine to have personal beliefs and opinions, but not to the point that you put down or offend others in your quest to be heard.

10. WHAT ARE MY ATTITUDE AND OUTLOOK ON LIFE?

Seeking a godly mate also involves constantly evaluating and developing your personal character and attitude toward life. A woman's attitude can create or destroy her opportunities to find a mate. The Lord can use the time that you are single to develop godly character, wisdom, and appreciation for life in order to make you a valuable asset to a future mate. Use this time to pray and ask the Lord for insight into who you are and in what areas your life may need improvement. Remember, you are seeking a mate who is also seeking you. You want the Lord to make you all that you need to be for His glory.

CONCLUSION

Seeking a godly mate can be a fun and rewarding experience. Nothing is more exciting during this time than watching the Lord unfold His blessings upon you because you are seeking His will. You will find that when the Lord is developing you and helping you to "grow up" in Him, a peace concerning His desires for you will become more and more evident. "For I know the plans I have for you," declares the Lord, "plans to prosper you and not to harm you, plans to give you a hope and a future" (Jeremiah 29:11). The Lord's greatest desire is to cover you in His love and to fill you with His purpose. When He made you, He gave you all that you need to be all that He called you to be, whether single or married.

The mate the Lord has chosen for you will be your complement, meaning your enhancement. A mate does not make you, but he adds to you, and you add to him. Each person has something that will make the other shine. When seeking a mate, it is not enough to know whether or not the other person will give you all that you need. You must also see that you can offer something as well.

One of the greatest joys in having a godly mate is being able to see that even in the relationship before marriage, you have grown spiritually. Overall, a godly mate should seek to bring out the best in you while you are seeking to bring out the best in him. Always ask the Lord for a godly mate who loves and honors the Lord first, then loves and honors you.

References

1984. *The holy Bible: New international version.* Grand Rapids: Zondervan.

Nave, O. 1986. *Nave's topical Bible.* Grand Rapids: Baker.

Michelle Obleton

The
Pastor's
Wife

MICHELLE OBLETON was born and raised in Detroit, Michigan. She has a bachelor of arts degree in religious education from William Tyndale College in Farmington, Michigan. She is the founder and director of WINGS Ministries (Women in Godly Service) and also founded the singing group Soaring Spirit. She teaches women's Bible study, has a ministry that trains women for leadership, and serves as a national speaker for women's organizations and churches. Michelle is a member of Waukegan Community Church in Waukegan, Illinois. Michelle and her husband, Fred Obleton, have two children, Shelby and Andrea.

Chapter 6

Michelle Obleton

The Pastor's Wife

A wife of noble character who can find? She is worth far more than rubies. Her husband has full confidence in her and lacks nothing of value. She brings him good, not harm, all the days of her life. (Proverbs 31:10–12)

The position of pastor's wife in today's society is challenging and complex. She is constantly faced with many family and church issues, the unrealistic expectations of the congregation and her husband, and also personal struggles and pressures. The pastor's wife is extremely important to her husband's ministry. Therefore, she is directly targeted by Satan. Pastors' wives need to understand that they are in spiritual warfare every day. If Satan could creep into the garden way back in Genesis and single out Eve to frustrate God's plan for humankind, he can still creep into churches and single out the pastor's wife to frustrate God's plan for the church.

As a pastor's wife, I would like to discuss seven complex areas in the life of a ministry wife: (1) her personal resentment toward the church, (2) criticism of her and her family (especially her husband), (3) her high-profile life, (4) the various expectations placed upon her, (5) her feelings of loneliness, (6) her own lack of preparation for the ministry, and (7) the "other woman" syndrome. In addition I want to offer some biblical solutions to these problems and to provide resources that will aide the pastor's wife.

PERSONAL RESENTMENTS TOWARD THE MINISTRY

Many pastors' wives resent the ministry because of the all-consuming hold it has over their husbands. They are aware of the many people who look to their husbands for daily guidance. It appears that their husbands eat, sleep, live, and breathe for the church.

I became aware of my own resentment toward the ministry during my husband's seminary training. My husband, now a pastor, was so excited about preparing for the ministry. It appeared he was always studying for some exam, some paper, or reading some book. Many times I can remember standing in the doorway of his study thinking how I hated watching the back of his head. I became aware of changes taking place between us, more in me than in him.

I was emotionally confused. My husband was becoming a leader for God. Didn't I want him to do well in his classes while in seminary? Yes, but not like this. I felt shut out, like I was losing my husband. Feelings of jealousy came over me. This new intruder was wedging its way between us. I had trouble expressing myself to my husband. I didn't understand my own negative thoughts and emotions. I knew I was wrong to interfere with my husband's desires to serve God, and I assumed God was disappointed with me, too. As I look back, I can't help but wonder how many other wives were feeling the same way as we watched our husbands prepare for ministry, not really understanding our position as pastor's wives.

Finally, after seminary, we packed our belongings and moved to our new church plant in the Midwest. By then we had a fourteen-month-old son. My husband was excited about finally pastoring. I was too . . . a little. But in six months the intruder had returned. I was in emotional turmoil again. The wedge between my husband and me was growing bigger.

My husband would wake up happy, singing as he dressed for the day. I would wake up with a sigh, knowing my day held caring for a crying baby, household chores, and a growing list of ministry responsibilities. When my husband returned home, his only conversation was about the church. The ministry had become our life. I was jealous. This new church plant was stealing my husband from me. "How can a church steal my husband?" I would ask myself repeatedly. I began to see the church as my husband's new mistress. She was very bold in her advances toward him. She came into our home and robbed us of quality time together. She was demanding of his time, his energy, and his affection. His thoughts were of her all the time. She was the last thing he spoke of before falling asleep and the first thing he mentioned in the morning. Some days my husband would be home physically, but mentally he would be miles away (with her).

I would try to share my frustrations with him and with others, but I didn't really know what to say. How do you tell your husband you see the church as a "husband snatcher"! How do you tell anyone that you hate the church and you want to leave it? I was a pastor's wife. I was supposed to be loving, sweet, kind, godly, and all that stuff. Satan's attack was fierce; a spiritual war was taking place within me, and I was losing the battle.

I also resented the fact that some people simply saw me as my husband's shadow and not as a real person. When members of the congregation would introduce me as "the pastor's wife," I felt like shouting, "Who is that? Is that me? Right now you are making me feel like the pastor's bathroom tile, or his kitchen rug. I really do have a name. My name is Michelle, and I am hurting inside. Can I tell you about it?" Instead, I put on a smile and greeted the visitors warmly. They would walk away seemingly pleased, as if they had really met me. My name was never mentioned.

As I searched the Scripture for answers to my personal struggle, I began to identify with Job's wife. She gave up on God, her husband, and even herself. She reached a dangerous point in her life where she simply didn't care anymore. She had lost everything that meant anything to her: all of their wealth plus her seven sons and three daughters, all in one single hour. Then she witnessed her husband develop painful sores from the top of his head to the bottom of his feet. Her husband went out and sat in an ash pile, scraping himself with ashes. She also lost faith and confidence in God. To her, God seemed unfair, cruel, and unjust to have let this happen. She even suggested to her suffering husband to give up on his relationship with God and just die. She said, "Curse God and die" (Job 2:9).

We should not be so quick to judge Job's wife as cold and uncaring. She may have been very tender and warm until she reached the point when all her human possessions and her children had been taken from her. The emotional shock of losing everything may have been more than she could handle. Obviously she responded to her adverse circumstances with bitterness and anger. Job's wife, however, could have chosen to react differently. She could have gotten in there alongside Job and weathered the hard times with him. Facing challenges together makes them more bearable. The remainder of the book of Job leaves him out on the ash heap with the failing comfort of three friends.

The pastor and his wife should go into ministry as a team, fighting the same battle. The Lord began to help me understand that He had not just called my husband to the ministry, He had also called me. I was part of His plan for the church and I needed to see the ministry opportunities that He had given me.

Each pastor's wife is different, equipped with differing spiritual gifts and abilities. Some pastors' wives do best by simply encouraging their husbands, while others take on some leadership within the church. Both positions are extremely important. The issue is really not what she does as much as her sense that she and her husband are together in the ministry and involved in a true partnership. In developing that partnership, it is important for the husband to recognize and acknowledge his wife's gifts and abilities. Too many pastors, perhaps due to their own insecurities, feel threatened by wives who may become very successful and, in some cases, surpass their husband's success (Briscoe 1990).

CRITICISM OF THE MINISTRY WIFE AND HER FAMILY

The words to this Negro spiritual are so true when it comes to the pastor's wife: "I've been 'buked an' I've been scorned. I've been talked about sho's you born." No pastor's wife is exempt from criticism, and few are criticized more than she. She is criticized simply because she *is* the pastor's wife. It comes with the territory. The pastor's wife will be talked about for the things she does as well as the things she does not do. She can never stop these attacks hurled at her. Someone will inevitably find something wrong with the way she relates to her husband, her children, and other people. They will probably talk negatively about the way she dresses, wears her hair, and her overall appearance. The standard of perfection held for the pastor's wife can be even higher than the one held for the pastor.

Along with criticism of the pastor's wife comes criticism of their children. They stand out like beacons in the church and are marked out as the "pastor's kids." Their behavior, good or bad, becomes the standard for the other children within the church. Raising emotionally healthy children in a pastor's family under the scrutiny of the church becomes a real challenge. The majority of this responsibility falls on the pastor's wife.

The worst criticism that most pastors' wives experience is when people speak disapprovingly of her husband. Pastors' wives usually find this hard to deal with because they know how hard their husbands have worked, prayed, and trusted God for various things within the church. The wife is aware of the many sacrifices he makes on behalf of the church and his desire to see the church glorify God. Every pastor's wife should be aware of the fact that just because you and your husband are doing a work for God does not mean that everyone in your church will love, support, and appreciate you. Many times, because you stand in a position of leadership, that becomes reason enough for resistance among members of your church.

In the book of Numbers we see a leader (pastor) and his wife who bore the brunt of some fiery criticism—Moses and his wife. The criticism was led by Moses' own sister, Miriam. Perhaps Miriam's criticism came out of her own insecurity over her brother's new wife. She no longer had the influence in Moses' life that she once did. She began to challenge Moses' authority because of her jealous attitude toward his wife. God was very displeased over the criticism of his anointed, as well as the anointed's wife, and He struck Miriam with leprosy.

God is able to handle those who criticize the pastor and his wife. It may not be as swift and obvious as striking them with leprosy, but we need to rest in the fact that God has greater ways of dealing with people than we ever could. The business of the church belongs to God. It was ordained by Him (Matthew 16:18). The battles in the church also belong to the Lord (1 Samuel 17:47). God cares about the church and He cares about the leaders. Our job as leaders is to be faithful to the things of God. His job is to do the work.

HIGH PROFILE

The pastor's wife, in some respects, has a tougher job than the First Lady of the United States. The President's wife does not have to appear before the same group of people each Sunday. She is free to travel around the world with her husband, share her ideas, and appear by his side when he makes public appearances. She also chooses activities, causes, and projects she wishes to be involved with. The pastor's wife, sometimes also referred to as "the first lady," has one major audience: the local church. It is here she must appear alongside her husband week after week.

In the book *Home Sweet Fishbowl*, Denise Turner states, "Pastors' wives live in a fishbowl. Some call it a house of glass, and she often resents being watched, pressured, and criticized by the parishioners who perceive it their duty to guard the pedestal position of the pastor's wife" (1982, p. 73)."

This fishbowl living can be very uncomfortable. During our first year in ministry the Lord blessed us with our second child, a little girl. There would be some Sundays when I knew I still had the smell of spit-up milk on me from the baby, and I couldn't get to the bathroom fast enough when I would hear voices coming in my direction, "Oh, there's the pastor's wife." Between trying to keep the baby quiet, chasing my two-year-old son, smiling, greeting people, looking cute, and acting spiritual, I was a basket case.

Once again I frantically searched the Scriptures for this "everybody's watching me" dilemma. God directed me to the book of Esther. Queen Esther was the wife of King Xerxes, who ruled the most powerful country in the world at that time. Her life as queen was one of high profile and also one of tremendous influence upon the king. She had replaced the former queen, Vashti, through a beauty contest (Esther 1:9). Here was the "first lady." Queen Esther was placed in a position of influence to change the course of history for herself and her people, the Jews. She took a big risk by going before the king to plead for the survival of the Jewish nation. This request could have cost her her life. Queen Esther's greatest strength was recognizing that her position as queen was God-ordained and that God was using her influence "for such a time as this." God used Queen Esther to save her people and to destroy the enemies' plan to eliminate the Jews.

A pastor's wife is not usually asked to risk her life like Esther did, although the challenging demands and daily grind of ministry are still known to be painful. The pastor's wife can use her influential position to be a great asset to her husband, but she first has to realize that she is serving alongside her husband as a calling from God. She is in this visible spot because it is a part of God's will for her life. He wants to use her in some significant way for his kingdom here on earth. The greatest asset a pastor's wife can have is to know her position (serving alongside her husband) is God-ordained. She is in God's will, and God is using her for such times as these. She has been given certain gifts and abilities for the advancement of the kingdom. Like Esther, she also has an enemy that wishes to destroy her and the people of her church. The pastor's wife can overcome the enemy as she stands on the fact that she is where God wants her, and that she will allow the Lord to use her as He sees fit.

EXPECTATIONS

When someone mentions the pastor's wife to you, doesn't it set off certain images in your mind: long dress, bun hairstyle, strong, devoted, and stoic? Within the local church the expectations of her vary from person to person. Each preconceived idea is based on one's church and cultural background.

During our first year of ministry I found myself floating around in a spiritual daze. It seemed like everyone had a separate agenda for what I was to do and to be. I actually taught Sunday school, worked in the nursery, and played the piano. Yet I heard so many voices surrounding me, telling me to do something more or something different. One Sunday when the church was pressed for a soloist I was enlisted. (They will never do that again.) I knew I had to define and understand my responsibilities. The following list helped me get this area into perspective. I realize each church is different, but I hope these thoughts will help other pastors' wives who are trying to figure out their role in their husbands' ministries:

Invest time and effort in personal spiritual training. The pastor's wife must also take time to study God's Word and show herself approved unto God (2 Timothy 2:15). This Scripture is not for just pastors, but for all believers. Your growth and relationship with God is the key to your fulfillment.

Work closely with your husband and help him to fulfill God's calling in his life. Working closely means sharing with each other and seeking to understand each other. It means spending time together in prayer for the ongoing ministry, for each other, and for the needed strength to get through a meeting, a particular situation, or a personal confrontation. Working closer is the result of seeing God work in the lives of people. This can become a great asset to any pastor.

Set both short-term and long-term goals for your family and develop creative ways to accomplish them. The pastor's wife can plan times for her family to take long vacations or short, meaningful trips that will get them away from the routine of the ministry. If left to the pastor these times will not come as often as they should, therefore a creative wife makes them happen and the entire family benefits. You should make these plans in advance so your husband can adjust his schedule.

Try to balance family time, ministry responsibilities, and personal development and improvement. You should be aware when the ministry is absorbing too much of your family's time and bring it to your husband's attention. You should also protect your husband from meaningless visits and phone calls that rob time. For example, a salesman who wants to sell something your family does not want or need or cannot afford should not be allowed to take up your husband's time. You should be aware of opportunities for your family that will allow for personal development, especially for yourself. Classes and seminars that will allow for more growth and more effectiveness should be seriously considered.

Encourage your children to love and cherish the church by speaking of it positively, even when you do not feel particularly affirmative toward the church. This includes the people, time sacrifices you and the children make, the governing boards, and the time your husband spends away from his family. Encouraging your children to appreciate and not resent the church allows them to grow up with a greater love for God, the things of God, and the people of God. Serving God has many rewards. It takes just a few minutes to reflect on the joys and speak to our children about the good things. Some of these benefits include enjoying friendships, seeing marriages saved, spending time together in God's Word, spending time together praising God, sharing love, welcoming new believers, and supporting those in pain.

Prayerfully assist your husband in evaluating the spiritual atmosphere of the church. God has given most women the ability to discern character and intent of others. The pastor's wife's ability to discern should be recognized by herself as well as her husband. It should be used for the glory of God.

Motivate other women to grow, mature, and develop. Here lies the secret in growing mature churches. Since women are discerners, influencers, and responders, they become catalysts for change. The pastor's wife is in a position to encourage women to study the Bible and grow in their faith. You do not have to be a gifted teacher or even the leader of the women's ministry. But you need to see that it gets done and be a vital part of the growth process yourself (Titus 2:4–5).

LONELINESS

Pastor's wives are some of the loneliest women in the world. The average church member simply does not want to hear about the pastor's wife's struggles. Yet she has needs, hurts, and disappointments unique to her own situation. The pastor's wife is limited as to whom she can really talk to, due in part to the fact that many problems faced by pastors' wives are complex.

I once received a phone call from a pastor's wife who discovered her husband was having an affair. I listened intently as she cried and shared her pain. She went on to say that her greatest problem was what to do in her situation. Whom could she turn to for counsel? Any decision she made regarding his affair would affect so many people, including her own children. Should she keep his affair silent so that he could maintain his career as a pastor? Should she let the affair be known, realizing it would destroy him as well as hundreds of other people?

> Most of the world's greatest souls have been lonely. Loneliness seems to be the price a saint must pay for his saintliness. The leader must be a man or woman who, while welcoming the friendship and support of all who can offer it, has sufficient inner resources to stand alone, even in the face of fierce opposition, in the discharge of his responsibilities. They must be prepared to have no one but God. (Tozer 1982, p. 145)

When women in the church have problems with the pastor, it affects their relationship with the pastor's wife. No other relationship between women puts as much emphasis on liking or disliking the mate.

The pastor's wife is often left out of casual social activities and is sometimes made to feel different. Whenever I took part in small group conversations with the women of the church I perceived that during the course of the week they were spending time together, shopping or going out for coffee. How I wished I could have joined them. But I wasn't asked. Was something wrong with me? Did they think pastors' wives didn't go shopping?

Hannah, whose story is told 1 Samuel, was a woman given to great loneliness. Her husband, Elkanah, was a wealthy, prominent man who loved her more than his other wife, Peninnah. Hannah, however, had two problems: She had no children, and she was constantly criticized by Peninnah. On one occasion Hannah had been criticized and provoked so severely she became seriously depressed. She cried constantly and refused to eat. Elkanah reminded Hannah of his great love for her and how he always gave her double portions of meat for sacrifices. Although she had all the love and devotion of her husband, Hannah still could not be comforted. Her need was greater than what her husband could meet. She needed supernatural strength and power. She needed God alone. Hannah went before the Lord in "bitterness of soul" and she poured out her grief to Him.

Many pastors' wives find themselves, at times, like Hannah, where they need to pour out their souls and it seems that even their husbands are not enough comfort. The ministry needs, personal needs, physical needs, family needs, and emotional needs seem to be overwhelming. Pastors' wives need to be able to find God in their pain. They need to retreat to that private place where they can lay out their cares and needs before God. This is also a place where crying and smeared makeup is totally acceptable.

Pastors' wives also need other female friends with whom they can share their feelings. A good starting place for developing friendships or mentoring relationships is to find other women with common interests or in a similar ministry position. Mary, the mother of our Lord, and her aunt Elizabeth developed a strong relationship based on the miraculous birth of both of their babies. Being the wife of a pastor can also make good ground for relationships with other pastors' wives. One caution though: if you both live in the same city or in close proximity to each other, it may not be wise to share church information. Many times comparisons have destroyed friendships, especially in church ministries. Develop your relationship as two pastors' wives who share some of the same pressures. Pray for each other and find the time to encourage each other often.

LACK OF PREPARATION

Most pastors' wives have not been prepared for the ministry. Many women have been told in so many ways that God called only their husbands to the ministry. The qualifications for the pastor are given up front and they are clear, but there are no spoken qualifications for his wife. She has strolled, smiling, into the church alongside her husband, only to find herself in serious spiritual combat. The recourse for some has been to lock their emotions into an "I don't care" mode and try to survive the onslaughts. Many pastors' wives become bitter due to a lack of preparation for and understanding of ministry. Not only do they find themselves resenting the ministry, but they also question if it is worth the effort. To avoid these pitfalls, how *does* the pastor's wife prepare herself for ministry?

Be sure you are a devoted believer with a sincere conviction and interest in spiritual things. When a pastor's wife is devoted to the things of God she also becomes devoted to the people of God. She is able to serve, encourage, and believe God in supernatural ways.

Ask God to give you a desire and show you how to be actively involved in the life of the church your husband will pastor. This does not mean you have to be absorbed in every activity and event in the church, but you need to realize the presence of the pastor's wife reaches so many people. You are the one who sets the standard. What you do stamps approval or disapproval on various activities. You need to be visible; however, you do not need to do everything.

Work on your "people skills." The pastor's wife should possess the ability to work with people in general. You must genuinely like people. This does not mean you have to become close friends with everyone in the church. But by your love and encouragement you are able to motivate others as well as yourself to get a job done.

Understand your calling. You must believe that God has called you to function as a pastor's wife; God has not given this potential to every woman. The sooner you accept the call from God for yourself the sooner you will be able to serve with a heart of gratitude toward Him.

Learn to be unselfish. The pastor's wife will have to make enormous sacrifices at times, yet not all the time. You should step in when you are able to support the demands of the ministry. Be aware that your husband may need you greatly on some occasions.

Learn how to communicate graciously. View yourself as a servant of God who is serious and dependable, who speaks the truth in love. Do not conduct yourself with looseness. Don't discuss others simply for the sake of gossip. When a pastor's wife discusses or talks with someone, she should not be a phony; she speaks the truth from her heart with love. She cares more of what God says about her than what people say.

These are some of the ways a woman can prepare herself to be a pastor's wife. I encourage you to seek additional sources for more help.

THE OTHER WOMAN

In every church there are people who have tremendous needs. Helping these people in their needs should be one of the goals of every church. These people can be very dangerous to the church body, however. If left alone and ignored, people with great needs can destroy a church. They have a way of knowing the other needy people within the church and will latch on to them and cause problems. They may form little groups and spend much of their time engaged in gossip and creating discord within the church.

A pastor's wife may have a keen radar to detect the needy people who come to the church, especially needy women who have great admiration for the pastor. While admiration for a member of the opposite sex can be healthy, there is a point where it leads to danger. The pastor is often viewed by many as a strong spiritual giant who is able to solve all their problems. Women who admire strong male leadership are attracted to the pastor. A pastor's wife is often aware of these attractions and knows that in the sexualized society we live in today, infidelity has become common-place. She realizes that a needy woman, better known as "the other woman," can pose a serious threat to her family as well as the church. Satan will use this kind of woman to destroy a man of God.

In the book of Judges, Delilah had but one quest in her relationship with Samson—total destruction. She had been hired to learn the secret of his great strength and how to overpower and subdue him. She was to be paid 1,100 shekels of silver (equal to thousands of dollars) for her infor-mation. In three attempts to get him to tell her the secret of his strength she used all of her feminine charm. On the second attempt, Samson revealed a lie that was closer to the truth. On the third attempt, Delilah used prodding and nagging day after day until he was tired to death and finally revealed the true secret (Judges 16:15–16). Samson had no secret magic but was supernaturally enabled by God. He became weak, not because his hair had been cut, but because he had disobeyed God regard-ing the cutting of his hair. The Philistines seized him, gouged out his eyes, bound him with bronze shackles, and made him their slave in one of their prisons. Finally, Samson became their live entertainer and performed for them at their command (16:25).

Extramarital affairs are portrayed on television and in the movies as an everyday thing. As such behavior becomes more accepted, Christians, unfortunately, are also becoming more tolerant of and vulnerable to affairs.

When a pastor has an affair and it becomes known, his entire career and life occupation can be destroyed. He also loses the trust of his wife and children. The pain inflicted upon loved ones creates deep wounds that take years to overcome. He no longer has the confidence of those who follow his leadership. Ultimately, he could lose his position as pastor.

Ministers are no less susceptible to the surging drives of sex and pas-sion than anyone else. If anything, they are more susceptible because they're exposed to every kind of emotional and spiritual sickness. Usually, needy women who turn to the pastor for help are reaching out for love and empathy.

Michele Buckingham (1986) takes the position that adultery occurs most often in marriages that are already in trouble. Infidelity intrudes when one partner attempts to fill a need for something that is missing in the marriage by finding an intimate relationship with someone else. It is suggested that couples who openly face their difficulties before they get out of control are seldom faced with this problem (Strom 1986).

Kay Marshall Strom has some suggestions for a woman (including a pastor's wife) should she suspect or find out that her husband has been unfaithful.

1. The pastor's wife should talk to her spouse. Perhaps the problem was not what she really thought it was, and through discussion of it, other needs and issues facing the marriage can surface.

2. Consult a qualified marriage counselor. Do not try to straighten out your own marriage problems. A trained counselor can serve masterfully as an objective party to the situation.

3. Don't put off dealing with the situation. The sooner the problem is dealt with, the greater the chance of saving the marriage.

4. The pastor's wife must come to terms with the way she feels. If she has strong feelings of anger and bitterness, she must deal with and express this pain in some way before she can make any clear, rational decision.

5. She must develop and utilize good communication skills, which are one of the keys to a healthy marriage. This type of communciation should take place on a regular basis.

6. She should refrain from overreacting when her husband expresses his feelings of love for her. The chances are good that he may still love her. The marriage may be in need of much healing but is not necessarily over.

7. The pastor's wife should not blame herself for her spouse's behavior. She must not feel that her reaction has caused the infidelity.

8. She must hold her unfaithful spouse accountable. His rights as a husband and father have been nullified by the adulterous affair. By virtue of his conduct he has relinquished his headship.

9. Divorce is never the automatic answer to the problem, even though Scripture permits it because of adultery. Divorce can create new problems that are even harder than the existing ones.

10. The pastor's wife should strongly consider the alternative of for-giveness before giving up completely on her marriage. Trust, once lost, is difficult to regain, but the marriage can be healed by the grace of God.

11. Many couples who have successfully worked out their marital dif-ficulties have found that the lasting results were well worth the struggle involved in reconciliation.

12. Focus on the need to forgive, because this is a biblical principle found throughout the Scriptures. When we refuse to forgive, we must understand that God will not forgive us. When we forgive one another, it frees us from bitterness and allows us to love oth-ers the way God loves us.

13. After the spouse has repented of his sin, restoration should become the objective. The past will not easily remove itself. The wound will heal, but the scar will remain. (Paraphrased from Strom 1986)

One final comment: Never use the children as a weapon against your spouse. Buckingham (1986) explains why.

> I used the children. I had no other weapon. I never confided in them, but on occasion, when I felt I was being ripped to shreds, I would say to them in his presence, If you only knew what a hypocrite your daddy is ... Instead of convicting him, my words would infuriate him. Sometimes he would leave the house, slamming the door behind him. When that happened I knew I had driven him into the arms of another woman, but the pain was so deep I seemed unable to keep from lashing out. (p. 155)

Your children are in a vulnerable situation and great care should be taken when considering life-changing situations. Remember, this does not have to be the death of your marriage.

CONCLUSION

The pastor's wife must come to know that the role she plays has its various perplexities. They are real and can be painful. Her focus, however, should be on much more than the difficulties. There is a privilege of being involved in ministry that a wise pastor's wife would not want to miss. The cure for many of her frustrations is tied into her allowing God to use her in her position as pastor's wife. No one has a greater opportunity to lead and influence others. When a pastor's wife allows God to lead her, she becomes strong, confident, and Christlike. She becomes rich in faith, patience, kindness, and love. Most of all, she reaps the greatest benefits from her growth in her own personal walk with God.

Recommended Reading

Briscoe, Jill. *There's Still a Snake in My Garden*. Wheaton, IL: Victor Books, 1990.

An honest, warm, funny, and realistic book as Jill shares her faith, her experiences as a mother of lively teenagers, her adjustments to a new culture (the United States), and her role as pastor's wife.

Briscoe, Jill; Laurie Katz McIntyre; Beth Seversen. *Designing Effective Women's Ministries*. Grand Rapids: Zondervan, 1995.

A comprehensive guide to reaching, teaching, and training women in the local church.

Buckingham, Michele. *Help! I'm a Pastor's Wife*. Altamonte Springs, FL: Creation House, 1986.

The voices of thirty wives who show what it is really like to be married to a pastor—and don't leave anything out. They speak candidly and movingly from their roles as wives, mothers, women, and leaders.

Dugan, Lynne. *Heart to Heart with Pastors' Wives*. Ventura, CA: Regal Books, 1994.

One of the best books for helping pastors' wives meet today's issues with confidence and clarity.

Heald, Cynthia. *Becoming a Women of Excellence*. Colorado Springs: NavPress, 1986.

A book that strikes at the heart of what the Bible says about becoming a godly woman. It includes eleven lessons for personal Bible study.

"Just Between Us." Brookfield, WI: Telling the Truth Media Ministries.

A timely magazine for ministry wives. Articles deal with the struggles of the ministry faced by women. (Write P.O. Box 1412, Brookfield, WI 53008–1412, for a subscription.)

Porter, Carol, and Mike Hamel. *Women's Ministry Handbook*. Wheaton, IL: Victor Books, 1992.

A comprehensive guide to reaching, teaching, and training women in the local church.

Sanders, J. Oswald. *Spiritual Leadership*. Chicago: Moody Press, 1986.

A book not only for pastors and Christian workers, but for anyone—including pastors' wives—who want to know something about God's leadership in their own lives.

Strom, Kay Marshall. *Helping Women in Crisis*. Grand Rapids: Zondervan, 1986.

A resource for people-helpers who want to be ready when a woman confides that she is facing a crisis. The author deals with ten common crisis situations, including child abuse, incest, infidelity, rape, and attempted suicide.

Tucker, Ruth A. *Private Lives of Pastors' Wives*. Grand Rapids: Zondervan, 1993.

Stories of fourteen women, married to men well-known in church history, and how they have played an essential role in the ministry of the church. This book appreciates the special calling of pastors' wives.

Whiteman, Thomas A., and Randy Petersen. *Becoming Your Own Best Friend*. Nashville: Thomas Nelson, 1994.

A book about loving, affirming, and supporting yourself that also helps you to see yourself the way God sees you.

ℛeferences

Briscoe, Jill. 1990. *There's still a snake in my garden*. Wheaton, IL: Victor Books.

Buckingham, M. 1986. *Help! I'm a pastor's wife*. Altamonte Springs, FL: Creation House.

1984. *The holy Bible: New international version*. Grand Rapids: Zondervan.

Strom, K. M. 1986. *Helping women in crisis*. Grand Rapids: Zondervan.

Tozer, A. 1982. *The pursuit of God*. Camp Hill, PA: Christian Publications.

Turner, D. 1982. *Home sweet fishbowl*. Waco, TX: Word Books.

Deneese L. Jones

Meeting the Faith Challenge of Rearing Our Sons and Daughters

DENEESE L. JONES is an Assistant Professor at the University of Kentucky in Lexington. Born and raised in Dallas, Texas, she received a bachelor of science degree in elementary education from Texas Women's University, a master's degree in education and a Ph.D. in curriculum and instruction from Texas A&M University. She resides in Lexington, Kentucky, with her husband, Steve, and their two daughters, Stephanie and Monica. Deneese attends the First Church of God in Lexington and serves as chair of the Board of Christian Education, as superintendent of the Sunday school, as a representative on the Church Council, and as Spiritual Life director.

Chapter 7

Deneese L. Jones

Meeting the Faith Challenge of Rearing Our Sons and Daughters

Many nights I prayed: "Lord, help me to build them up to be all that You designed them to be."

That day of reconciliation for me seems just like yesterday, although it has really been more than seventeen years. My then-three-year-old marriage was in the midst of difficulties as my husband and I struggled to find our purpose in life. We had a three-month-old daughter who seemed to be the joy in our lives. Yet, somehow, I felt empty and incomplete. As a twenty-four-year-old, unemployed public school teacher with a strong desire to make a difference in this world, I had been worrying a lot. We had just moved back to Texas from California where my husband had recently been discharged from the Navy. Money was tight. We had a tiny, cheap student apartment, and I had thirty cents in my purse without any backup in the bank.

On this memorable evening, I sat at the table in the dining room of people that I hardly knew as they attempted to share the gospel through Scripture readings to another young woman who seemed totally uninterested. As I sat listening and reading from the little New Testament that I kept in my purse, I felt as though a heavy weight was pressing against my heart. I pulled my nursing daughter closer to my chest and swallowed hard as I tried to absorb the words that were being spoken and the Scripture passages that were being read. They seemed hauntingly harsh, but I could not escape the truth that surrounded me. Someone read, " ... if the righteous scarcely be saved, where will the ungodly stand ..." Those words hit me like a ton of bricks. Suddenly, I saw myself as I envisioned God must see me and I did not like what I saw. The earth seemed to shift under my feet, but the Scriptures drew me in deeper.

A powerful force seemed to be guiding me as I clung helplessly to the now-sleeping child who lay at my bosom. The sermon that I heard in the discussion and admonitions that evening was unlike any that I had ever known. It seemed to be a sermon given to me and me only, directly from God. For the first time in my life, I knew that if I did not accept the Lord as my personal Savior, my life was headed toward a dead end. As I spoke the words, " ... excuse me, ... but I need to ask Jesus to come into my life, now ...," little did I know that I was taking the first step toward replacing my fears with faith. I was breaking a negative cycle that had so engulfed me that I could not see life's beauty. It was the beginning of my realiza-tion that our thoughts create our reality because of the power of God's Holy Spirit who teaches us when we are open and teachable.

As the people in that room rejoiced aloud, I felt lighter and a bit freer. A tremendous weight seemed to have been lifted from my heart. But beyond these feelings, there was a refreshing sense of trustworthiness in God and His Word. Instead of mourning the things that I felt were miss-ing in my life, I began counting my many blessings. As I looked across the room at a husband who I knew loved me, I paused to silently give thanks for my life, my healthy child, and the roof that was being provided over my head. Even in the bewildered eyes of my spouse I could see nothing but desire for a new hope.

In the weeks, months, and years to come, the women sitting around this table and others from this unique congregation became key instru-ments in the life of my family. They, along with their empowered African-American Christian men, nurtured me, encouraged me, admonished me, and disciplined me by their words and deeds. They taught me a love for God's Word, His people, and His service, but most importantly, they taught me—by precept and example—the power of faith. The positive, life-affirming thoughts inspired by the Scriptures changed me. They served to lift my faith and equip me. Now I was focused on the beauty of a life in God, on my God-given talents and gifts, and the power of God within me. I began to step into the world expecting good things to happen. I learned that without faith it is impossible to please God.

FAITH FOR POSITIVE CHANGE

As the mother of two daughters, I have experienced that having this kind of faith means being active, not sitting back bemoaning life and waiting for change. It means loving and believing in ourselves and using the transforming power of God's Holy Spirit to move our lives and the lives of our children forward. The truth seems simple, but living it is not so simple. As time has gone by, I have seen the work of the Holy Spirit in my life as well as His saving grace in my husband and my two daughters. Times have been difficult financially, physically, mentally, and spiritually, but faith in God has begun a revolution in my life.

This chapter is meant to encourage African-American women to cultivate their personal faith in God as they undertake the difficult task of child rearing. Faith will allow us to hold a positive vision of what we want for ourselves and for our children and to put the energy behind that vision to make it a reality. Our enemy is not the system or those who foster it. Our enemy is fear: fear that blinds us to truth, fear that keeps us bitter with anger, and fear that leaves us without power. This is the kind of fear that keeps us focused on what we do not want rather than on what we need to lead us and our families toward a harmonious, abundant way of life as promised by Jesus Christ.

Christian mothers are never alone. We must realize that in Christ we have everything we need to overcome any of life's challenges. There may have been countless times when we have felt the earth shake beneath us or the weight of life pressing in on us. This is happening to African-American people today and to people throughout the world. It is one of the many ways in which the Holy Spirit speaks to us and encourages us to change. There are times when it seems as if our face must hit the ground before we listen to and heed heavenly wisdom.

Traditionally, as African-Americans, we are a spiritual people. I believe that current hard times are awakening us to a new reality and a reaffirmation of purpose. It is important to remember that faith played a large part in the lives of our ancestors and the legacy which they have left us. We must continue to be champions of faith—both when it's easy and when we are in crisis. It is certain that life will bring sorrow, broken hearts, health problems, financial difficulties, and much, much more. But our life with the Lord will bring dependence, maturity, refreshment, refuge, redemption, righteous judgment, and many other rewards. In addition, He will restore our hearts, minds, and souls. Let us keep our expectations and our visions high as we endeavor to meet the challenge of rearing our sons and daughters of color.

Whatever we focus on is what we are moving toward. By directing our minds, we direct our lives. The Lord wishes to give us life in abundance and we must remember that truth. His name is Wonderful, Jesus my Lord. His name is full of wonder, miracles, excitement, fulfillment, peace, and joy. There is something about that name! Our thoughts must be positive—always looking for the good and wonderfulness of the Lord. He is Almighty God who parted the Red Sea, raised Lazareth from the dead, and lives today in our hearts, wanting to be a miracle in our lives and the lives of our children. Today is ordained by God for you to draw near to Him and allow Him to be near to you in child rearing.

THE LEGACY OF AFRICAN-AMERICAN MOTHERHOOD

> I can see no reason why the mother who produces the children should have less say in their upbringing than the man whose role is only that of initiator. And, after the fertilization for nine months, the period of gestation goes on inside the woman. And this role is extremely crucial, in fact it is the most crucial factor in the reproduction of the species and the maintenance of society. But for some reason this most crucial work performed by woman is the basis for woman's position of inferiority. And if anything was rational, this should be the basis for the respect of woman. (Cleaver 1971, p. 144)

Motherhood

There was a time when motherhood had a place of honor in this country. A national day honoring mothers was even established as the bearing of children was a woman's highest aspiration. But times have changed, and motherhood has become one of the victims of changing times. The women's movement seems to have made motherhood out to be a tool of sexist oppression. And while there are some African-American women who have become disenchanted with the maternal role, the pervasiveness and the magnitude of their rejection of motherhood differs significantly from that of Anglo women. In part, they differ because of the unique position they hold as caretakers of the African-American race. To understand the reasons why this is so, we must look to the past.

African Mothers

Although some people assume that motherhood became important for African-American women during the slave era, there are indications that the maternal role was also emphasized strongly by African women. The available historical evidence reveals that antedating the slave experience, Black women in Africa had an unbreakable bond with their children. In fact, the African social structure patterned the mother's attitude toward her child. Tribal customs emphasized the importance of the maternal role in the social organization of the group and certain cultural artifacts, such as art, conveyed the importance of the place of motherhood. Such symbolic information indicates a concern for the continuity of life during the earliest times. In fact, in ancient African societies, children were carefully protected by the extended family system and, during their formative years, children began to learn their role requirements and responsibilities. Moreover, African society placed a high esteem on the mother's role as child bearer and guardian of the tribal legacy (Murdock 1959).

Slave Mothers

When the African mother arrived on this continent in chains, there were not any ceremonies to commemorate her role as a mother. Her task was primarily to labor in the fields of the plantation with the men. Producing children was important only in that they constituted future slaves or capital for the slave-holding class. Hence, the development of maternal feelings were dependent now on physiological and emotional responses of mother to child rather than cultural mores and tribal customs. Yet, none of the brutalities suffered or the humiliations encountered could destroy the fundamental impulses and instinctive maternal feelings a mother had toward her child.

The slave mother's burden began in childbearing. Other slave women served as midwives for the delivery of her child. The slave owners believed that slave women needed very little care during this period, which may partly account for the high rate of infant mortality. After bearing her child, the slave mother was unable to care for it because of her obligations as a worker (Stampp 1956). Older extended family members cared for the child during the long days while the mother worked in the fields. Thus, slave children, in contrast to their African counterparts, did not have a protected childhood. By the time the children reached puberty, they could be taken away from their mothers and sold on the auction block. This meant that African-American children were thrust into adulthood and the continuation of their involuntary servitude (Bontemps 1969).

It was this practice of selling away their children that provoked the most courageous acts of African-American mothers. The heroic acts of the slave mother are legendary. Frederick Douglass, the great abolitionist, recounts how his mother walked twelve miles to see him and had to return the same distance before the morning sunrise (Quarles 1960). Even the children of the slave master received the devotion of the African-American mother. She attended her mistress during pregnancy and took care of the infant as soon as it was born. Frequently she, in place of the mother, nursed and weaned the child. If the child was female, the African-American woman slave was never separated from the child until she was an adult (Frazier 1966).

African-American mothers who were slaves seized upon any opportunity they had to be with their children and to give them love and affection. After a hard day's labor in the field, they could find warmth and sympathy among their children and their kinfolk. It was in this environment that the African-American mother could express her tender feelings and kindly impulses. Booker T. Washington writes that one of his earliest recollections is that of his mother cooking chicken late at night and awakening her children for the purpose of feeding them (Frazier 1966).

To the contrary, the practice of using African-American male slaves as breeding instruments meant that their role was biological only. The slave father, if present, had little authority. His function was as a field worker or a house servant. Many times the father's name was not indicated on plantation birth records; the children were listed as belonging to the mother, and whatever authority the mother did not have belonged to the slave master (Davie 1949). Consequently, the slave mother was the most consistent person in the young child's life. Within this environment, she played a strategic role. African-American women provided all the vital functions in the absence of a consistent husband/father figure and all the child's familial ties were traced to the mother. Finally, although motherhood was clothed in scant dignity due to the vicissitudes of slavery, the African-American mother represented the highest ideals of motherhood in any culture.

Post-Slavery Motherhood

After the legal demise of slavery, African-American women were still faced with the challenges of motherhood. The cumulative effects of slavery had left the African-American family in disarray. Fathers had been sold away from their families, paternity was sometimes unknown, and countless numbers of children had Anglo slave masters as unacknowledged fathers. These factors, along with the problems of Reconstruction, left many African-American mothers with unilateral responsibility for the care of their children (Staples 1971).

But African-American women met their maternal responsibilities faithfully. They tilled the land and provided subsistence for themselves and their children. One anthropologist who studied the conditions of life in the African-American community reported that

> Even where husband and wife share responsibility for maintaining and directing the family, the woman is likely to contribute the larger share of the income and to assume the larger share of the family responsibility. The economic disparity is most evident in town, where employment is so much more available to the women than to the men.... In many cases the woman is the sole breadwinner. (Powdermaker 1939, p. 145)

Although she faced problems maintaining her family in the rural South, the African-American woman supposedly encountered greater and different problems when she moved to the city. Because of the different environment, the reduced effectiveness of kinship ties, and her greater economic dependency on public institutions, she lost control of her children. Many African-American women had to seek work outside the home, leaving their children without parental supervision. The children in some of these families filled the ranks of juvenile delinquents. Women who did not work were forced to turn to public assistance agencies to help support their families (Frazier 1966).

African-American women may be the only group that ever had to rear children and support them too. Yet for generations they have reared their children effectively, in spite of many hardships. Although having children has never been as simple for African-American women, children have traditionally been regarded as a value in themselves, whether they were economic assets or liabilities. In America today, motherhood is still of great importance to African-American women.

FAITH FOR THE CHALLENGE FROM INFANTS TO TEENS

"Train a child in the way he should go, and when he is old he will not turn from it" (Proverbs 22:6). At the heart of each child is a prayer, "Please take time to know me. I am different from anyone else. My tenderness of heart, my likes, my dislikes, and my sensitivities are different from my brothers and sisters." The key verse for this section uses the word "train." In Hebrew, this word originally referred to the palate (the roof of the mouth) and to the gums. In Bible times, the midwife would stick her fingers into a sweet substance and place her fingers into the infant's mouth, creating a sucking desire in the child. The child would then be delicately given to the mother, whereby the child would start nursing. This was the earliest form of "training." The age of the child mentioned in Proverbs can fall between a newborn and a person who is of marrying age.

The second part of this verse says, "when he is old he will not depart from it." At first, I thought this meant an older person who had become wayward yet finally returned to the Lord. Little did I know that this word "old" meant "bearded" or "chin." Solomon is talking about a young man who begins to grow a beard when he approaches maturity. For some it might be in junior high and for others it might be college. The concept is that we, as African-American parents, are charged to continue training our children as long as they are under our care. For me, as a young mother and novice Christian, the Word of God was what I learned to cling to in difficult times and in times of great joy. From it I was able to continue the process of the development of faith. Certainly it was during these earlier years of new adjustments and additional stress that I began to really study the Scriptures and my faith was tested.

Harried Times

Do you have the type of home where nothing seems to get done? Where each room would take a bulldozer just to clean up the mess? Do you rush around all day or after work never completing any one job, or if you do complete a task, is there a little one behind you, pulling and messing everything up again? There is not one mother alive who has not experienced these feelings! In reading Proverbs 3:6 (KJV), "In all your ways acknowledge him, and he will direct your paths," young mothers would benefit from the act of falling to their knees and praying, "Please God, direct my path. I acknowledge You to help me, Lord. I'm going to allow

You to lead me and not lead myself in my power. I want your power and direction. Lord, I'm tired. I'm on overload with a husband, a job, a home, and children. I do not have time left over for me or anyone else. I can't even do any of us justice. Please help me to put it all together and make it work to glorify You and Your children. Amen."

The Lord will honor your prayer and the faith with which you pray. He can make a change but individual mothers must make changes, too. I suggest that you begin a program in which you can commit fifteen minutes (at least) per day to a quiet time of prayer, reading the Bible, and meditation with the Lord. If necessary, get up earlier each morning while the house is quiet and talk to the Lord, read His Word and pray. God will redeem your time with him. As you learn better how to lean on the Savior, the cloud of overload and stress can be lifted. Expect dramatic changes for a newer direction. When we learn to look to God for help and comfort in all the ways of our life—our families, our home, our finances, our commitments, and our careers—God's promise to us is that He will direct our path.

The Power of Prayer

> I got up early one morning and rushed into the day;
> I had so much to accomplish that I did not have time to pray.
> Problems just tumbled about me, and heavier came each task.
> "Why doesn't God help me?" I wondered. He answered, "You didn't ask."
> I wanted to see joy and beauty, but the day toiled on, gray and bleak;
> I wondered why God did not show me. He said, "But you did not seek."
> I tried to come into God's presence; I used all my keys at the lock.
> God gently and lovingly chided, "My child, you did not knock."
> I woke up early this morning, and paused before entering the day;
> I had so much to accomplish that I had to take time to pray.

Author unknown

The development of our faith will demonstrate God's examples and principles to our children. The story is told of a young mother who was having a talk with her young son as they were preparing dinner together. The mother was telling the boy what Christians should be like and how they should act. When the mother had finished describing the attributes of a Christian, the young boy asked a stunning question: "Mom, have I ever seen a Christian?" The mother was aghast. What kind of an example am I? she thought. How would you feel if your child asked you the same question? The writer of Psalm 78 reminds us that there are some patterns for parenting—patterns that we can use to help our children know the things of God and to realize that we are God's children:

- Tell the next generation the praiseworthy deeds of the Lord (Psalm 78:4).
- Teach your children the statutes and laws of God (Psalm 78:5).

Only then will our children see by our words and examples that we are Christians.

Discipline and Nurturing

With all the media attention given to child abuse, many Christian parents become confused regarding discipline. The book of Proverbs, fortunately, contains some specific verses which offer good biblical principles for rearing children. In this game of tug and war, the natural tendency is to throw in the towel and give up. Far too often, African-American mothers have given up the task of gently but firmly shaping their child's will, much as a trainer of an aggressive animal or as the potter would shape a piece of clay.

James Dobson, in his book *The Strong-Willed Child*, gives some insight into this area as he discusses the contest of the wills between generations. He believes the parental response is very important. When a child behaves in ways that are disrespectful or harmful to self or others, the hidden purpose is often to verify the stability of the boundaries. This testing has much the same function as a policeman who turns doorknobs at places of business after dark. Though he tries to open doors, he hopes they are locked and secure. Likewise, children who assault the loving authority of their parents are greatly reassured when their leadership holds firm and confident. Children find their greatest security in a structured environment where the rights of other people (and their own) are protected by definite boundaries.

It takes a special kind of mother with godly wisdom to provide this kind of balance. How can a novice mother accomplish this?

1. We must note the difference between abuse and discipline. Proverbs 13:14 tells us that if we truly love our children, we will discipline them diligently. Abuse is unfair, extreme, and degrading. This action does not grow out of love, but from hate. Abuse leads to a poor self-image that will often last a lifetime. Discipline, on the other hand, upholds the child's worth and is fair and fitting for the infraction.

2. It is important that the child understands the discipline. When we disciplined our children, we spent some time with them talking about what they had done and made sure they understood what the infraction was. The object of these discussions was to make our children know the importance of immediate obedience. We learned that each child was different, so the way we approached them would be through knowledge of that child. There were many times when a spanking was applied to the legs or beefy part of the buttocks, and they did hurt. This was not done in anger, but always in stern, tough love. One of the main purposes of this discipline was to have the children remember that they are responsible for their actions and must be accountable for their behavior.

3. There is a need to shape and not crush a child's spirit. You can look into the eyes of children around you to see those who are being crushed and those being shaped. Our youngest daughter was a strong-willed and stubborn child. She knew what she wanted and did not have a problem demonstrating that desire—even if it meant hitting another child or screaming to get her wishes fulfilled. Today, as a young woman, she still knows what she wants, but in an assertive manner, she has channeled her energies into better ways of demonstrating it. My goal as a mother was to build her up with solid direction and self-assurance that would see her throughout a lifetime. The child who is shaped will have a love for life, but a crushed spirit produces a child without any hope for the future.

4. We must always keep balance in our lives with God as a focus. We do not want to be so rigid that we do not allow our children to make mistakes, or so loose that children are bouncing off the walls trying to find their boundaries. Children must know where the boundaries are and what the consequences are if they choose to go beyond these limits. In Scripture we read about physical discipline, such as using the rod. "Folly is bound up in the heart of a child; but the rod of discipline will drive it far from him" (Proverbs 22:15).

5. We must strive to be consistent in our approach to guiding and directing our children. Make sure that youngsters have a clear understanding of the rules. Discipline in private; if you're in a public setting, wait until you can be alone. Be firm in your discipline, but assure your child of your love and concern. As I look back over those training years, I am reminded of the many mistakes we made. But when mistakes were made, we were the first to admit them to our children. Even when the mark is occasionally missed, remember that you are still moving in a proper direction. Be encouraged. Your children want to know their boundaries. There is self-assurance in knowing.

God spoke through Moses and said, "These commandments that I give you today are to be upon your hearts. Impress them on your children. Talk about them when you sit at home and when you walk along the road, when you lie down and when you get up" (Deuteronomy 6:6–7). As parents, we are to reflect God to our children. As they look into our faces, and our lives, they are to see a man or woman of godly desires and actions. In America today, we earnestly need more African-American parents who will stand up and do the right thing. Christian growth is a daily process of taking off the old self of attitudes, beliefs, and behaviors which reflect the dark side of our nature (sin) and changing to those characteristics that reflect the presence of Christ in our lives. The only way to grow and succeed is by being renewed in the spirit of our mind (Ephesians 4:2–24).

These are some helpful ways in which we as Christian African-American women can rear and nurture our young children:

- Teach them to pray from the moment they learn to speak.
- Set examples by praying aloud for them and with them.
- Require children to ask God's blessing on their food or offer them an opportunity to ask God's blessing on the food for everyone seated at the table.
- Read Bible stories to them daily and discuss how this information relates to their real-life habits.
- Teach children and young people responsibility by allowing them to help (selecting a menu, shopping for food, preparing food, setting the table, serving food, removing the dishes when the family is finished eating, and cleaning the dishes).
- Develop a consistent time of family prayer or study that is relevant to things in their everyday lives.
- Develop a conscience in young children by making them accountable for their actions and behaviors.
- Take them to Sunday school and church regularly and let them see your consistent participation as well.
- Talk to your children about spiritual things.
- Establish guidelines and principles for courtship/dating early in their young lives and remind them of these periodically. (In our

home it was established that as saved young women they would not be allowed to date unsaved young men. This was taught early and has never created a problem for us—even in the dating years).

- Write your teenage child(ren) a note letting them know how much you love them. Give a few specific traits you like about them.
- Make a point to spend quality one-on-one time with each of your children.
- Teach them that the uniqueness of their heritage is a gift from God.
- Instill Black pride, self-confidence, and appropriate assertiveness by sharing traditional cultures, Black heroes and heroines, and techniques essential for successful adaptation in the modern world (teaching our children strategies to deal with racism and the negative feelings about being Black).

In these ways, they can begin to know what a Christian is, because they would have known you—a reflector of God's grace.

Finally, note that we are to train a child in His way—not our ways, our plans, our ideas. It is important to see that the verse in Proverbs is not a guarantee to parents that rearing a child in God's way means they will return back again when they are old. I honestly do not believe this is the proper principle for us as African-American mothers.

When we train our children according to "His way"—the way in which the child has been created by God—we approach each child differently. We do not compare them one to another. Each child is uniquely made. Mothers of infants, toddlers, young children, and teens should learn to design different approaches for each child. My older daughter is certainly not like her younger sister, even though they are only fifteen months apart in age. I believe that each child had her own bent and was already established when God placed her in our family. It takes wisdom, however, that can only come from God, to understand who they are and to be an encouragement to them. Many nights I prayed: "Lord, help me to build them up to be all that You designed them to be."

FAITH AND GROWTH OVER THE YEARS

"Then they can train the younger women to love their husbands and children" (Titus 2:4). When I was younger, I wanted to cross Titus 2:4 out of the Bible. I thought, I will never be an older woman! Today I consider it a privilege to be an older woman. To have the opportunity to teach another is an honor. It does not matter how old we are; we will always be older to someone. I have many times overheard my older daughter teaching her younger sister to play a game, read a book, or count her money. The experience has been interesting to observe as they learn to depend on each other.

I have learned much from other women. Those women in my early Christian experiences, who were mentioned previously, have been a beautiful example to me. I watched how they loved their husbands with a soft spirit. And I thank them today for the way they reared such fine sons and daughters as examples of what needs to be done and effective ways of doing this. Actually, most of what I am today I learned from the older women in my life. It's now my joy to teach those very things to other women God puts before me.

"Sons are a heritage from the LORD, children a reward from him. Like arrows in the hands of a warrior are sons born in one's youth" (Psalms 127:3–4). In the book of Psalms, verses 127:1–128:4 provide an overview of what it takes to make and develop a healthy family. We first must examine the foundation of the home: "Unless the LORD builds the house, its builders labor in vain. Unless the LORD watches over the city, the watchmen stand guard in vain" (v. 1). The protective wall surrounding a city was the very first thing to be constructed when a new city was built. The people of the Old Testament knew they needed protection from the enemy, but they were also smart enough to know that walls could be climbed over, knocked down, or broken apart. Ultimately, the people knew that their real security was the Lord guarding the city.

Today, we must return to that faith in the Lord if we are going to be able to withstand the destruction of our fortifying "walls"—our families. In an effort to provide all of the material things desired for our children, we rise early and retire late. But as in Psalm 127:2, we find this is futile. Our faith must be that the Lord has His hand over our families. Our job is to rear them according to His Word for their lives. In 127:3 it says, "Children are a reward [gift]" from the Lord. In the Hebrew, "gift" means "property," "a possession." Truly, God has loaned us His property or possessions to care for and to enjoy for a certain period of time. As we think about growing vegetables, we cultivate the soil, sow seeds, water, fertilize, weed, and prune; in like manner, rearing children takes a lot of time, care, nurture, and cultivation. We cannot neglect these responsibilities if we are going to produce good African-American fruit. Left to itself, the garden—and our children—will be overgrown with weeds.

Moving on to Psalm 127:4, we see a picture of how to handle our children. They are compared to arrows in the hand of a warrior. Skill in handling an arrow is vital. Wise parents will know their children, understand them, and examine them before they shoot them into the world. In the last section of this passage, Psalm 128:1–3, we dwell upon the importance of the Lord's presence in the home.

- The Lord is central to a home's happiness (v. 2).
- Through the Lord, wives and/or mothers will be a source of beauty and life to the home (v. 3).
- Through the Lord, children will flourish like olive trees, which generously provide food, oil, and shelter for others (v. 3).

CONCLUSION

Each day that I am in God's Word, I better understand what the fullness of God is all about and some basic principles for praying for our own family. Oh, how we need families where people really love each other. We see so much evil that originates from the family. African-American women need to ask God to protect their families from evil and put a big hedge of protection around each member. Continually, we must be on guard for the lion that tries to enter and devour members of our families.

Today, with the lack of commitment, lack of faith, lack of life in relationships, we must pray that families will begin to grasp the vastness of Christ's love for them individually and collectively. We cannot comprehend this love that goes beyond our knowledge. But with a great leap of faith, we believe and live the gospel message first within our own life and then share this love with our family members. "By wisdom a house is built, and through understanding it is established; through knowledge its rooms are filled with rare and beautiful treasures" (Proverbs 24:3–4). I will pray for you and your family that, as an African-American woman, you may grasp these principles and that your rooms will be filled with the rare and beautiful treasures called children.

References

Cleaver, K. 1971. The joy and pain of motherhood. *Black Scholar* 16 (7): 40–48.

Bontemps, A. 1969. *Great slave narratives*. Boston: Beacon.

Davie, M. 1949. *Negroes in American society*. New York: McGraw-Hill.

Dobson, J. 1985. *The strong-willed child*. Wheaton, IL: Tyndale House.

Frazier, E. F. 1966. *The Negro family in the United States*. Rev. ed. Chicago: University of Chicago Press.

Murdock, G. P. 1959. *Africa: Its people and their culture*. New York: McGraw-Hill.

1984. *The holy Bible: New international version*. Grand Rapids: Zondervan.

Powdermaker, H. 1939. *After freedom: A cultural study in the Deep South*. New York: Viking Press.

Quarles, G. 1960. *Narrative of the life of Frederick Douglass, an American slave*. Cambridge, MA: Harvard University Press.

Stampp, K. 1956. *The peculiar institution*. New York: Vintage.

Staples, R. 1971. *The Black family: Essays and studies*. Belmont, CA: Wadsworth.

PART 3

LIVING
ALONE

Jacqueline Tilles

Singleness and the African-American Woman

JACQUELINE TILLES is a Professor in the College of Education at Wayne State University in Detroit, Michigan. Born and raised in Detroit, she has a bachelor of science degree in elementary education and a master of education degree in English. She has a specialist degree from Hunter College in New York City and a Ph.D. from the University of Michigan in Ann Arbor. She is the founder of Christ the Lord Christian Church in Grosse Pointe Park, Michigan, and the founder of the citywide Christ the Lord Christian Bible Study for Detroit and Grosse Pointe Park. She is a national speaker at Christian conferences and at academic institutions.

Chapter 8

Jacqueline Tilles

Singleness and the African-American Woman

For in him dwelleth all the fullness of the Godhead bodily. And ye are complete in Him, which is the head of all principality and power. (Colossians 2:9–10)

So many things in life come in twos—two eyes, two ears, two lips, two arms, two parents, two sets of grandparents, American History I and American History II, Algebra I and Algebra II. Twoness seems to pervade our lives so much so that oneness, aloneness, and singleness seem quite strange. The media certainly try to make us believe in this strangeness, for they constantly write about "the hottest couples," famous celebrity twosomes, and eligible bachelors who are not content—but who are on the lookout for women who will dispel their singleness.

Rare indeed (and perhaps nonexistent) are the articles, television shows, or videos about the joys of oneness, aloneness, or singleness.

In fact, singleness is often viewed as a kind of modern-day curse that leaves feelings of loneliness, rejection, lovelessness, and a longing for sexual intimacy in its wake. Even the Bible, that timeless book of practical wisdom, says that "it is not good that the man should be alone" (Genesis 2:18). Statistics tell us, however, that in spite of all of this "twosome" encouragement, "currently, only twenty-two percent of young black women marry" (Reynolds 1994). Statistics also tell us that "black women out-pace black men educationally; for every one hundred black women who complete their college education only sixty-seven black men get college degrees" (Reynolds 1994). Such educated women are reluctant to marry beneath their status. Statistics further reveal that "today 500,000 black males inhabit U.S. prisons, further depleting the availability of young marriageable males" (Reynolds 1994). All of this suggests that most single African-American women will either remain single for the rest of their lives, become involved in occasional sexual liaisons, or "shack up" with live-in companions in order to satisfy their longing for companionship, love, sex, and intimacy.

Since Jesus clearly prohibits such behavior by those who follow Him, the question arises, What is a single, African-American woman who loves Jesus to do? On the one hand, the Bible tells her to "flee fornication" (1 Corinthians 6:18), to "be content" (Hebrews 13:5), and to "be holy" (1 Peter 1:15). On the other hand, her inner desires tell her that she needs a man.

This chapter deals with some of the emotional and practical dilemmas faced by the single, never-married African-American woman who wants to please the Lord—dilemmas involving loneliness, self-image, love, and sex.

LONELINESS

The famous author Thomas Wolfe has said, "Loneliness, far from being a rare and curious phenomenon peculiar to myself and a few other solitary men, is the central and inevitable fact of human existence" (Wirt & Beckstrom 1974). The psychologist Erich Fromm states that "the deepest need of man is the need to overcome his separateness, to leave the prison of his aloneness" (Wirt & Beckstrom 1974). A study conducted by Siminaur and Carroll, entitled *Singles: The New Americans,* revealed that the most pervasive problem faced by singles is the problem of loneliness (Koons & Anthony 1991).

Loneliness is a feeling of unhappiness, desolation, or depression because of one's aloneness. Loneliness is a feeling of unconnectedness *to* and isolation *from* the people with whom one may be surrounded. Loneliness is a longing to link one's heart with the heart of another. Loneliness is the inward sense that no one on earth really cares. A person may be alone and feel lonely. A person may be with other people and feel lonely. A person may be married and feel lonely. In each instance, loneliness occurs because of a lack of loving connectedness to other people.

Feelings of loneliness often arise at night when the single person would like to share her day with someone, talk through some problem, delight in some special joy, or simply cuddle up with someone and be loved. But there is no one with whom to share, thus, loneliness descends upon the soul.

Feelings of loneliness sometimes appear on birthdays, holidays, and at other times when couples, families, or groups get together and enjoy each other. Feelings of loneliness often occur at unexpected times, while sitting alone in a restaurant, while walking alone at a mall, while on a picnic surrounded by many couples, while working at your job, while sitting in church, or when listening to an innocent remark by a friend.

Carole Greene (1985) describes this unexpected way in which loneliness descends in her poem "The Circle":

It happened at a party, Lord,
an outdoor party,
not so different perhaps from that long ago wedding
at Cana.

They formed a circle,
all the married ones,
and somehow forgot to include me.
Immediately this became for me
a powerful symbol
of so much that has happened in my life.
I felt rage, bitterness,
and—yes, Lord—hatred.

One single once told me that being alone on special days was like being locked in a closet: "You feel dark and isolated, and yet you know that somewhere beyond your closet there is light and activity, fun and fellowship, but you can't quite get to it all. So you settle down in your dark closet and you get busy, or you sleep, or you walk, or you curse, or you cry."

Another single once described her loneliness this way: "I feel like a flower that no one wants to pick. *I* know *I'm* beautiful and fragrant, but no one else knows, and no one even wants to know. When I get that feeling of unbelievable sadness, I know that I am lonely."

When loneliness descends, it often produces feelings of sadness, grief, anger, depression, bitterness, rage, or some combination of these. Loneliness, for some singles, is an on-again, off-again emotion. Loneliness, for other singles, is a constant, unending state of being. When these strong emotions arise, we seek solutions: something (or someone) to heal the loneliness. Sadly, many of the solutions that we seek fail to really eliminate the loneliness. Thus, they might be described as false solutions.

False Solutions

Women who are lonely very often try to eliminate (or at least mitigate) the feeling in ways that are less than helpful. At times the lonely person will simply *pretend*. She will tell herself that things are fine, that there is no problem, and that she has a full life. Despite such thinking, she often begins to work longer hours, take on more responsibilities, become involved in more activities, all in an attempt to manage the loneliness that she pretends is not there.

Often the lonely person will *eat* and *eat* and *eat* in order to try to feel better. Food becomes a salve for wounded feelings, or it becomes a reward that says, "You are worthy. You are just fine." At times the lonely person will sleep, watch TV excessively, drink, or use drugs in an attempt to *escape* the pain of loneliness. Women who call themselves Christians are not immune to such behaviors and often permit loneliness to drive them into these self-destructive habits.

Spending is sometimes used as a way of handling loneliness. A woman subconsciously thinks: "If I can buy enough clothes, enough furniture, a sharp enough car, or enough 'adult toys,' I can build enough happiness into my soul to push the loneliness away."

Travel is another false solution to loneliness. A cruise to the Bahamas, frequent trips to New York, a tour of the Southwest, fifteen days in Europe, these will help me meet new friends and perhaps even the man of my dreams. It will also help me to get away from my stifling loneliness.

Frequenting bars and clubs is often used as an antidote for loneliness. "This puts you in touch with exciting people, people with good jobs, prestige, and connections. They may not be Christians, but they're fun. And when I'm with them, I forget about my loneliness," says one single, churchgoing woman.

Casual sex is also used a solution to loneliness. "If I sleep with him, I won't lose him. Then I'll have somebody and I'll no longer be alone," is the reasoning of many single women. All of their Christian teaching regarding sexual purity and all of the Bible's warnings about the dangers of sex outside of marriage are pushed to some obscure corner of their minds. Salving the terrible loneliness becomes the major concern.

Unfortunately, none of these solutions achieves the intended purpose. None of them removes the loneliness. Yet, the solutions continue to be explored, often, throughout a woman's entire life. In the end, such solutions leave the sad legacy of resentment, bitterness, increased loneliness, and despair. If loneliness is to be well managed, false solutions must be seen for what they really are: barriers to wholeness, happiness, and true contentment.

The Way of Jesus

If loneliness is to be eliminated or alleviated, the way of Jesus must become the way of the single Christian woman. Jesus understands loneliness because He experienced loneliness.

- He knew loneliness during his forty-day temptation in the wilderness.
- He knew loneliness in His relationships with His family, for they never seemed to understand Him.
- He knew loneliness in His dealings with His disciples, for they always seemed to see things differently from the way that He saw them.
- He knew loneliness in the Garden of Gethsemane, for the disciples seemed incapable of giving him the prayer support and the comfort that He so desperately needed.
- And certainly, Jesus knew loneliness as he hung on the cross and experienced separation from people and separation from God. His cry, "My God, my God, why hast thou forsaken me?" (Matthew 27:46), certainly attests to this.

Yes, Jesus experienced the awful depths of loneliness and yet He triumphed over it. Thus, He is eminently qualified to help single women triumph as well. In order for Jesus to bring victory over loneliness, a woman must be certain that she has entered into a *friendship with Jesus*. She must be certain that she is not merely a church member or one who has merely been baptized or one who has merely performed good works. A woman can do all these things and still not have a friendship with Jesus. Friendship with Jesus is achieved when a woman

- Confesses her sins.
- Believes that Jesus died to pay the death penalty for her sins.

- Believes that Jesus arose from the dead and is alive and can help her.

Once a woman confesses these heartfelt beliefs to Jesus and invites Him to live in her heart, she enters a true friendship with Jesus. Her soul is saved and she becomes a Christian in the truest sense of the word.

Once a woman enters a friendship with Jesus, whenever loneliness knocks at her heart's door, she can pray to her friend, Jesus. She can call on the One who understands her loneliness because He has been there. She can beg Him to fill the lonely places in her soul with His love and His peace. Each time she prays such prayers, quietly and surely, peace will come and loneliness will be lifted. Victorious prayer such as this is possible only for the woman who has entered a personal friendship with Jesus.

The woman who has become a personal friend of Jesus can also read the Bible and find a lifting of her loneliness. She can read Psalms 23, 34, and 91 and pray the words of these psalms into the lonely crevices of her heart. Once the time spent in the Bible is over, loneliness will either be lessened or be eliminated.

Loneliness can also be dealt with by developing intimate prayerful friendships with other single Christian women. Meeting weekly to pray or study the Bible together; having lunch or dinner; going to the theater; discussing books or issues; going shopping, or simply sharing hopes, dreams, joys, pain, and Jesus with another Christian woman (or several Christian women) on a regular basis can do wonders toward eradicating one's sense of loneliness.

Making time for such sharing is imperative if a single Christian woman is to ever develop the kind of support system, friendships, and relational joy that help to push loneliness out of the heart.

Jesus, prayer, and the Bible can go a long way toward eliminating loneliness, but warm relationships with other Christians must also be consciously and lovingly cultivated. Loneliness in the life of a single woman must be tackled, wrestled, fought, and pinned to the ground through the power of Jesus. It cannot simply be ignored, for when it is, loneliness will seep into the corners of our lives and rule our emotions, our thinking, and our choices.

SELF-IMAGE

Self-image refers to the way in which a person perceives herself. Whether we see ourselves as homely or pretty, capable or inept, good or bad, useful or useless grows out of the image we have of ourselves. All too often, the image that single African-American women have of themselves is less than positive.

Single Black women often see themselves as not good enough, not pretty enough, or not sexy enough because there is no man in their lives to give them the affirmation their womanliness craves. One single once told me, "Unless *a man* tells me I look good, I never really believe I do. Unless *a man* notices me, I feel lumpy, old, and ugly. Unless *a man* is a part of my life, my sense of self-worth is very small."

All too many single African-American women either consciously or subconsciously hold such views. Their lives and their thinking are dominated and defined by how men see them (or fail to see them). As a result, their self-images teeter, totter, and drag.

The self-image of African-American singles is also often affected by the media hype of our age. According to the media, women who are tall and thin look better than women who are short and fat. Women who have flawless skin and curvaceous figures look better than women with pimples and few curves. Women who have large breasts and shapely legs look better than women with flat chests and chunky legs. Single women who already feel bad about not having a man tend to feel even worse when they fail to measure up to media definitions of prettiness.

In addition, despite the fact that the year 2000 is almost here, long-held views regarding the ugliness of Blackness are still with us, and they are still all too often believed.

Thus, many single African-American women feel that if they were only lighter in skin color, if they only had keener features, and if they only had longer, straighter hair, they would be seen as beautiful. A twenty-year-old recently poured her heart out to me and told me that she knew that a certain young man would like her if only she were light-skinned and if only she had long, pretty hair. Despite the fact that we live in the 1990s, such thinking is not uncommon.

Add to these reasons for poor self-image the ordinary human feelings of inadequacy due to our day-to-day failures and mistakes and the sheer human inability to reach certain goals and fulfill certain plans, and is it any wonder that the self-image of African-American single women is all too often lower than low?

Jim Towns (1990) suggests that persons who have a poor self-esteem tend to demonstrate it in a variety of negative ways:

1. The person develops a critical and jealous nature; nothing ever pleases him.
2. He reacts negatively to criticism or laughter; he becomes paranoid because he feels that everyone is always picking on him or ridiculing him.
3. He becomes very uncomfortable when alone; he must always have someone around him; he has never learned to be alone without being lonely.
4. He places great emphasis on the accumulation of material possessions; he believes that he has value because of what he has rather than who he is.

African-American women whose self-images are so affected often begin to operate out of what Reynolds refers to as the Sapphire Syndrome (after the nagging wife of George Stephens in the *Amos 'n' Andy* radio and television show). Such Black women spend

> a great deal of . . . time shopping at malls and looking at soap operas. Her self-esteem is measured on the basis of how close she can match her perception of what the white woman has. Any black man available to be used for this purpose is her potential target. In an attempt to get what she wants, the black woman has learned to use whatever is at her disposal. Her body and sex are her ultimate weapons. These black women seem compelled to scheme about ways to get gifts and money from men. (Reynolds 1994)

This suggests the tragic lengths to which a poor self-image can carry a woman.

False Solutions

Women with poor self-images try to solve this problem in a variety of subconscious ways. Perhaps the major "solution" to the poor self-image problem is *anger*. African-American men often ask, "Why are Black women so mean, so angry, so mad all the time?" The answer is that subconsciously they don't feel good about themselves, and they feel compelled to lash out at others. The harsh tone of voice of many African-American women results from sad and negative feelings about *themselves*. The "chip-on-the-shoulder" attitude, the "don't-mess-with-me" stance, the streams of profanity, or the angry words that sometimes spew forth for no apparent reason are often the result of a deep inner sadness that is rooted in a poor self-image. Instead of solving the problem, anger usually only makes it worse. Angry behavior causes others to perceive us negatively; we then often internalize that negativity and we end up having a poorer self-image than we had before the angry display. Anger generally catapults us into a vicious cycle that makes things worse.

Another way in which single African-American women try to solve the poor self-image problem is to attempt to *dress, look, and act "sexy."* Somehow, if jeans are tight enough or a skirt is short enough or a blouse is low enough, this will "prove" that "I'm as good as anybody who has a man and maybe even better." Somehow, if I can interest a man or "turn him on" (whether I care about him or not), this proves that I'm as good as the woman who has found a man. Sad to say, such "sexy" behavior is exhibited by Christians and non-Christians alike. And, more often than not, it only results in anger, rejection, grief, and an increase in poor self-image.

A third way by which many African-American singles try to solve the poor self-image problem is to throw themselves into *their education and their work.* The thinking is that somehow, "If I can just be smart enough; if I can just get enough A's; if I can just get enough degrees; if I can just get enough promotions; if I can get a Ph.D. behind my name; or if I can just become CEO of a company—this will prove that I'm as good (or better) than the woman who has found a man." Certainly this kind of thinking is not true of all women who achieve in academics or in the world of work—but it is true often enough to suggest that it is a common false solution to the problem of poor self-image.

Still another way of dealing with a poor self-image problem is *denial.* The woman in her twenties or thirties who says "I know I look good. I'm already fulfilled. I don't have a man; I don't need one, and I don't want one!" often feels terrible about herself, precisely because there is no man in her life. Single women in their forties or fifties have often arrived at the point of sincerely believing that no man is needed in order for life to be fulfilling. But women in their twenties or thirties who claim such fulfillment are often denying their true feelings.

Denial is a problem because it prevents a woman from looking at life realistically, from dealing with true feelings and from achieving inner wholeness and peace. The single who lives in denial is in a dream world of her own making and she will never see life or herself as they really are as long as she refuses to face the truth.

Coping with the problem of self-image by resorting to these false solutions always leaves heartache and trouble. It also intensifies the poor self-image and proves emotionally detrimental to the woman involved.

The Way of Jesus

If self-image is to be improved, the single woman must look to the way of Jesus. When a woman gives her life to Jesus, He cleanses away the past with all its sins, mistakes, regrets, and foolish thinking. Jesus gives a woman a brand-new start. Jesus accepts a woman for who she is and gives her a position of value and importance before God Almighty. Certainly this builds her self-image in a refreshing and exciting way. As a woman continues to follow the way of Jesus, she discovers assertions and promises in the Word of God that build her self-image. Assertions such as these make a single woman feel accepted and loved just for herself:

> *The LORD hath appeared of old unto me, saying, Yea, I have loved thee with an everlasting love; therefore with loving-kindness have I drawn thee. (Jeremiah 31:3)*

> *He hath made us accepted in the beloved. (Ephesians 1:6)*

> *But God, who is rich in mercy, for his great love wherewith he loved us, even when we were dead in sins, hath quickened us together with Christ ... and hath raised us up together, and made us sit together in heavenly places in Christ Jesus; That in the ages to come he might show the exceeding riches of his grace, in his kindness toward us through Christ Jesus. (Ephesians 2:4–7)*

Promises such as these give a woman the intense inner confidence that she can be deeply fulfilled even if she lives her entire life without a man:

> *Being confident of this very thing, that he which hath begun a good work in you will perform it until the day of Jesus Christ. (Philippians 1:6)*

> *I can do all things through Christ which strengtheneth me. (Philippians 4:13)*

But my God shall supply all your need, according to his riches in glory by Christ Jesus. (Philippians 4:19)

For in him dwelleth all the fullness of the Godhead bodily. And ye are complete in him, which is the head of all principality and power. (Colossians 2:9–10)

One of the best ways for a single African-American woman to enhance a flagging self-image is to read such assertions and promises from the Word of God and pray them into her soul. Reading Christian books about the value of singleness and the joys of singleness can also boost the self-image. Books such as Bobbie Reed's *Learn to Risk: Finding Joy As a Single Adult;* Harold Ivan Smith's *Single And Feeling Good;* and Mary Whelchel's *Common Mistakes Singles Make* are written from a Christian perspective and can be extremely helpful. *A Singular Devotion*, also by Harold Ivan Smith, is a fine devotional book—one that can encourage singles to look to the Word of God and be encouraged by the lives of singles who have lived fulfilling lives.

Discovering one's spiritual gifts and using them to build the kingdom of God can also enhance the self-image. When a person accepts Jesus, the Holy Spirit gives that person one or more spiritual gifts. Teaching, preaching, mercies, helps, and organization are some of these gifts (see Romans 12:6–8; 1 Corinthians 12:27–28; and Ephesians 4:11–12). While spiritual gifts are mainly given to build the body of Christ, the use of them can be personally fulfilling to an individual. Simply knowing the Lord is using you in an eternal endeavor is humbling, exciting, satisfying, and joy-inducing. A woman feels valued and valuable as she devotes herself to the building of the Kingdom for which Jesus died.

Self-image can also be enhanced if a woman will only learn to celebrate herself. This, too, is an activity that is a part of the way of Jesus. Celebrating yourself is done by

- Making and keeping your surroundings beautiful even though you may live alone.
- Getting your hair done regularly and wearing coordinated clothing that fits your body build and age.
- Setting the table fancy just for yourself as you eat your meals.
- Treating yourself to dinner out or a trip to the theater as a reward for a job well done.

- Celebrating your birthdays, talking about your age, and seeing each year as a reason to praise God for His kindness to you. After all, a birthday is simply a day to rejoice because the Lord sent *you* into the world. It is not a day to remember the so-called curse of aging; it is a day to celebrate blessings.
- Getting a like-minded group of single women together to study what the Bible has to say about self-image can also be helpful. Such a session can conclude by having each woman rejoice in all that the Lord has made her to be. A time of celebration (singing, sharing Bible verses, sharing testimonies) can then ensue.

Nothing can enhance a woman's self-image like a deepened relationship with both Jesus Christ and other committed women of God.

LOVE

Victor Hugo has said, "The greatest happiness of life is the conviction that we are loved, loved for ourselves, or rather, loved in spite of ourselves" (Doan 1968). This suggests that every human being longs (indeed *needs*) to be loved by some other human being and, certainly, single African-American women are no exception. Thus, whether we have a man in our lives or not, we each need desperately to be loved—loved *for* ourselves and loved *in spite* of ourselves.

Every single African-American woman needs to have someone in her life who will on occasion say, "I love you" with words, with a card, with a note, with an affirmation, or with a compliment. It may be that no man will ever say "I love you" in any of these ways, but if *someone* expresses love, the soul can be nourished, the heart can be warmed, and the sense of completeness that comes from being loved can settle deep within.

Certainly it is true that nearly every single African-American woman longs for a man's touch, a man's caring, a man's companionship, and a man's "I love you," but if this cannot be, then sincere, true, upright love from *any* source can sustain the human need to be loved.

One single who regularly visits elderly people in a nursing home commented, "I get the feeling that they *like* to see me coming and that they're sad when I don't come. I get the feeling that they genuinely *love* me."

Another single who teaches in a nursery setting remarked, "These babies love me just for myself. I don't have to do or be or perform well in order for them to love me. They love me freely and totally just because I'm me."

A single who had been estranged from her family for years once called me and reported, "It's taken me forty-two years to discover that my family really loves me, and all the time I've been looking for that kind of love in a man."

Love, acceptance, affirmation, and warm regard can be found in many people and places: in the elderly, in children, in one's own family, in friends, and in fellow Christians. But love will never be found unless we

1. Admit that we need love.
2. Freely give love to others, for if we do, the Lord will see to it that love, in some form, is returned to us.
3. Accept the love that others give to us and never demand that they love us beyond their capacity to do so.
4. Accept love no matter what its source may be. (If it is from a child, accept it and be glad. If it is from an elderly person, accept it and be glad. If it is from a mentally impaired person, accept it and be glad. I once had a wheelchair-bound person with a speech impediment dearly and deeply love me. What a heartwarming experience!)

Many single African-American women miss out on love because they neither know nor follow these guidelines. Instead, they conclude that their lives are lacking in love because of the absence of a man and sexual fulfillment. What a false conclusion! Sexual fulfillment and love are not necessarily the same. There may be no man and no sex, but life can be rich in the love of friends, the love of children, the love of the elderly, the love of the needy, or the love of young people if we will only open our hearts to the love that is waiting for us in someone's heart.

False Solutions

Perhaps the most common modern solution to the love problem is *"living together."* A young, single African-American woman falls in love with a man, decides that she can't live without him, and begins to live with him without benefit of marriage. More often than not, a child is produced from such a union. The man eventually leaves, and the woman, who did all of this in the name of love, is left alone and is still unloved.

Living with a person to whom one is not married is wrong because the Bible tells us that sex outside of marriage is wrong. It is wrong also because it looks bad, and the Bible tells us to avoid even the appearance of evil (1 Thessalonians 5:22). In addition, living together is foolish because the woman is generally the one who is left with children who need raising, bills that need paying, and a broken heart that needs mending. The woman tends to be the loser in "living together" situations for she becomes spiritually bankrupt, emotionally devastated, sometimes physically abused, and often financially overwhelmed. Generally, at such times the woman realizes that what she thought was love was really only infatuation, lust, or loneliness.

Single African-American women also attempt to satisfy their need for love by entering *sexual relationships* with men. Such women stop short of actually living with men to whom they are not married, but they long for closeness, intimacy, and sexual fulfillment, so they "give in" and have sex, often with one man after another. Usually such women are used, degraded, and abused by the men with whom they have sex. Yet they continue to enter into sexual liaisons—often with the same type of man that they just broke up with. Rarely do they see their relationships as sinful, wrong, or psychologically damaging. They are simply looking for love, and society has repeatedly told them that this is the way to find it.

Single African-American women may try to satisfy their need for love by entering *ill-advised marriages*. More and more, Black women will marry men who have no jobs, men who have no education, men who have no potential, and men who have no future simply because these women want a man to love them. In recent years, I have known beautiful African-American women who had excellent careers and were highly educated to marry drug addicts, convicts, men who were unemployed (and didn't want to be employed), men who were high school dropouts, and men with no future. None of the marriages lasted and each brought far more heartache than surely would have occurred if the woman had remained single. Thus, the basic problem of single African-American women with regard to love seems to be mistaking sex, lust, infatuation, or simply male attention for love.

The Way of Jesus

Those who follow the way of Jesus have a startlingly authentic example of what real love is like. This example is found in Jesus Himself. Jesus was single all His life long and yet His life was full of love. He found love in intimate friendship with Peter, James, and John as well as with Mary, Martha, and Lazarus. He found love as He worked, fellowshiped, and served with His twelve disciples. He found love as He taught, helped, rescued, and involved Himself with all kinds of people. He found love as He reached out to children and permitted them to be a part of His life. Even when Jesus was mocked, abandoned, and forsaken, He continued to reach out in love and forgiveness. Despite being deeply hurt, Jesus continued to build loving relationships with others.

If single African-American women are to have love in their lives, they must follow the way of Jesus and give love to all kinds of people. Amazingly, when love is given, love somehow is returned. It is not always returned from those to whom it is given, but it will be returned. Jesus will see to it. At various times in my life, I have given love to

- Nursing home residents
- Housing project residents
- Shut-ins
- Groups of teenagers
- Groups of children
- Disabled persons

In each instance, I have met regularly with them, shared gospel devotions or Bible studies, given gifts, shared myself (my feelings, thoughts, and activities), taken them on outings, and planned parties. Inevitably, either those with whom I shared, or their relatives and friends, have become my friends and have filled my life with love.

Single African-American women must also learn to cultivate friendships with other women. So often women allow competitiveness, jealousy, suspiciousness, or ill will to dominate their relationships with other women. As a result, they miss the richly loving relationships that women can have with other women. If African-American women would only form support groups, Bible study groups, fellowship groups, and prayer groups with other women who face similar concerns, they would find that loving relationships will begin. Such relationships can then be cultivated through two-by-two visiting, phoning, card-sending, lunching, and opening the heart during times of prayer. Instead of fighting each other, single African-American women must learn to share with each other. Real love would then fill hearts and warm lives.

Above all, single African-American women must learn to wrap themselves up in the love of Jesus. This can be done by

- Doing a personal Bible study on the "love verses" in the New Testament (for example, John 3:16, 1 Corinthians 13, 1 John 4, and others).
- Spending a day (or half-day) with Jesus on a personal retreat. (Praying, singing, and reading Bible passages and chapters from Christian books can leave a woman feeling close to Jesus and on deeply intimate terms with Him.)
- Doing a two-to-three-month-long study of Charles Colson's book *Loving God*. (For example, read a few chapters a week until your heart senses the love that God has for you and that you can have for Him.)
- Meditating on Christian hymns and songs that speak of the Lord's love—one song a week or one song a month. Songs such as "Loved With Everlasting Love," "O How He Loves You and Me," "Love Lifted Me," "The Love of God," "Love Divine, All Loves Excelling," "What a Friend We Have in Jesus," and "Jesus Is Always There" can flood the heart with the conviction that Jesus really cares.

Love is all around the single African-American woman and it is waiting to be grasped. Black women must learn to identify the many faces of love, and they must reach for it wherever they find it.

SEX

We live in a society that is obsessed with sex. Nearly every issue of the various popular magazines has at least one article on sex. Many daily newspapers have columns that answer questions about sex. More and more, prime-time TV shows, films, and videos feature explicit conversations about sex as well as hot and heavy bedroom scenes. And, sadly, most TV talk shows deal regularly with perversions of sex (priests who have sex with young boys, barbershops with topless female barbers, bisexuality, etc.). When a single is surrounded by such lewd conversation and such erotic sights, it is very difficult to keep one's thinking, values, and activities sexually pure.

Add to the influence of the media the ways in which African-American girls are socialized, and it is not difficult to see why the sexual thinking of many women is confused. Many girls are still taught (by unspoken messages if not in words) that sex is dirty, degrading, or bad. More often than not, it is still true that no accurate sexual information is given to African-American girls. Dr. Jawanza Kunjufu (1993) states: "Studies indicate that [African-American young people] become sexually active between 11 and 14 but parents begin discussing sex education with them when they are 16." He further states that inaccurate sexual information is dispensed in the African-American community through mythological statements such as "If you really love me then [you must] show me," "I want to marry you someday and we should find out if we are sexually compatible," "Everybody is doing it but us," or "Don't worry, you can't get pregnant for the first six months. God gives a grace period." Such mythological statements often cause African-American girls to engage in sex outside of marriage with the thought that there will be no enduring consequences.

In addition, engaging in premarital sex and having children outside of marriage are no longer frowned upon as they once were. There is no stigma attached to such activity. Thus, single African-American women feel that the people who matter to them (mother, father, friends, relatives) will have little to say about their premarital sexual activity other than to encourage them to use a contraceptive. If a child should be born out of wedlock, everyone will accept it and love it, so unwed pregnancy is really not a problem. Finances, health care, time management, and the multitudinous concerns of parenting seem never to enter the young woman's mind.

Years ago, African-American women who were victims of sexual abuse, incest, and rape often suffered in silence. In our day, however, our society speaks openly and specifically about such matters. Sadly, though, more and more African-American women reveal that they have been subjected to these tragic sexual experiences. Dr. Marilyn J. Munson (1991) reports that

- One of five women has been sexually assaulted.
- In a recent survey, twenty-nine percent of women who were abused sexually before age eighteen identified their father as their first abuser.
- Sixty percent of rape cases involve a perpetrator known to the victim.

Thus, through the influence of the media, through misinformation, through lax values regarding sexual behavior, and through the harsh realities of sexual abuse, incest and rape, African-American girls acquire sexual information that follows them into adulthood and influences their sexual behavior. Koons and Anthony (1991) report: "Few published studies have examined the sexual behavior of unmarried adults, but a 1983 National Institutes of Health study of the sexual practices of 1,314 never-married women concluded that 80 percent of single American women in their twenties have engaged in sex. One third of those women had become pregnant at least once, and 40 percent of those pregnant aborted their first pregnancy." Howard and Wanda Jones (1992) report that "at the end of the '80s, more than half of all black babies were born out of wedlock." All of this suggests that the sexual climate among single African-American women is, by and large, permissive, confused, and tragic.

False Solutions

Because of the confused sexual climate in our society, many single African-American women simply "go with the flow" and *do as those around them.* They become sexually active at an early age and either have a child out of wedlock or have an abortion. Often, this is repeated with man after man. As the members of our church go into the homes of those in the surrounding community to share the gospel, it is not uncommon to meet single (never-married) African-American women in their late twenties or early thirties with four, five, and six children. In more instances than not, women who have children out of wedlock end up having to deal with the problems of unemployment or underemployment, substandard housing, a lack of health insurance, loneliness, and depression, as well as all of the problems involved with raising children alone.

Other women resort to *sexy behavior and appearance* in order to try to "catch" a man and develop a satisfying sexual relationship. Such women become sex objects in their own thinking, and instead of developing their minds and souls, they spend an inordinate amount of time and energy enhancing and dressing their bodies and flirting with and pursuing men, always in the hope that they will find a husband who will make their sex lives satisfying and thrilling.

Many African-American women feel that since there are few single men available to meet their sexual needs, the only sensible alternative is to become *involved with married men.* Such women often begin such a relationship with casual conversations. They then move to having lunch with the man, engaging in long phone conversations, sympathizing with him over problems in his marriage, hugging, kissing, petting, and eventually intercourse. Before a single woman realizes it, she has become "the other woman," and she often justifies her illicit relationship with such excuses as "but we really love each other."

Relationships with married men always come to a bad end. The single woman always loses, and generally, the man returns to the "terrible" wife whom he spent so much time berating.

Many single African-American women deal with their longing for sex by resorting to *envy, resentment, or bitterness.* They refuse to admit their sexual needs and claim to have few problems in this area. Yet, they refuse to attend bridal showers and weddings, consistently making negative remarks about people who date and about married couples. When such attitudes are allowed to persist, they result in a deep resentment and an ugly bitterness that infect nearly every aspect of a woman's thinking and feeling. In the end, the only person who is hurt is the woman harboring the bitterness.

Some single African-American women handle their desire for sex by developing *negative feelings toward all men.* They make such statements as "All men are dogs," "All they want to do is get you in bed," "They don't really care about you," or "They only want to use you." Such remarks are often made by women who harbor resentment or bitterness because no man has chosen them. Consequently, they develop an antipathy for all men and become walking stereotypes of the statement, "Hell hath no fury like a woman scorned." Many a "mean" Black woman is simply a rejected Black woman who longs for a satisfying sexual relationship.

The Way of Jesus

Over and over again in the New Testament, we are commanded to be chaste:

I beseech you therefore, brethren, by the mercies of God, that ye present your bodies a living sacrifice, holy, acceptable unto God, which is your reasonable service. (Romans 12:1)

Flee fornication. Every sin that a man doeth is without the body; but he that committed fornication sinneth against his own body. (1 Corinthians 6:18)

What? Know ye not that your body is the temple of the Holy Ghost which is in you, which ye have of God, and ye are not your own? For ye are bought with a price: therefore glorify God in your body and in your spirit, which are God's. (1 Corinthians 6:19–20)

Now the works of the flesh are manifest, which are these: Adultery, fornication, uncleanness, lasciviousness. . . . (Galatians 5:19)

For this is the will of God, even your sanctification, that ye should abstain from fornication. (1 Thessalonians 4:3)

If a single African-American woman is to live her life according to the way of Jesus, she must not have sex outside of marriage. She must not commit fornication. She must live a life of celibacy through the grace and power of Jesus Christ. God's Word permits no ifs, ands, or buts in this area of life. The standard is high, holy, and unyielding, and the resurrection power of Jesus Christ is available to all who desire to live by that standard. Once a woman invites Jesus to live in her heart and rule her life, Jesus remains there forever to give her the grace and power needed to remain sexually pure. Certainly, since we live in a society that is obsessed with sex, sexual purity will never be easy but it is definitely possible. Were it not possible, Jesus would never have established it as our standard.

In order for a woman to maintain the standard of Jesus in a happy, emotionally healthy way, she would do well to remember the following guidelines:

- Realize that there are worse things than being single, alone, and celibate. Being married and unloved is worse. Having children to raise alone is worse. Being in an abusive relationship is worse.
- Believe that the single life and the celibate life is good, acceptable, and can be fulfilling. Singleness, according to 1 Corinthians 7:7, is a gift from God and surely all of God's gifts are good.
- Realize that sexual intercourse is not a must in order to be fulfilled. Fulfillment can be obtained through a deep relationship with Jesus and through warm, loving, intimate human relationships.
- Resolve that by God's grace you will remain sexually pure. At age twenty-five, I made the decision on my knees before the Lord to be a happy sexually pure single. After that moment, whenever temptations have come I've been able to return to that decision,

pray for grace, and remain victorious. If we make no such decision, we tend to get caught up in the turbulent passion of the moment and forget that we have an anchor that can keep us steadfast and true to the Lord whom we claim to follow.

- Realize that sex is good and beautiful as long as it is used within the bounds of marriage. It is extremely important that a single woman realize that God's gift of sex is beautiful whether she has the privilege of using the gift or not. Such a realization is emotionally healthy and helps to prevent bitterness from settling in the heart.

- Pray with utmost sincerity, review Scriptures that you have memorized, and read the Bible when you are filled with sexual desires. It really does help.

- Build your spiritual life and ask the Lord to keep your desires under control. Daily, as you pray and read God's Word, pray for purity, joy, inner peace, and godly control.

- Pray as though you are having a warm and intimate conversation with a friend. Such daily times spent with the Lord will prepare you to deal victoriously with sexual temptation when it comes.

- Read as much as you can about sexuality and commit all that you know to Jesus. Knowledge is power when it comes to sexual purity.

- Keep productively busy. Productive busyness refers to doing things that are meaningful, helpful to others, and useful to the Kingdom of God. Productive busyness refers to doing things that build the mind, the body, the soul, and the spirit. Wandering about the mall, watching soap operas and talk shows, or gossiping on the telephone is not productive busyness.

- Avoid intimate relationships with married men. Involve yourself with an entire family and not merely the husband. Many single women have had affairs "sneak up" on them while they were innocently involved with a friend's husband.

- Resolve by God's grace to never allow negativity, resentment, or bitterness to rule your thinking and your behavior. In sexual matters, pray for the ability to say the opposite of that which is negative and always do the opposite of that which bespeaks resentment or bitterness.

The way of Jesus with regard to sexual matters is a way of purity but it is also a way of joy, a way of inner peace, fulfillment, and spiritual wholeness.

CONCLUSION

The life of the single African-American woman is often filled with problems related to loneliness, self-image, love, and sex. As she deals with these difficulties, the Black woman often reaches for "solutions" that compound the problems instead of alleviating them. If such women could only learn to follow the way of Jesus in dealing with these matters, each problem could be turned into an opportunity for growth and development. The problem of loneliness could become an opportunity for deep fellowship with the Lord. Self-image problems could become an opportunity for intellectual, emotional, social, and physical improvement. The need for love could become an opportunity to achieve selflessness and to fill one's life with authentic, honest friendships. Unfulfilled sexual desire could become an opportunity for achieving intimacy with Jesus, inner resolve, and deepened holiness.

Michael Green (1982) writes:

> A parent once described how her three children would respond to a spider web in the garden. The first child would examine the web and wonder how the spider wove it. The second would worry a great deal about where the spider was. And the third would exclaim, "Oh, look! A trampoline!" There was only one spider web in the garden—but that web was perceived differently by each child. To the first child, it was an object of fascination. To the second child, it was an object of fear; and to the third child, it was an object of joy. It was all a matter of perspective.

In the same way, the single life can be viewed in various ways. It can be viewed as something to be endured, feared, and cursed, or something to be embraced. The way in which we *choose to perceive* the single life will determine how it is viewed and how it is lived. *It is all a matter of perspective.* May Jesus grant us as single African-American women the grace to view singleness with *His* eyes.

Recommended Reading

Caldwell, Genevieve. *First Person Singular*. Nashville: Thomas Nelson, 1986.

June, Lee N., ed. *The Black Family: Past, Present, and Future*. Grand Rapids: Zondervan, 1991.

Majors, R., and J. M. Billson. *Cool Pose: The Dilemmas of Black Manhood in America*. New York: Simon & Schuster, 1992.

Purnell, Dick. *Free to Love Again*. San Bernardino, CA: Here's Life, 1989.

Reed, B. *Learn to Risk: Finding Joy As a Single Adult*. Grand Rapids: Zondervan, 1990.

Smith, Harold I. *A Singular Devotion*. Old Tappan: Fleming H. Revell, 1990.

_____. *Fortysomething and Single*. Wheaton, IL: Victor Books, 1990.

_____. *Positively Single*. Wheaton, IL: Victor Books, 1986.

_____. *Single and Feeling Good*. Nashville: Abingdon, 1987.

_____. *Singles Ask: Answers to Questions About Relationships and Sexual Issues*. Minneapolis: Augsburg, 1988.

Terkel, Studs. *Race: How Blacks and Whites Think and Feel About the American Obsession*. New York: Doubleday/Anchor Books, 1992.

$\mathcal{R}$eferences

Colson, C. 1987. *Loving God*. Grand Rapids: Zondervan.

Doan, E. 1968. *Speakers sourcebook II*. Grand Rapids: Zondervan.

Greene, C. 1985. *I am one: Prayers for singles*. Minneapolis: Augsburg.

Green, M. 1982. *Illustrations for biblical preaching*. Grand Rapids: Baker.

Jones, H., and W. Jones. 1992. *Heritage and hope: The legacy and future of the Black family in America*. Wheaton, IL: Scripture Press.

The King James version of the Bible.

Koons, C., and M. Anthony. 1991. *Single adult passages*. Grand Rapids: Baker.

Kunjufu, J. 1993. *The power, passion and pain of Black love*. Chicago: African-American Images.

Mason, M. 1991. *Making our lives our own*. San Francisco: HarperCollins.

Reynolds III, A. 1994. *Do Black women hate Black men?* Mamaroneck, NY: Hastings House.

Towns, J. 1990. *Single space: Victorious living for the single adult.* Tulsa: Honor Books.

Whelchel, M. 1989. *Common mistakes singles make.* Tarrytown: Fleming H. Revell.

Wirt, S., and K. Beckstrom. 1974. *Living quotations for Christians.* New York: Harper & Row.

Annie Roberson
and Norvella Carter

When Your
Mate Is Absent:
Handling Your
Emotions

ANNIE ROBERSON is a native of Mineola, Texas. She is a second-year student at Southern Bible Institute. She is the founder of Women Who Fear God International. Annie was formerly director of housing for Alternative Community Development Service, Inc. She is the mother of three daughters: LaShamond, LaShonda, and Shermelia. She is a member of Oak Cliff Bible Fellowship in Dallas, Texas, and served as administrative assistant to Pastor Tony Evans. Currently, she is Director of Evangelism and Coordinator of the Ladies Fellowship ministries; she is also a volunteer chaplain at the Lew Sterrett Justice Center and is involved with the Bill Glass Prison and Prison Fellowship Ministries.

NORVELLA CARTER is Assistant Professor of Education at Illinois State University. She was born in Detroit and raised in Inkster, Michigan. She received a bachelor of science degree in special education and a master's degree in administration and supervision from Wayne State University in Detroit. She received a doctor of philosophy degree from the Graduate School of Arts and Sciences at Loyola University of Chicago. She resides in Normal, Illinois, with her husband, William Charles Carter Sr. They have seven children: Tracie, Camille, China, Crystal, William Jr., Kellie, and Victoria. Norvella is a member of Christian Family Center in Peoria, Illinois. She is a former Christian education director and currently serves as a deaconess and member of the Outreach ministry.

Chapter 9

Annie Roberson
and *Norvella Carter*

When Your Mate Is Absent: Handling Your Emotions

"For I know the plans I have for you," declares the LORD, *"plans to prosper you and not to harm you, plans to give you hope and a future." (Jeremiah 29:11)*

M arriage in today's society is under extreme attack and there are various reasons that cause the African-American woman's mate to be absent from the home. The primary reasons appear to be separation and divorce. Other major reasons include: incarceration, desertion, placement of a mate in a nursing home, and death. The most recent social tragedy is incarceration.

THE CONSEQUENCES OF ABSENCE

The absence of a mate is not an "African-American problem." *All* women have been at the center of dramatic demographic, social, and economic changes during the past few decades. One of the most glaring changes is the increase in marital disruption through separation and divorce. By 1990, marital dissolution had become so common in the United States that one out of every two marriages ended in divorce (Wineberg 1990). In contrast to the 1950s and 1960s, millions of families are currently headed by females. In terms of numbers, White women head more single-parent households than any racial group in the country (Bureau of the Census 1992).

From the 1970s through the 1990s, numerous studies found that separation and divorce had detrimental economic effects on all women and their children (Bane & Weiss 1980; Chideya 1995; Duncan & Hoffman 1985; Espendshade 1979; Smith & Beninger 1982). Separation and divorce account for much of the change in the economic well-being of families, particularly women (Duncan 1984; Weitzman 1985). The average family on welfare consists of a woman and two young children. Contrary to media portrayals, the majority of welfare recipients are White (U.S. Department of Health and Human Services 1993).

The plight for African-American women is critical, however, because most Black couples must have both spouses work in order to escape poverty. On the average, a Caucasian husband alone earns only ten thousand dollars less than what a Black working wife and her husband earn combined (Chideya 1995). Separation and divorce are the most prevalent causes of poverty for African-American women (Mauldin & Koonce 1990; Kniesner, McElroy, & Wilcox 1988).

One of the most recent social tragedies that contribute significantly to the loss of the African-American woman's mate is incarceration. There are 525,000 African-American men nationwide who are absent from their families for this reason (King 1993; U.S. Department of Justice 1991a, 1991b). During the past twenty years, the destruction rendered by this particular circumstance has reached slavery proportions and has become a serious threat to African- American people and their families. When a Black man is sentenced to prison, his entire family (spouse, children, and extended family members) suffers tremendously. According to the U.S. Department of Justice (1991a, 1991b), 46 percent of the men incarcerated in state prisons were either married, widowed, divorced, or separated. Seventy percent were supporting two or more persons at the time of conviction (King 1993). These statistics are reflective of the fact that African-American males, married or not, were actively involved in the lives of nuclear, extended, or non-blood related family relationships before their incarceration. This means that wives, mothers, aunts, grandmothers, children, siblings, companions, and others suffer a great loss upon confinement of the African-American male.

In addition, the woman and her family must live with degrading myths and false perceptions about Black men that are generally accepted by society. For example, an ongoing misconception that is prevalent in the media and repeated over and over by people who hear it is, "There are more African-American men in prisons than in colleges and universities." This is not true, in terms of college-aged men, but it is rarely challenged by most people who hear the statement. In fact, in 1991, there were 136,000 Black males aged eighteen to twenty-four in prison (Chideya 1995) while 480,000 Black males in the same age group attended colleges and universities (King 1993; Evangelauf 1992). Comparing all African-American men ages fifteen to eighty years old who are incarcerated with one "college-aged group" is misleading. This seemingly minor error promotes negative stereotypes about Black men and adds to feelings of hopelessness in African-American families.

For the African-American woman, incarceration causes economic, psychological, emotional, and physical losses similar to those experienced by the death of a family member. This is a time when the presence of the Lord is particularly vital in the life of the African-American woman. It is a time when an abundance of emotions threatens to engulf her life.

The purpose of this chapter is to explore the emotions women experience when their mate is absent, to present strategies for dealing with those emotions, and finally, to share the personal testimony of a Christian African-American woman that reflects the emotions and strategies identified in the chapter.

EMOTIONS: BEWARE

During your mate's initial separation from the home, you will most likely experience what feels like intolerable pain. This pain can be compared to the labor pains of childbirth. To you, it is worse than childbirth because you cannot see deliverance. You are in a state of shock which numbs your physical body. You may move blindly about, trying to accomplish those necessary and routine chores, or you stop functioning altogether.

After the initial shock, you may experience anger, fear, uncontrollable crying, evil thoughts, hatred, depression, and possible suicidal tendencies. Yes, you feel like you've been run over by a series of Mack trucks. During this time of pain, you are vulnerable and Satan has a way of magnifying this crisis. To alleviate the pain and feelings of hopelessness, you might look immediately for love from another person. It is possible that you may grow deeply bitter and want your mate or others to pay for hurting you. You want to somehow avenge the wrong that has been done to you. Usually, you learn through experience that following this path is fruitless and leads to a dead end.

You become an emotional wreck. You have feelings of insecurity. You find yourself asking, "How will I make ends meet?" When you sit down and take a look at your economic, social, and psychological picture, you become even more anxious. You experience self-condemnation and a feeling of failure. You feel that you should have tried harder at making your marriage work or that you should have been able to avoid trouble. You feel that perhaps you could have prevented the loss of your mate. Your one and only companion in the intimacy of marriage is gone. Low self-worth and self-esteem overpower you. You feel like another statistic. You are embarrassed to go to church, you are embarrassed on your job, and you dread talking to your children. Day after day you evaluate your circumstances and eventually discouragement and hopelessness will set in as you wrestle with getting through the day.

The loss of a mate is a tragic circumstance that evokes powerful emotions. These emotions are so strong that often they are difficult to control. Emotions express our feelings but can become serious barriers to overcoming painful situations; emotions must be handled properly and brought under control because they do not always reflect the truth. Strategies for handling your emotions fall into two different phases. The first phase deals with the inner woman, which is vital for survival. The second phase deals with external activities, which improves your quality of life.

Strategies for Handling Your Emotions

The Inner Woman

Phase one begins when you decide to meet your inner needs by engaging in *serious, consistent, and earnest prayer* to God. Prayer is communication between you and God. "The effectual fervent prayer of a righteous [person] availeth much" (James 5:16 KJV). God is the only one who truly understands your feelings and is anxious to provide healing and comfort for your soul. Talk to Him in prayer and know that He will hear you. "Evening, morning and noon I cry out in distress, and he hears my voice" (Psalm 55:17 NIV). "The LORD is near to all who call on him, to all who call on him in truth. He fulfills the desires of those who fear him; he hears their cry and saves them" (Psalm 145:18–19 NIV).

In prayer, God invites you to commune with Him. Prayer offered in faith is your most powerful resource. It is important because you can communicate your desires, but it is even more important to ask Him to give you the desire to do His will. If you commit your life daily to God, you will be able to move forward day by day, then week by week, and you will feel the pain lifting as you grow stronger in the Lord.

The next part of phase one is to take *refuge in the Word of God.* Study the Scriptures daily and allow them to minister to your inner needs. "All scripture is given by inspiration of God, and is profitable for doctrine, for reproof, for correction, for instruction in righteousness" (2 Timothy 3:16 KJV). The Scriptures will strengthen you, provide you with wisdom, guide you in godly living, and illuminate the personal path that you should follow in your life.

> *I would have despaired and perished unless your laws had been my deepest delight. I will never lay aside your laws, for you have used them to restore my joy and health. (Psalm 119:92–93 LB)*

> *Nothing is perfect except your words. . . . They make me wiser than my enemies, because they are my constant guide. (Psalm 119:96, 98 LB)*

> *Jesus replied, "Are you not in error because you do not know the Scriptures or the power of God?" (Mark 12:24 NIV)*

> *Thy word is a lamp unto my feet, and a light unto my path. (Psalm 119:105 KJV)*

God's Word helps you to live a life that is pleasing to the Lord in spite of your circumstances. Although your mate is absent, God still has a plan for you. Many women make major mistakes in their lives because they do not know how to live godly lives and are unaware of the position the Lord takes on major issues. Study of the Bible will reveal that God has the answer to all of your questions and problems. He is the only one who can minister to your inner needs.

The third step in this phase is to develop your *faith in God.* After prayer and study of the Scripture, you must have faith (believe) in what He says and trust Him in every area of your life. This step is very important because in order to do this you must abandon all thoughts of self and trust only in God. In this phase, reliance is shifted from yourself to complete reliance on God. Can you trust Him to deliver you in your deepest hurt? If not, ask Him to increase your faith and to show you how to trust Him. Through these circumstances, He will develop your faith, endurance, and Christian character.

The benefits that you have as a Christian woman are infinitely greater than anything humankind could ever produce. Faith in God will allow you to shed all of your anxieties, fears, and insecurities because you know with great confidence that you can depend on Him and He will take care of you in every circumstance.

Cast all your anxiety on him because he cares for you. (1 Peter 5:7 NIV)

God has said, "Never will I leave you; never will I forsake you." (Hebrews 13:5 NIV)

Trust in the LORD with all your heart and lean not on your own understanding; in all your ways acknowledge him, and he will make your paths straight. (Proverbs 3:5–6 NIV)

We live by faith, not by sight. (2 Corinthians 5:7)

Do not allow your circumstances to rule your emotions. Develop your faith in God and believe that you will come out of this situation stronger and wiser because of your relationship with Him. Your faith will enable you to handle your emotions in a way that you never dreamed possible. Remember that God is able to transform your life and is willing to do it. Confirm in your inner self that you are fearfully and wonderfully made (Psalm 139:14). You are valuable to God and He loves you with an everlasting love.

External Activities

The second phase of handling your emotions deals with external activities. These activities are important because they help you focus on the spiritual and positive aspects of life while you go through the healing process. During your time of pain you may not feel like becoming involved with other people, but that is exactly what you need to do. Find a women's Bible study, support group, or a women's prayer group where you receive encouragement and will be held accountable for living the Christian life. This is a time when you are vulnerable. You need to fellowship with mature women of God who can lift you up in prayer, listen to your concerns, and offer wise counsel from the Word of God.

Seek *support from women* who are reverent in their behavior. Look for godly women who love the Lord and know Him as their personal Savior. Look for women who are honorable and respectful as characterized in their daily walk and lifestyle. Talk to women who are controlled by the Holy Spirit. You need support from people who can provide a positive influence in your situation. You want to be with people who will assist you in handling your emotions and aid you in the healing process.

Do not be afraid to seek *professional Christian counseling, if necessary.* As you go through the healing process, there are times when you may need professional help. If you recognize that you are not making sufficient progress or you stop functioning in day-to-day routines, ask your pastor or a Christian friend to assist you in finding a counseling center. Do not allow pride to stop you from getting the help you need. Professional counseling has assisted many women in recovering from the emotional traumas of life.

Next, as you go through your crisis, turn your attention toward *self-improvement.* Search for opportunities to attend classes that are of interest to you. Join an aerobics or other exercise class, take a course at the community college or local university, seek job-training opportunities that might help you advance at your job. Activities such as these will keep your mind off the negative aspects of your situation and will provide benefits that will improve your mental, physical, intellectual, and, possibly, your financial stability.

Another way to engage in self-improvement is to give time and *service to others.* Helping people has a marvelous effect on morale and self-esteem. Contributing your time will allow you to focus on the positive things in life rather than the negative circumstances you are facing. Try to reserve some of your time so that you can serve your church, or volunteer in a community service program or charitable organization. If you work well with children, volunteer to assist with functions or programs at your local school. Your contributions will be appreciated and you will be able to see the blessings that you are able to give to people and your community.

Finally, as you begin to get a grip on your emotions, seek ways to *help your children adjust* to the situation also. Allow them to talk about their problems so that you will know how to deal with their frustrations. Provide them with much prayer, study of the Word, support from extended family members and friends, plus many activities that will boost their self-esteem and keep them busy. Children are very resilient and can "bounce back" as long as you are loving, supportive, and full of hope in the Lord. Enroll your children in groups that will be helpful to them and seek professional counseling for them if you determine that it is necessary.

Many women across the nation are handling their emotions successfully as they recover from the trauma of living without their mate in the home. An example of that success is shared next by co-author Annie Roberson, who is from Dallas, Texas.

A Personal Testimony

In my situation, I left my mate after nineteen-and-a-half years of marriage because of a gambling addiction that he refused to recognize as a financial problem for himself and our family. What do you do when your mate refuses help and denies that he has a problem? Do you stay in the struggle and have a nervous breakdown or become despondent with life as a whole? You can't force him to seek help or to quit gambling. Neither can you help your mate by continuous fussing and nagging. But you can seek help for yourself.

As a Christian woman, I consulted with spiritual advisors at my church. Even when I was counseled that I had grounds to separate, I did not. I was still waiting on a miraculous change in my mate. I wanted to see him value the marriage and the family as a whole.

Confronting

My mate did not respond to verbal interaction regarding the addiction's impact on the family or to letters I wrote seeking to clarify the family crisis. Home was a place where he ate his meals, got his clothes washed, and met his personal needs. My children and I were basically on our own to take care of our own business. There was no unity, partnership, nurturing, sharing, caring. We were merely cohabiting in the same house.

Leaving

Leaving was not a fly-by-night decision. It was something I wrestled with for several years. As a matter of fact, in 1984 I heard a sermon entitled "The Portrait of a Fool." In this sermon, the pastor talked about a woman being married to a fool. A foolish man could be blessed with an excellent wife who carries out all the domestic responsibilities of a godly woman caring for him and the children, but he would not value or respect her. The preacher did not recommend divorce, but did state that there was a time when a woman had to leave a fool in order for the children to live with at least one sane person in a household of peace.

Leaving my mate was a decision bathed in much prayer. Some women have lost their lives after such a decision. Know your mate. Even more, know God! Use godly wisdom in all your decisions. Some family situations are so traumatic and abusive that a mate must seek safety for herself and her children outside of the unwholesome environment.

Again, leaving for me was not an easy decision because I am a Christian. God blessed us with our three beautiful daughters, and I never wanted them to experience not having a father in the home as I had. As my husband's addiction worsened, however (as most addictions do), I decided to leave on the basis of 1 Corinthians 7:10–11: "But to the married I give instructions, not I, but the Lord, that the wife should not leave her husband (but if she does leave, let her remain unmarried, or else be reconciled with her husband), and that the husband should not send his wife away" (NASB).

The option, as I understand the Scripture, is that if the wife leaves, she is to remain unmarried or else be reconciled with her husband. Scripture also says, "God hates divorce" (Malachi 2:16). Therefore, I must hate it too. I chose to leave based on the Scripture in Corinthians, anticipating that my husband would then seek family counseling.

Reconciliation

To my great disappointment, that counseling has not happened, even though it is what I desired. I would like our relationship to be reconciled. Two people, however, must want reconciliation and work at making it happen. If there is not cooperation between the two parties, your hands are tied. Only God can make the two one if they are obedient to the Word. He is not going to force either party. He loves them both. God will bless the one who is obedient. "For this cause a man shall leave his father and his mother, and shall cleave [*stick like glue*] to his wife; and they shall become one flesh"(Genesis 2:24 NASB). Can we force our mates to cleave to us? The answer is no. Our only recourse is to pray, live holy lives, and wait on deliverance from God.

Support

I sought help from Gamblers Anonymous and the Alanon organization. I carried my girls with me to counseling sessions so that they would understand the situation that our family was going through. I received much satisfaction from these support groups. They understood the situation. I found out that our family was not alone in this crisis. I found out that people of all races share in this common problem; I heard testimonies of people who were walking in my shoes. They had come to the realization that they needed help and were seeking that help. When our mates made bad decisions we were the ones who tried to correct the problem. I learned that adults have to be responsible for their own behavior and suffer the consequences of that behavior.

With the help of these support groups I was able to let go and to be satisfied with my decision to be separated after almost twenty years of marriage. I continue to pray for my husband's salvation and surrender to the Lord. I think of the longing expressed in Scripture: "O Jerusalem, Jerusalem, ... how often would I have gathered thy children together, even as a hen gathereth her chicks under her wings, and ye would not!" (Matthew 23:37 KJV). Only God holds the future and knows how this will end.

Since that time (now two and a half years), I have received one telephone call from my husband and no efforts toward reconciling our relationship. In spite of this, I felt compelled to invite my mate to attend counseling sessions, couples' retreats, and Gamblers Anonymous for support and direction. His response was that they couldn't be worked into his schedule and he doesn't need help.

Am I sitting in a dark room biting my fingernails, pulling my hair out, or raiding the refrigerator? Heaven forbid! My God is sovereign! I hold onto the Scripture in Philippians: "I have learned the secret of being filled and going hungry, both of having abundance and suffering need. I can do all things through Him who strengthens me" (Philippians 4:12 NASB).

Has it been easy? Of course not. The separation has been very painful for me and my girls. They did not want to leave their dad, their home, their friends, and their school district. Adjustments are always painful. But by the grace of God we've made them.

I sought the help of my godly mother and actually moved in with her for one year. I was able to save a little money. I used her car while I prayed for my own transportation. Eventually I was able to purchase a used station wagon in good running condition. As a matter of fact, the week I purchased it, I needed to take my daughter to Austin, Texas, to test for her cosmetology license. I asked the car's seller if the car would make it. He said, "Sure, take your time." By faith we went off to Austin from Dallas. We did not have any problems with the car and it is still running. I prayed, but God knew what I needed even before I asked. Tough decisions are tough to us, but they are not tough for God.

Over time, we were able to move into our own apartment. Even though I do not like being absent from my mate because it feels like a bad witness before the watching world, I have honored God in my Christian walk and conduct. I love God and wait for Him to move on my behalf.

Parenting Alone

As I weather the storm of parenting alone, I seek to keep my children the center of my focus by providing them tender love and care; I affirm them in every way possible because they must get over the hurt and feelings of blame they have for my mate not being in the home. I let them talk about their feelings of hurt and the fact that we had to live with their grandmother for a while because of circumstances.

Since the separation, two of my daughters have graduated from high school. My youngest daughter is still at home and is involved in the youth ministry and the youth choir at our church. The church provides trips, skating parties, and bowling activities throughout the year. These programs help a lot when parenting alone. My church also provides wholesome activities for my entire family. We have a single parents' support group that meets on Fridays for women (and men) who are parenting alone. Free child care is provided. Throughout the year, courses and seminars are set up to address specific needs through the Christian education ministry.

I feel it is important to take advantage of ministries at church and activities at recreation centers in the community. These resources have helped my children's growth and self-esteem. For example, I enrolled my teenager in an etiquette course held at the local mall to boost her morale. She enjoyed it. I look for things that my youngest daughter and I can do together. We started an exercise class together and from time to time we walk to her high school for more exercise.

Perseverance

Finally, I do not isolate myself or retreat into the dark for pity parties. I pray, study the Scriptures, keep the faith, and stay involved in life. I pursue help from Christian people, especially my mother, sisters, and pastors. I also sought assistance from a Christian counseling center.

I often think of my friend and sister in the Lord, whose mate was incarcerated for five years. She was very bitter and angry with him. Her few visits to the prison resulted in explosive, angry encounters. She was at the point where she really hated her husband. For emotional reasons, she found it hard to care about herself and to dress attractively. After months of counseling and encouragement, she walked into the church one day, completely transformed. Why was she transformed? She found an older woman to counsel her. She was able to vent her frustrations in a weekly women's support group. Her attitude change enabled her demeanor to change. As she made progress, she was able to take advantage of an opportunity for a better paying job. The Christian counseling was the key to enable her to receive healing and success.

Parenting alone, letting go of the past, and moving on toward God's promises: it can be done. Whether your mate is absent because of incarceration, desertion, or your own leaving, the pains are the same. You will need support, encouragement, and direction. Look for wisdom in the Word of God and God's people.

CONCLUSION

There is little doubt that the African-American woman who has lost a mate will have to deal with the emotional trauma that stems from this situation. As she deals with the adjustments, stress, and hardships it is comforting to know that others have emerged victorious by utilizing the strategies that minister to the inner woman: prayer, study of the Word, the development of faith in God. It is also encouraging to avail oneself of those things that promote a positive outlook and improve the quality of life: Christian counseling, self-improvement opportunities, and support for your children. Remember, one of the greatest benefits of being a Christian is that you will never have to "go it alone," especially to handle your emotions, because the Lord will always be with you as you go through the healing process.

Take the advice of Annie Roberson: Do not sit in a dark room and bite your fingernails, pull your hair out, or raid the refrigerator. Do not give yourself a pity party. Instead, claim the promises of God and remember, you can do all things through Christ who strengthens you.

Recommended Reading

Ashker, Helen. *Jesus Cares for Women*. Colorado Springs: NavPress, 1987.

Dobson, James C. *Emotions: Can you Trust Them?* Wheaton, IL: Tyndale House, 1992.

_____. *Love Must Be Tough*. Dallas: Word Books, 1993.

Evans, Anthony. *Marriage God's Style*. Chicago: Moody Press, n.d.

Foh, Susan. *Women and the Word of God: A Response to Biblical Feminism*. Grand Rapids: Baker, 1980.

Kraft, Vickie. *The Influential Woman*. Dallas: Word Books, 1992.

Lockyer, Herbert. *The Women of the Bible*. Grand Rapids: Zondervan, 1988.

McGee, Robert. *The Search for Significance*. Houston: Rapha Publishing, 1990.

Richards, Larry. *When Life Is Unfair*. Dallas: Word Books, n.d.

Richmond, Gary. *The Divorce Decision: What It Can Mean for Your Children, Your Finances, Your Emotions, Your Relationship, Your Future*. Waco, TX: Word Books, 1988.

Rodger-Rose, LaFrances. *The Black Woman*. Beverly Hills, CA: Sage Publications, n.d.

Springle, Pat. *Codependency: A Christian Perspective*. Waco, TX: Word/Rapha, 1990.

Swindoll, Charles. *Living on the Ragged Edge*. Cassette tape LRE 10-A. Fullerton, CA: Insight for Living, n.d.

_____. *The Quest for Character*. Portland, OR: Multnomah Press, 1987.

References

Bane, M., and R. Weiss. 1980. Alone together: the work of single-parent families. *American Demographics* 2 (May): 11–14.

Chideya, F. 1995. *Don't believe the hype: Fighting cultural misinformation about African-Americans*. New York: Penguin Books.

Duncan, G. 1984. *Years of poverty, years of plenty: The changing economic fortunes of American workers and families*. Ann Arbor, MI: Institute of Social Research.

Duncan, G., and S. Hoffman. 1985. A reconsideration of the economic consequences of marital dissolution. *Demography* 22 (November): 485–97.

Espendshade, T. 1979. The economic consequences of divorce. *Journal of Marriage and Family* 14 (August): 615–25.

Evangelauf, J. 1992. Minority-group enrollment at colleges rose 10% from 1988 to 1990, reaching record levels. *Chronicle of Higher Education*, A33–A37.

1984. *The holy Bible: New international version*. Grand Rapids: Zondervan.

King, A. 1993. The impact of incarceration on African-American families: Implications for practice. Families in society. *Journal of Contemporary Human Services* 10 (March 1993): 145–53.

The King James version of the Bible.

1971. *The living Bible*. Wheaton, IL: Tyndale House.

Kniesner, T., M. McElroy, and S. Wilcox. 1988. Getting into poverty without a husband, and getting out, with or without. *American Economic Review* 78 (May): 86–90.

Mauldin, T., and J. Koonce. 1990. The effects of human capital on the economic status of divorced and separated women: Differences by race. *Review of Black Political Economy* 18 (Spring): 55–68.

1984. *The new American standard Bible*. Nashville: Thomas Nelson.

Smith, J., and E. Beninger. 1982. Women's nonmarket labor: Dissolution of marriage and opportunity cost. *Journal of Family Issues* 3 (June): 251–65.

U.S. Bureau of the Census. 1992. *The Black population in the United States*. Washington, DC: U.S. Government Printing Office.

U.S. Department of Health and Human Services. 1993. *Characteristics and financial circumstances of AFDC recipients: Fiscal year 1991.* Washington, DC: U.S. Government Printing Office.

U.S. Department of Justice. 1991a. *Correctional populations in the United States, 1991a: Jail inmates, 1990.* Office of Justice Statistics Bulletin (NCJ–129–756). Washington, DC: U.S. Government Printing Office.

U.S. Department of Justice. 1991b. *Jail inmates, 1990.* Office of Justice Statistics Bulletin (NCJ–130–445). Washington, DC: U.S. Government Printing Office.

Wineberg, H. 1990. The timing of intermarital fertility. *Social Science Quarterly* 71 (March): 175–83.

Weitzman, L. 1985. *The divorce revolution: The unexpected social and economic consequences for women and children in America.* New York: Free Press.

Jean Jackson-Swopes

From Marriage to Singleness: Coping with Widowhood

JEAN JACKSON-SWOPES is a native of Gainesville, Florida. She holds a bachelor's degree in pre-medicine from Bennett College in Greensboro, North Carolina, a master's degree in microbiology from the University of Kansas, and a doctorate in microbiology specializing in immunochemistry from the University of Florida at Gainesville. Jean is a College Relations Manager for Abbott Laboratories. Jean resides in North Chicago, Illinois, with her husband, Sherman, and their five children. She is a member of Waukegan Community Church in Waukegan, Illinois, and is a Sunday school teacher and the director of the children's ministry.

Chapter 10

Jean Jackson-Swopes

From Marriage to Singleness: Coping with Widowhood

There is a time for everything, and a season for every activity under heaven: a time to be born and a time to die. (Ecclesiastes 3:1–2)

One might ask, why this chapter in a book written about African-American females? Physical death is the destiny of every human. We cannot conquer death. We can produce it and delay it, but we cannot stop it. It appears that the destiny of death occurs earlier in the lives of African-American males as a group than for males of any other ethnic group (Chideya 1995). When death strikes, mates of African-American men are left behind to suffer the loss. The rule of relational permanence holds that when two people love and marry each other, they should always remain together. When we love someone, we come to identify with that person. To be suddenly thrust into singleness due to the loss of a loved one, whether by death, divorce, or other tragic circumstances, can be devastating. When death strikes, the loss is permanent. The person as we knew him in this life will never exist again. What is left? Shock and intolerable pain.

IN THE FACE OF DEATH AND BEREAVEMENT

Most of us know that death, like birth, is a normal and inevitable phase of the human experience. A grieving widow can be either an ugly reminder that this too might happen to other wives or she can be a lifting monument of a God who provides divine protection.

Books on death, dying, and grieving are numerous. Widows have written guides for other widows to assist them through the long and painful process of recovery (Gates 1990). Many women have suffered this loss and have been left to go it alone. In 1993, there were 11.2 million widows in the United States, of which 12 percent (1.4 million) were African-American (Statistical Abstract of the United States 1994); additionally, of the 11.2 million widowed, 8.6 million were over the age of sixty-five (Census 1994).

This portion of our chapter is dedicated to African-American females who have lost or may lose a mate to death. It is a message of encouragement and love. God does provide for widows and holds them in high regard. It is as if before creation, He knew that the journey of the widow would be a lonely, desolate, and painful one. From Genesis to Revelations He has ensured her provision and protection. Women should know this, especially African-American females, because the way is already difficult. Throughout the Old and New Testaments, God is adamant about the treatment of widows. The word "widow" appears in numerous passages. God uses widows in very special ways to demonstrate His compassion and will for people's lives. It is also interesting to note that there is no similar biblical treatment for widowers.

The widow is no longer so isolated today. Bereavement groups and clubs offering support are readily available (Taves 1981). How a widow deals with the pain of loss depends fundamentally upon the relationship she has with God and her understanding of the new role and responsibility that comes with widowhood. Most Christian females know that when death strikes, they don't have to go it alone. They know that there is a God who can and will sustain them through this rite of passage. Much has been written about grief and widowhood, but little attention has been given to God's perspective on widowhood. African-American women need to know that the greatest dignity to be found in mourning the loss of a loved one is the dignity that can be found in the life one lives afterward.

GRIEF AND MOURNING

"Blessed are those who mourn, for they will be comforted."
(Matthew 5:4)

When death strikes, the bereaved are thrust into a state of emotional stress which has all the physical and psychological effects of severe physical trauma. It is this state of stress and emotional injury that precipitates grief. If recovery is to take place, there must first be a period of mourning. Mourning is the way of managing grief and restoring the wounded spirit to wholeness. Intervention in the mourning process can have devastating consequences. Sickness and death may even result (Margolis 1975). Those women who experience the untimely deaths of their spouses are more vulnerable than those who experience an anticipated death. Studies have shown that the bereaved are more prone to death and even physical disease within the first year after the death of a spouse than similar age-matched groups who have not suffered loss by death. Some studies have found an increased incidence of hormonal imbalances in bereaved individuals, often leading to physical diseases such as cancer and tuberculosis, and affective disorders such as depression (Margolis 1975). Seven stages of grief are identified and described below (Caine 1988). For each woman, the order and duration may differ, but the stages are all the same.

Numbness and shock. The initial news of the death of a loved one is like a heavy weight. When it comes unexpectedly it can leave one listless and without emotion. This is a period when the death is recognized but is neither accepted nor fully integrated into the realm of reality (Ginsburg 1987). On the outside a widow may appear rational and calm, and even emotionally under control. This initial numbness is the body's way of dealing with the intense initial agony and pain.

Denial. This is a period when the bereaved refuses to accept that a mate is truly dead. It is a defense against reality (Raab 1989). If we deny that something takes place, we shift it to the back of our minds. This brings about a belief that if we don't accept it then it isn't happening. Denial may actually serve as a cushion to allow for time to readjust while functioning through the process of arranging and planning the funeral.

Anger. This is misdirected blame and is one of the more prominent stages of grief. The bereaved may become angry at the doctor, friends, family members, the person who died, and even God. It isn't uncommon to hear comments like "Why me?" or "Why did he leave me with all these problems?" Anger is a common human emotion rooted in feelings of rage, helplessness, and guilt (Mason 1988). The danger of anger is that if it persists, it can and does become debilitating.

Disorientation. When the mind is overloaded with demands and decisions, the bereaved may lose all sense of direction or relationship with surroundings. This period is marked by bouts of forgetfulness, irrational thoughts, and in some instances, irrational behavior.

Depression. This feeling of gloominess and loneliness results from the realization that one's mate truly is gone (Brothers 1990). These melancholic feelings may be based on real or imaginary concerns and usually go unrecognized. Most women are able to work through this form of depression, but some do not succeed. Many women suffer great depression and are afraid to seek help. When identified, clinical depression can be treated. In some instances, if clinical depression goes unchecked, it can and does lead to physical illness and even death by suicide.

Guilt. Feelings of self-blame and self-recrimination are also experienced by most widows (Ginsburg 1987). Many women express disbelief and anger in being left alone, particularly those who have no job skills and are left with minor children. This is often manifested in "if only" thoughts, such as "if only I had insisted that he see a doctor," or "if only I had made him exercise more, then he would still be alive." Many times the bereaved may overcompensate for feelings of guilt by holding an elaborate and expensive funeral. What she failed to give a husband in life, she tries to give in death.

Acceptance. This the final acknowledgment that the death has occurred and that the person's life is finished. He is gone. This stage also brings about the realization that one has to go on with life. It may take a considerable amount of time to reach this stage, but until then healing cannot start.

Grief does not have a timetable and each widow must allow the stages to unfold in her own time and way. The process of mourning as a reaction to the loss of a loved one must be carried out to completion. The intensity and duration of the mourning period are related to the depth of the sense of loss. The funeral ritual, the laying to rest of the body, is the most accessible and valid resource for meeting the full range of emotional issues that are encountered in grief (Margolis 1975). For African-Americans, the disposition of the body and a need to involve the community in the ceremony is a very important part of the our culture (Mathabane 1994). To have the *proper* funeral is almost as important as living. For many, the disposition of the body reflects the dignity and worth of the deceased. It is an opportunity for many widows to demonstrate the reverence and, in some instances, the awe with which the spouse was regarded in life.

AFRICAN-AMERICAN WOMEN AND GRIEF

The process of grieving for African-American females is deeply rooted in the African heritage. In many African cultures, the funeral ritual lasted for days and involved the entire community. Although death was considered a private affair, it was also at the same time an affair of the community. This public expression of grief brought healing and help, not only for the bereaved wife and family members, but also for the people of the community. It was a chance for all to celebrate the loss of a soul and to heal. As with Western cultures, death was not seen as the end, but as a transition. For this transition to take place, everyone had to be involved with the dead: the immediate family, the extended family, and the community. The suspension of normal activities was not only required but considered necessary if the dead were to traverse to the land of the ancestors and if the living were to heal.

The strict death etiquette that is imposed on African-American females in some communities is also deeply rooted in ancestral rituals. The body had to be handled properly. In some cases this required a process, assisted by the elderly women of the tribe, of baths in magical potions of animal blood and various medicinal herbs and roots (Mathabane 1994).

The custom of African-American widows to isolate themselves and adorn themselves in black clothing during and after the funeral is another example of this ritual. Even today, in some African cultures a widow is viewed as unclean, contaminated, and an object of bad luck.

From a Christian perspective, we know that Christ knew and understood the pain and anguish associated with death and grief. Nowhere is this more evident than in the Beatitudes, when He said, "Blessed are those who mourn, for they will be comforted" (Matthew 5:4). The Greek word used here for "mourn" is the strongest word known for mourning in the Greek language (Unger 1978). It is the word used by Jacob in his expression of grief when he believed that Joseph, his son, was dead (Genesis 37:34). It is the kind of grief that cannot be hidden. It is the kind of grief that brings deep pain to the heart and unrestrained tears to the eyes. This kind of sorrow can do either one of two things for us: it can bring us to our knees or it can take us to our graves. To mourn is normal and the funeral ritual is therapeutic. Women must remember that the goal of the grieving process is not to forget the person who is lost but rather to embrace them in death, and accept that grief is inevitable.

A widow should gain a deeper dependence on God and know that He values her. He is in control, and He is big enough to handle the anger and guilt. She should recognize that she is not alone in her pain and she should establish a deeper connection with other people. It is time for her to fully embrace the promise of heaven and know that God will fulfill His promises. When things go well it is possible to live on the surface for years; but when sorrow comes, such as that experienced when a loved one dies, one has to go deep into the things of life. It is there that we find solace and new strength. It is there that through the comfort and compassion of God, beauty enters the soul.

A DIFFERENT DESTINY: A ROLE ADORNED BY GOD

A father to the fatherless, a defender of widows, is God in his holy dwelling. (Psalm 68:5)

Widows and widowhood are referred to almost a hundred times in the Bible. God is very succinct and clear on his expectations and treatment of the fatherless and widows. Old and New Testament coverage provides a complete code of conduct for widowhood, which covers God's instruction to the widow, the family, the church, and the community. Widows are repeatedly used as examples of God's expectations of us and of His divine power to protect and provide for us. In Exodus, Deuteronomy, and Leviticus, God states over and over again His beneficial provision for widows: "Every forgotten sheaf in the harvest field was to lie; the olive tree was not to be beaten a second time; nor were the last of the grapes to be gathered but rather were to be left behind in order that the hearts of strangers [aliens], the fatherless and widows might be gladdened by the bounty of Providence" (Deuteronomy 24:19–21, paraphrased).

God has never indicated that a widow is unclean or contaminated. In fact, quite to the contrary, He clearly states: "Do not oppress the widow or the fatherless, the alien or the poor. In your hearts do not think evil of each other" (Zechariah 7:10).

By definition, a widow is one who has survived the loss of a husband. There is, however, a significant difference between the younger widow and the older widow (Nudel 1986). The difference is not in the pain they suffer, but in their rite of passage. Generally, the death of a younger person is more difficult to accept. Most people do not wish to believe that a young person can die. It brings death too close to home. (If a younger person dies, it implies one's own vulnerability to death.)

In many instances, the younger widow may find that she is avoided by friends and family. Her life is temporarily placed on hold. The dreams and visions that she and her husband may have shared will never be. If there are children, the way for her is even more difficult. She has the added responsibility of going beyond herself to assist them in their grief. If they are preschoolers, caring for them may limit her contact with older adults, lessening the opportunities to talk through the pain and the grief.

By contrast, the older widow today is much more familiar with death and dying. She also has had many more years of living and coping during which to develop and refine basic survival strategies (Nudel 1986). Over the years, she will have most likely already experienced numerous losses of friends and family: some to nursing homes, some to better climates, and some even to death. Those older widows who have enjoyed happy marriages have memories of the good and the bad times to sustain them in their hour of grief.

For older widows, sex may or may not be important anymore. For the young widow, this is a different story. Life has dealt her a dirty blow; in the peak of her sexual life she has been robbed of the one man who chose to honor and cherish her for the rest of her life.

Solace comes in knowing that in the New Testament, God gives a deeper meaning to widowhood. He also distinguishes between the needs of the true widow, the older widow, and the young widow. For each, He has made provisions. He defines the true widow as one who is in need and alone, without living children or grandchildren. He has placed these women in the responsible care of the church. For the true widow without a church family, who dedicates her life to Him through daily prayer and petition, God has promised direct divine protection and provision.

Widows who have living children or grandchildren are to be cared for by their families. Families and churches who fail to provide for their own are considered to be worse than unbelievers. Younger widows, with normal and healthy desires, are encouraged to remarry to prevent them from entering into sinful relationships or engaging in the temptations associated with idleness. Widows who live ungodly lives are considered spiritually dead and do not qualify for either the support of the church or God's divine provisions.

GOD'S REGARD FOR THE WIDOW

The LORD watches over the alien and sustains the fatherless and the widow, but he frustrates the ways of the wicked. (Psalm 146:9)

Biblical narratives about widows are both instructive and important for our guidance. Through the widows of the Bible, God powerfully demonstrates His divine care and protection of all of His children. In the Old Testament, God's most prominent use of widows was to insure the genealogy of Jesus Christ through the lineage of David and for the edification and building up of two of His strongest prophets, Elisha and Elijah. Tamar, a Canaanite, is considered a woman with a pathetic history. Through incest, trickery, and debauchery, this widow became the mother of Perez, a son of Judah and thus an ancestor of Jesus, the Messiah (Genesis 38:12–30). Another widow, Ruth, a Moabite, through her marriage to Boaz, a Hebrew, was blessed with a son, Obed, who became the father of Jesse and the grandfather of King David. Ruth was awarded a place in the chosen line through which the Savior of the World appeared (Matthew 1:3–6).

These two examples show two widows opposite in character, one a wretched sinner, the other a loyal and loving friend, both used by God to affirm that His son would bear the burden of sin for all and redeem both the Jews and Gentiles. Ruth's unselfish loyalty and love is a monument to all young widows, for such is the foundation of true friendship and happiness today. Tamar is God's reminder to us that we all sin and fall short of God, but through him there is the offer of forgiveness and eternal life (Lockyer 1988). God's way of accomplishing His plans and His high regard of widows can be seen in the story of the widow with her port of oil (2 Kings 4:1–7). In her hour of greatest need, this widow was able to help God's prophet Elisha. Her faith, belief, and obedience enabled her to experience God's power and divine provision. She was given "over and above" the amount requested.

The widow of Zarephat is but another example of how God used a widow to demonstrate His will for humankind. Through a synergistic relationship with the prophet Elijah, God provided for this widow and her son during severe famine and drought. The life of her son was restored, the first recorded instance in Scripture where God used the restoration to life of one who had died to authenticate His power. Additionally, through her faith she came to prove, like the widow with her jar of oil, that "little is much, if God is in it." Her sharing with another in need did not impoverish, but greatly enriched, her life. In the New Testament, Jesus immortalized the widow Zarephat as a symbol of the dispensation of God's divine grace.

In the New Testament, God continued His admonition to the church to care for and protect the widow. It was clear that the early church heeded this command, for Scripture records great concern and care shown for widows, particularly when there had been previous neglect (Acts 6:1). When we consider the widows of the New Testament, we see that God continued to provide lasting lessons on sacrificial living and giving.

Consider Anna the prophetess, the only female in the New Testament to have that title (Lockyer 1988). Anna was a "true" widow. Married for only seven years, she was still a widow at the age of eighty-four. Upon the death of her husband, she was left alone and desolate. But Anna did not bury her hope in a grave; rather, she devoted herself completely to the service of the Lord through daily fasting and prayer at the temple. Hers was a life of godly control. Through her faith and long years of devotion she was awarded the distinction of being the first female to announce to all those who were looking forward to the redemption of Jerusalem that the Messiah had come (Luke 2:36–38).

Consider, too, the widow of Nain (Luke 7:11–18). Like many other widows in the Bible, she was the recipient of a special dispensation from heavenly hands. Hers is an example of the millions of bereaved mothers whose sorrows have been resolved through divine intervention. When Jesus encountered the funeral procession of her only son, He was deeply moved. He touched the coffin and the widow's son was restored to life. This was the first manifestation of Jesus' divine power to raise the dead. The widow of Nain didn't seek Jesus—He came to her out of love and compassion.

Jesus taught us, through the parable of the widow with only two mites, that it is not what we give, but how we give (Mark 12:41–44 ; Luke 21:1–4). Jesus used this lonely widow to show us that "the eyes of the Lord are in every place, beholding the evil and the good."

In the parable of the importunate widow (Luke 18:1–8) Jesus taught us the importance of continuous prayer and petition. The objective of this parable was to teach us patience and perseverance through prayer.

CONCLUSION

Godly widows operate in this world under the protective, loving, divine plan of God. When death strikes her mate, and the pain seems unbearable, the widow should seek refuge at the feet of the Father. The pain and suffering are inevitable, but God gives the widow the ability to choose to trust in Him. If she stays in His will, her choices will be His choices and He will do great things through her. His plans will be carried out in His own time. The African-American widow, in her pain and sorrow, must go deep into the things of life. If she lives a godly and obedient life, faithful and submissive to God, she will come face to face with the Savior, and He will provide her with divine protection. This is her blessed assurance.

$\mathcal{R}$eferences

Brothers, J. 1990. *Widowed*. New York: Simon & Schuster.

Caine, L. 1988. *A helpful guide to the problems of being a widow*. New York: Morrow/Arbor Houser.

Chideya, F. 1995. *Don't believe the hype: Fighting cultural misinformation about the African-American*. New York: Penguin Books.

Gates, P. 1990. *Suddenly alone: A guide to widowhood*. New York: Harper & Row.

Ginsburg, G. 1987. *Suddenly to live again: Rebuilding your life after you've become a widow*. Los Angeles: Jeremy P. Tarcher.

1984. *The holy Bible: New international version*. Grand Rapids: Zondervan.

Lockyer, H. 1988. *All the women of the Bible*. Grand Rapids: Zondervan.

Margolis, O., et al. 1975. *Grief and the meaning of the funeral*. New York: MSS Information Corp.

Mason, J. 1988. *Stress passages: Surviving life's transitions gracefully*. Berkeley, CA: Celestial Arts.

Mathabane, M. 1994. *African women: Three generations*. New York: HarperCollins.

Nudel, A. 1986. *Starting over: Help for young widows and widowers*. New York: Dodd, Mead.

Raab, R. 1989. *Coping with death*. New York: Rosen.

U.S. Department of Commerce, Economics and Statistics Administration. 1994. *Statistical abstract of the United States, 114th edition*. Washington, DC: Bureau of the Census.

Taves, I. 1981. *The widow's guide*. New York: Schocken Books.

Unger, M. 1978. *Unger's Bible dictionary*. Chicago: Moody Press.

PART 4

FACING ISSUES AND MANAGING RESOURCES

Millicent Lindo

Balancing Home and Career

MILLICENT LINDO is the Executive Director of Westside Holistic Family Services in Chicago, Illinois. Born and raised in Armadale, Jamaica, she has a bachelor of science degree from DePaul University in Chicago and a master's degree in social work from George Williams College in Aurora, Illinois. She and her husband, Lloyd, live in Oak Park, Illinois, and have three children: Ruth and twins Donna and Gale. She is a member of the Keystone Baptist Church, where she serves on the Advisory Board and Outreach ministry.

Chapter 11

Millicent Lindo

Balancing Home and Career

... a woman's identity and self-worth should not be based solely on what she does. A woman needs a whole life perspective which is founded on who she is as the individual God has made her to be with her unique background and experiences, gifts and qualities, and opportunities for expressing them. (Conway and Conway 1983, p. 69)

It is quite evident in today's society that the work force has changed drastically over the past three decades or so. More women have joined the labor force, stimulated by economic needs and a belief in their capabilities and rights to pursue opportunities. A clear and increasing majority of women believe that both husband and wife should be able to work, should have roughly similar opportunities, and should share household responsibilities and the tasks of child rearing. The majority of mothers of preschool children now work outside the home (Hamberg 1993).

A working woman is most often trying to handle three jobs at once: career, mother, and wife. This is truly emotionally draining, besides placing great demands on her time. As a result, she often wrestles with guilt at not being able to do all three of them well. Working mothers also have to deal with how the demands of family impact their jobs. For instance, it is the mother who is usually notified when a child becomes ill. Must she remain at home to nurse a sick child? Employers are not always flexible or tolerant with this arrangement.

A working mother must consider her husband's attitude toward her work outside the home: "Some men are threatened with the possibility that their wives may become independent from them in everything—from the use of money to making decisions and having outside stimulation. The need for strengthening the marriage relationship is always present whether both are working or only the husband is" (Conway & Conway 1983, p. 69). The rise of the divorce rate has caused changes in the law regarding child support. Women of the '90s are seeing a need to develop their career in order to be prepared for the possibility of having to take sole responsibility for the care of themselves and their children. Of great significance is the increased number of single-parent families. The African-American community has seen a dramatic increase in the number of teenaged parents. These single parents have one of two choices: become trapped in the welfare system or go to work.

These changes that have been taking place in our families and our society as a whole are not new. This is especially true for the African-American woman. It is interesting to review the historical struggles of women of color, because balancing career and home is not new for us. This chapter will look at these issues within the context of our history as African-American working mothers. In addition, some helpful hints for both the working married and single woman will also be shared.

A HISTORICAL PERSPECTIVE

Paula Giddings, in her book *When and Where I Enter* (1985), gives us a historical perspective on African-American women and work. She points out that following the abolition of slavery, "free black women of the North had to struggle with consequences of being perceived as a different kind of humanity." Giddings writes:

Abolition had not erased the taint of their alleged immorality, and the converging social economic forces in the 1830s added a new challenge. With the emergence of a self-conscious middle class, black women had to overcome notions about the relationship of class, as well as color, to morality.

Northern industrialization brought about by the textile mills was reaching new heights in this period. The consequent flow of capital created a new middle class striving for upper-class status. For women the vehicle for these aspirations was what became known as the "cult of the lady" or the "cult of true womanhood." The idea of the cult was not

new. What had changed was the cult idea, its elevation to a status symbol. (p. 46)

According to historians such as Gerda Lerner, after abolition a woman
had to be true to the cult's cardinal tenets of domesticity, submissiveness,
piety, and purity in order to be good enough for society's inner circles.
Failure to adapt to any of these tenets, which the overwhelming number
of Black women could hardly live up to, made one less than a morally
"true" woman.

Domesticity held a central position in the cult idea. The true woman's
exclusive roles were homemaker, mother, housewife, and family tutor of
social and moral graces. Leisure (formally scorned as idleness) rather than
industriousness was the measure of social standing. Middle-class women,
who were contributors to the family economy, became models of conspic-
uously unproductive expenditures:

> In an increasingly industrial economy, many White men left the farm
> to work in factories. During the early rise of the factory system, it is
> reported that the main source of the labor force was proud, or needy,
> Puritan girls who viewed their work as a stopgap until they married.
>
> This work, though strenuous and with low pay, carried a certain status.
> With the coming of the cult, however, work outside the home lost its
> prestige, and women like the Puritan girls were no longer expected to
> be in the labor force but to stay at home and reproduce the labor force.
> These women were replaced by poorer immigrant women, a cheaper,
> more permanent, and more exploitable source of workers. (Giddings
> 1985, p. 48)

During this period, when increasing numbers of poorer women left
their homes and became factory workers, the slogan, "A woman's place is
in the home!" took on a certain aggressiveness and shrillness. It also
occurred when the abolition of slavery brought African-American women
into the wage labor force. African-American women, however, were
excluded from the industrial labor force for more than a century and their
work was confined to menial labor. Giddings (1985) supports this observation by citing an 1847 census which reveals:

> Close to half of the female Black population of Philadelphia consisted
> of washerwomen and domestic servants. About 10% were needle

women; 5% were involved in trades like hairdressing and dressmaking, jobs that could be performed in their own homes. Black women, both married and single, were forced to work though single women tended to be domestics and married women who needed to care for children and family were most often washerwomen.

Black women activists on the one hand agreed with the fundamental premises of the Victorian ethic. On the other hand, they opposed its racist and classist implications. At the same time they were conscious of the pressure on free Blacks to prove they could be accultured into American society. (p. 48)

Kari Torjesen Malcolm, in her book *Women at the Crossroads* (1982), expresses the feeling that

Christian women of all cultures have experienced discouragement when it comes to investigating career goals. The university is usually seen as a place to seek a spouse rather than a time to draw near to God and develop relationships through a career. And there is an unspoken threat if a woman steps outside of her sphere (homemaking, nursing, typing). (p. 189)

She also states that women have been trained to hide their talents and, "consequently, some of them have denied the Lord's call to action" (p. 189).

It is true that a part of God's plan for most women is motherhood. This does not preclude women from developing a career, since most families consist of only two or three children and full-time motherhood, before children start school, occupies less than ten years of a woman's life.

It is, therefore, possible for women to develop a career, especially after their children leave home for college. I do not subscribe to the notion that a woman's place is in the home. If the woman chooses, however, to remain at home with her children while they are young, she can also continue to develop her intellect and her own identity aside from her husband and children. If these areas of her life are not developed, when the children leave home she often experiences a great sense of loss and emptiness which her spouse cannot fill.

Then as now, the African-American family had to struggle to maintain middle-class status. The majority of middle-income African-American families have dual careers. This is due primarily to the comparatively lower wages of the African-American males to that of their White counterparts holding similar positions.

Therefore, for African-American women, working outside the home is often not a choice, but a necessity. On the rare occasion when the choice is made not to work, the woman usually finds ways, such as caring for children in her home, to earn additional income.

For unskilled low-income families, fewer choices exist. Even with both parents working they barely manage to live above the poverty level and many barely subsist below the poverty level. Given these dynamics, how can the African-American mother, whether married or single, manage to balance her home and career effectively?

MY PERSONAL EXPERIENCE

Following the birth of our children, I remained at home for the first seven years. We had twin daughters and a third child before the twins were two years old. Needless to say, I had my hands full. That period of time was a struggle for me in two ways. First, it was difficult making ends meet and, second, I had plans on hold to complete my education and develop a career. My husband's position in those early years was that the care of our children was our first priority and that we could manage on his salary and so we did for the first seven years.

Let me state here that it was important to the peace and security of our home that my husband and I did not oppose each other. Therefore, I went along with my husband's view, but I never gave up my dream. With much prayer and many discussions, coupled with love and respect for each other, we made it work.

The years at home were years of sacrifice. Living on a missionary's salary, I shopped out of the missionary barrel, resale shops, and garage sales. Those were also happy and fulfilling years, as I learned to be creative by making most of the children's clothing as well as my own while remaining active in the church and community.

While I enjoyed caring for the children and have never regretted the years I spent with them, I was also restless to get on with my education and career. For me, making money was not as great an issue as the need to be productive outside the home. Not all women experience this need, but for me it was real.

The children were ages six and seven when I accepted my first position outside the home at a mental health center a couple of blocks from our home. The children were enrolled in a private school that provided bus transportation. It was convenient and my husband and I were able to arrange our schedules so that one of us would be home to receive them.

I also remember that the first year or so I tried to compensate for working by being a supermom. I tried to maintain both jobs at the highest level. It soon became clear that I could not continue to do so. Caring for the children's needs became a shared responsibility between my husband and me. Granted, it was more me, but he did help.

Because I was always prayerfully seeking God's will for my life, I believe He opened up the opportunity for me to return to school. It was there that I began to discover what my gifts were and to continue my education.

Looking back, I am grateful that I spent time with the children during those formative years. If it is at all possible, I recommend it to parents with young children, for the children's survival as well as your own.

After entering the work force, careful planning of our time was important. Meals for the week had to be carefully planned; grocery shopping was sometimes done during my lunch hour, only because I worked close to home; and house cleaning got done on Saturday mornings. Day-camp arrangements had to be planned for the summer months.

My husband and I always managed, every other year, to take a three-week vacation with the children in Jamaica, which is our birthplace. Those were very special times. We also managed a few long weekends and outings just for him and me. Our system was called *survival*. As the children grew older, they were given a share of the household chores. My heart goes out to parents of young children in today's society. The pressures on the job and away from the job are so much greater. This is true for African-American families who are raising children in the inner cities as well as the suburban areas of our nation. We have an ever-present fear of gang activity, the whole drug culture, and many other environmental influences that impact our children's lives.

I am personally grateful that I had the opportunity to develop my career. When my last child entered college, I was free to enter fully into my career. God has blessed it and has given me many fruitful years with three well-balanced children, two of whom are now raising their own families and also balancing their homes with their careers. It is important to differentiate between working for money to pay the bills and working in a career. A career not only brings monetary rewards, but also brings the satisfaction of knowing what you are capable of doing as the unique individual God created. You must understand the gifts and abilities that God has given to you and bring your career in line with those talents.

A SCRIPTURAL VIEW

What was God's plan for the man and the woman when he created them? In Genesis 1:27–28 we are told that God blessed them and told them to "multiply and fill the earth and subdue it; You are masters of the fish and the birds and all animals" (LB). It is clear from the beginning that God was not anticipating a passive role on the part of the wife. Along with helping to multiply, she was also given co-responsibility of managing all aspects of the earth.

In addition, many other female leaders in Scripture achieved national status: women such as Deborah, the chief executive officer of the nation of Israel (Judges 4:4–5:31), and Esther, whose wisdom and assertiveness saved her people from destruction (Esther 2:5–9:32). In the New Testament we have Priscilla, who worked alongside her husband in ministry in the early church. She contributed to the spiritual development of the apostle Paul and Apollos and seems to have been the stronger half of the couple (Acts 18; Romans 16:3; 1 Corinthians 16:19; 2 Timothy 4:19). Also, we have the example of the contribution of Phoebe, whose leadership Paul places on a par with his own (Romans 16:1). The Old and New Testament examples suggest that a woman's work should be related first to who she is as a person before God and then to the norms of society.

Neither the career woman nor the woman who feels she wants to remain at home with her children should be ridden with guilt. We are not all alike and God's plan for each of us is not the same. Seek His will and He will guide you in the path that is best for you and your family.

HELPFUL HINTS FOR THE MARRIED COUPLE

Make sure there is agreement that you will be a dual career family. Count the cost and develop a plan for the nurture of the children. This plan should include

- Spending daily quality time with the children when you give them your full attention.

- Playing with the children if they are young. Get down on the floor with them for something as simple as a pony ride on Mom's or Dad's back.
- Reading stories and having discussions around their main themes.
- Having planned devotional times, maybe right after the main meal of the day.
- Taking special trips to the park, the museum, or the zoo, when weather permits.
- Taking a planned, extended vacation with the children annually.
- Making time for yourselves. This may include dinner out or a weekend retreat alone if you can arrange a sitter (or the assistance of your extended family). Do not neglect your relationship with your husband out of guilt for spending more time with the children. One of the best gifts you can give your children is your own secure relationship with their father.
- Deciding together how the additional dollars earned will be spent.
- Developing a budget and deciding who is responsible for managing the payment of the bills, based on the abilities of each partner.

HELPFUL HINTS FOR THE SINGLE PARENT

- Develop surrogate parental relationships with people in your church who have children. Enlist the assistance of the extended family, grandmothers, aunts and uncles, sisters and brothers; but don't abuse the relationship—be fair.
- Develop a support group with peers with whom you can socialize and have adult conversations and rotate baby-sitting services.
- Make use of special after-school and summer camps for your children. Be sure to check them out carefully.
- Develop friendships and interact with married couples in your church. Often they will include your children in activities they have planned for their own children and give you a break.
- Plan at least one week of your vacation to spend time with your children doing fun activities and creating meaningful memories.
- Teach your children early to participate in household chores, such as making their own beds, cleaning their rooms, taking out the garbage, and other chores.

- Plan time for your own recreation.
- Remember, you cannot do it all and you do not have to be a super-mom, but rather just an ordinary, loving, nurturing mom.
- Choose child care wisely and carefully.
- Give yourself time to unwind (after work) before you deal with the children's needs and problems. Take a short nap before preparing dinner and helping with homework.

CONCLUSION

The subject of the African-American woman's dedication to a career, whether Christian or secular, is still a matter of motives and perspective. For the Christ-centered woman, life's work should not be categorized as either Christian or secular. When we are doing whatever is right for us, it is Christian, even though it may not be funded by a Christian institution. A woman may have a secular employer, but she is in full-time Christian service if her motivation is in line with God's. The important key is that at every stage a woman should evaluate who she is and where she wants to go with her life. Since life is always changing, we continually need to fine-tune our goals and motives so that they are in line with God's purpose for our lives.

$\mathcal{R}$eferences

Conway, J., and S. Conway. 1983. *Women in midlife crisis*. Wheaton, IL: Tyndale House.

Giddings, P. 1985. *When and where I enter*. New York: Bantam Books.

Hamberg, D. 1993. The American family transformed. *Society* 3 (January/February): 60–69.

1984. *The holy Bible: New international version*. Grand Rapids: Zondervan.

Malcolm, K. T. 1982. *Women at the crossroads*. Downers Grove, IL: InterVarsity Press.

Ward, P., and M. Stout. 1981. *Christian women at work*. Grand Rapids: Zondervan.

Lisa Fort

Robbing Peter to Pay Paul: Breaking the Debt Cycle

LISA FORT, born and raised in Detroit, Michigan, is a Certified Public Accountant. She and her husband, John, live in Detroit, where they are partners in a consulting and marketing enterprise, Fort & Associates. She has a bachelor of business administration degree in accounting from the University of Michigan in Ann Arbor. Lisa and John have four children: Christian, Charity, John Wesley III, and Joshua. She attends the Afro-American Mission in Detroit, where she serves as coordinator of the prayer chain ministry. She is a former staff member of Campus Crusade for Christ, where she discipled women on the campus of Spelman College in Atlanta, Georgia.

Chapter 12

Lisa Fort

Robbing Peter to Pay Paul: Breaking the Debt Cycle

Praise be to the God and Father of our Lord Jesus Christ, the Father of compassion and the God of all comfort, who comforts us in all our troubles, so that we can comfort those in any trouble with the comfort we ourselves have received from God. (2 Corinthians 1:3–4)

Sometimes when we're in the midst of a crisis, it is hard to imagine that the crisis will someday end, and that we will, by the grace of God, emerge victorious. As a certified public accountant, I have received years of educational training and varied exposure to many aspects of financial management. Yet, it is my personal experience with debt, along with the experiences of those I've counseled, that has best prepared me to share the insights that follow.

My mother raised four daughters alone. As the oldest daughter, I assumed many responsibilities at an early age. I acted as a surrogate parent to my sisters, and did all that I could to help ease my mother's load. I took pride in my position in the family. My mother worked hard to make sure that we always had the best of everything. The houses we lived in, the clothes we wore, and the cars my mother drove gave no indication that there was a major financial crisis in progress. All holidays were celebrated in grand fashion. My sisters and I even received an individual box of candy, a card, and a nice gift every Valentine's Day and Sweetest Day. We never missed the circus or Ice Capades when they were in town. We had a family night out about once a week, and we always got to see the latest Disney movies (with popcorn and soft drinks, of course). We even took family vacations once each year.

My mother's intent was wonderful. She wanted to demonstrate to us in both tangible and intangible ways that we were loved, and the apples of her eye. As a result, she made many unwise financial decisions based on emotion. As a matter of fact, patterns were set in our lives that we are still trying to break. So, how did one person do all of the things just described, on an executive secretary's salary, with no other means of support? By "robbing Peter to pay Paul."

By the time I was eight years old, I had mastered the concept of "robbing Peter to pay Paul." I understood that trying to pay the bills meant juggling limited resources. Money that should have been paid to one creditor was routinely applied to a more *urgent* bill (one subject to "shut-off").

After school, while my mother was still at work, it was often my responsibility to make "arrangements" for our bills. I loved it. I felt like an adult. I was my mother's "righthand girl." My mother coached me well. I knew just the right words to use, and how to maintain a mature posture throughout the process. I was never to lie. My job was to assure the creditors who had not received a payment that they would be a priority the next paycheck. I remember one such arrangement when I was about nine years old. After talking with the creditor for about five minutes, he asked me if I could pay the bill for my mother. When I told him that I was only nine years old, the man was amazed. My reputation for handling adult responsibilities was also known among the teachers in my elementary school. On one occasion, after I had finished my class work early, my sixth-grade teacher gave me a dime and a hall pass to go to the pay phone to make arrangements with one of her creditors. These were some of my early experiences with money mismanagement and the debt cycle. Throughout this chapter, where appropriate, I will relate the rest of my story and the stories of countless others. It is my hope that these experiences and insights will be of value to anyone struggling with debt.

DEBTS

Most people have financial freedom as a goal. Breaking the debt cycle is the first step towards financial freedom. A typical chapter on financial freedom might include information on investments and retirement funds.

I'd like to focus, however, where most people are: in debt. The average American overspends. One debt is paid off just as another one is created. The process is then repeated over and over again, with no relief in sight. "Robbing Peter to pay Paul" is a way of life. In the following pages we will evaluate different aspects of the debt cycle, and learn some practical steps that can be taken to break that cycle.

We live in a country where the national debt runs into the trillions, and where minimum payments on consumer debt are the norm. Debt has become a way of life, rather than something to shun. Credit is glamorized. How much a company will loan you, signified by a gold card, for example, represents status in our society. It's been proven that those who use credit cards tend to make more frequent and higher priced purchases than those who use cash. Financial mismanagement affects us both collectively and individually. Many of our communities are in bondage. Much of the financial bondage has come as a result of our turning away from God's laws and decrees. Collectively, we have the resources, but it seems to slip through our hands and rarely benefits our communities. Deuteronomy 28:43–44 could have been written for the inner-city of any major city: "The alien who lives among you will rise above you higher and higher, but you will sink lower and lower. He will lend to you, but you will not lend to him. He will be the head, but you will be the tail."

Sadly, churches and other ministries often do not fare much better. In recent years many churches have become financially bankrupt because of mismanagement. If the money is not there, they are unable to do the work of ministry or meet the needs of saints. Benevolent funds are virtually non-existent in some places. In many cases, the government has taken the role that the church should have. Finances and money management are rarely thought of in terms of their spiritual ramifications. What type of testimony does a pastor have when asking a bank manager for an extension on a loan? Does he say, "My God can do anything but provide for this bill"? On a personal level, how many of us would feel comfortable sharing our faith with a bill collector after missing two promised payments? A neutralized testimony is Satan's goal.

Kinds of Debts

There are many categories of debt: mortgage, investment, educational, auto, and more. No one category, however, seems to have such an increasing vise grip on so many people as credit card debt. The credit card industry is one of the fastest-growing, most prosperous businesses in our nation. Everyone is getting in on the act. Even fast-food restaurants are beginning to accept credit cards for payment. Why? Because they know that instead of purchasing the $1.99 special, you're more likely to spend $5.00 with your credit card. If you eat out twenty times a month, that's $60.00 extra you're spending. Then, if you don't pay your balance in full that month, you'll actually pay interest on top of that.

The credit card industry has become so competitive that, in many cases, cards are no longer offered based on credit worthiness or the ability to handle credit. Credit cards are being offered to teenagers, and even to children as young as twelve years old. My own initial experience with credit cards was classic. At the ripe old age of twenty, I graduated from the University of Michigan Business School with a degree in accounting. Before I graduated from college, I received very enticing letters from banks notifying me that I had been "pre-approved" for several credit cards. I chose the one with the most exciting offer. A few weeks later I received my first national-brand card. The card had a $1,500 limit and came with a check in my name for $500. It was, in effect, a blank check with no rules. Before the ink on the back of my new card was dry, I was $500 in debt. I used the money for living expenses while I was in Colorado in training for a campus ministry to which I had made a two-year commitment to serve full-time.

After a very exciting and profitable summer of training, I returned home to begin raising financial support. It would be necessary to have a support team in place before I would be allowed to report to my assignment at Spelman College. Raising financial support was not an easy task. Although I had returned home to live with my mother, I did not have a financial base from which to begin working. My mother was in a major financial crisis at the time, and I found myself using the credit card to buy groceries and to pay outstanding telephone bills. My four-year accounting degree did not prepare me for personal financial stewardship. I learned fast how not to use a credit card.

Still, it was not until I realized that I was responsible for my debt that the cycle began to be broken. I remember being very humbled by the fact that I, not the collection agent, needed mercy. Sure, I deserved to be treated with respect, but the real issue was that I owed the money. My creditor deserved to be paid. "The wicked borrow and do not repay" (Psalm 37:21). That really hit home. After that realization, I began making decisions that would eventually help me break free from the bondage of debt. I committed my finances to the Lord and saturated my plans with prayer. It was then that I truly began to understand that God owns it all.

GOD OWNS IT ALL

How would your actions change if you knew that all the money that you've had in the past, possess today, and will have in the future did not belong to you? Well, that is exactly the case. The money that we have is not our own. It belongs to God. He has simply allowed us to use it. We are not required to repay it, we are just responsible to be good managers of it.

The earth is the LORD's, and everything in it, the world, and all who live in it. (Psalm 24:1)

For by him all things were created: things in heaven and on earth, visible and invisible, whether thrones or powers or rulers or authorities; all things were created by him and for him. (Colossians 1:16)

In other words, we can't go anywhere or see anything that God doesn't own. We are merely caretakers entrusted with the authority and responsibility to use the Owner's resources for His purposes. Since He owns it all, we have a responsibility to have His approval whenever we spend His money. Does this mean that you have to pray before you buy a pack of bubble gum? Maybe it does. It all depends on the desires of the Owner. If you have been convicted by God about your poor spending habits, and you find yourself constantly operating out of a deficit, you may need to do just that. I'm not talking about legalistic, insincere, prayers. Remember, God knows our hearts. I'm talking about sincerely asking God to help you to get to the root of the problem.

Prayer

For a while, getting at the problem may involve maintaining very strict spending guidelines. You may need to pray about every purchase until God's spending criteria for your life are established. Once you have a sense of how God would have you to manage His money, you can more confidently make management decisions. It's like starting a new job at a new company. In the beginning, making the transition to the new company's policies may seem tedious and time-consuming. You may have to consult the policy manual on items that seem incredibly insignificant. As you become more familiar with the way the company is run, you can relax a little as the rules become second nature. Becoming familiar with the guidelines, however, never exempts you from being governed by them.

The Bible is the policy manual for believers. God has many things to say about money and how we handle it. There are numerous Old Testament passages that deal with financial matters, and two-thirds of Jesus' parables deal with financial issues. Why would God devote so much of the Bible to these issues? I believe Matthew describes it best, "For where your treasure is, there your heart will be also" (Matthew 6:21). Since God places such significance on our money management, why shouldn't we?

I've often heard people say that they don't like to bother God with these kinds of issues. Well, with what kind of issues ought we to consult God? Since prayer is simply talking to God, why not talk to Him about the very thing that causes our blood pressure to go up in the daytime, and sleep to elude us at night? 1 Thessalonians 5:17 says, "pray continually." This seems like an impossible task until we realize that God wants us to talk with Him at all times about all things. Since this is the case, why feel silly asking Him about a pack of gum?

Tithe

Once we understand that God, in fact, owns it all, it's important that we make every effort to demonstrate this truth in our lives. The tithe is a clear and tangible way in which we can acknowledge God's ownership. The word *tithe* means tenth. Genesis 14:20 first introduces the concept of the tithe. It is here that Abram paid tithes to Melchizedek as a praise offering for the victory God has just given him over his enemies. Thus, the tithe was established before the law as an act of thankfulness and worship. The tithe was maintained and followed by the children of Israel after the law was given. As a matter of fact, under the law the Jews gave much more than a tenth of their income back to the Lord. The tithe was simply the starting point for giving. It was also upheld by Jesus in the New Testament as He rebuked the Pharisees for not being sincere in their worship of God (Matthew 23:13 and Luke 11:42). Thus, those of us who are under grace should adhere to the practice of tithing. This is not a menial act of worship; as an act of praise it should be done cheerfully.

In establishing the tithe, God wisely chose to use a percentage of income rather than a set amount so that the amount given would be fair to all. This is true whether you are wealthy or living on a fixed income. It is always difficult for me to hear people negotiate the tithe amount. If "tithe" means 10 percent, how can we rationalize tithing 5 percent? That is a contradiction in terms. You can *give* 5 percent, but you cannot *tithe* 5 percent. As mentioned above, the tithe is simply a starting point for our giving. "Bring the whole tithe into the storehouse ..." (Malachi 3:10). That same chapter of Malachi also encourages us to bring both our tithes and our offerings.

Tithing reflects an attitude and a belief. Not only does the tithe help maintain a proper perspective on God's ownership, but God also makes some promises along with His admonishment for us to tithe. God says, "Test me in this and see if I will not throw open the floodgates of heaven and pour out so much blessing that you will not have room enough for it" (Malachi 3:10b). When God offers a challenge with a promise, you can be sure that He will deliver.

Some people make the mistake in thinking that the verse in Malachi 3:10 says that if you tithe, God will multiply your money. Many people tithe with the sole intent of receiving financial return. That is not what the verse says. It says that He will pour out so much blessing that we won't be able to handle it. God's blessings are many, not merely financial. "I will prevent pests from devouring your crops, and the vines in your fields will not cast their fruit" (Malachi 3:11). Has God been rebuking the Devourer on your behalf? I've counseled people who say they cannot afford to tithe. But I ask, can we afford *not* to tithe? I hear of cars needing major repairs, refrigerators needing replacement, and a host of things that devour current income, making a bad situation worse. "One man gives freely, yet gains even more; another withholds unduly, but comes to poverty" (Proverbs 11:24). God will honor our right attitude in giving.

God will use our finances to teach us many things. Sometimes He allows financial difficulties to get our attention and cause us to focus on other areas in our lives that need to be dealt with. However, I would be remiss if I did not acknowledge that a financial crisis may be the result of injustice. "A poor man's fields may produce abundant food, but injustice sweeps it away" (Proverbs 13:23). Even then, we can pray and boldly beseech the Lord for deliverance. He is a just God who has promised to maintain the cause of the oppressed. Whatever the cause of our financial crisis, we can be assured that God is sovereign. We can rely on Him to supply all our needs according to His riches in Christ Jesus. Knowing this helps free us from our fears and weaknesses.

WHAT YOU DON'T KNOW MAY HURT YOU

Often when we are struggling to make ends meet, we feel so overwhelmed that we decide not to deal with the problem at hand. We look for ways to alleviate the pressures that our circumstances bring. There are many ways that we can fall into patterns of financial irresponsibility. The following are a few of the more common means that we use to try to escape reality:

- Unopened mail
- Unreturned phone calls
- Unbalanced checkbooks

Some people have become experts at analyzing when a bill has to be opened. Perhaps you've become resolved to open bills only when absolutely necessary: such as when the shut-off notice is enclosed.

This method of coping creates major problems. It places a person in a reactive rather than a proactive mode. When this happens, you're more likely to resort to desperate measures rather than to pray and plan your way through your problem. When this path is taken, you will often find yourself in a bargaining position with the creditor. At this point, the creditor may be less than willing to negotiate. If, however, the creditor is contacted before the deadline, you are more likely to be able to set up a payment plan.

Payment Plans

Try to set up a realistic payment plan. Creditors usually look more favorably at small consistent payments rather than larger sporadic ones. Avoid having your bills turned over to a collection agency. The job of the collection agent is to aggressively pursue payment. You don't need the additional headaches this may involve. Keep in mind that the original creditor would also like to avoid turning your account over to a collection agency. Why? Because the company must pay the collection agency 35 percent of the unpaid balance in order for the agency to take the account. In any event, be honest in your dealings. Your word and commitment to do something should mean more than a way to get out of the hot seat. Your attitude and faithfulness in carrying out your commitment is a testimony to the Lord's work in your life. Unopened letters may also include unanticipated information, such as a new policy toward those with overdue balances or notices of intent to pursue legal measures. Do not ignore these types of notices!

Many of the same principles apply when dealing with phone calls from creditors that go unreturned. I would strongly caution against having children get negatively involved in this process. How many times have our children been instructed to say "she's not home"? When we do this we are, in effect, teaching that there are acceptable times to lie. God will hold us accountable for this faulty teaching. If the children are to be involved in this process, it is important to take advantage of the teachable moments that financial crises can bring. It is at these times that we can (1) explain the mistakes that we have made; (2) ask forgiveness of God and our family where appropriate; (3) involve everyone in prayer; (4) and demonstrate the proper ways to respond in difficult circumstances. These are the kinds of lessons that our children will never forget.

The Checkbook

The unbalanced checkbook is a source of many problems. People guesstimate how much money they have in their account and, inevitably, they overestimate. This, of course, causes a chain reaction. A check is written and not recorded. The check bounces, and the bank charges a fee. The business that the check was written to also charges a fee. Somehow, you make a deposit to cover the check. You never record the fees, however, and at the end of the month you don't balance your checkbook, so you never take the fees into account. The next month you bounce other checks and perhaps lose check-writing privileges at several establishments.

The financial strain that bounced check fees can cause is intense, not to mention the emotional embarrassment. Why do so many people go from month to month with unbalanced checkbooks?

I believe there are two main reasons: (1) they don't know how to balance their checkbooks; and (2) they don't want the discipline that properly maintaining a checking account requires. The back of most people's bank statements explains how to reconcile your monthly statement and your checkbook. Do this faithfully every month. I also suggest that as you write each check, you record the check in the ledger before tearing the check out of the book. It would be best to calculate your new balance at the end of each transaction. Make it a point never to write a new check until the balance has been calculated. Make sure you also record any trips that you make to the automatic teller machine. Record each withdrawal and deposit in your checkbook ledger. Finally, one additional note of caution. There are some people who will write checks knowing that the money is not available to pay for the purchase. Never do this. This ultimately is a problem of integrity. Purchasing without the intention of paying is stealing.

KNOW YOUR WEAKNESSES

One very important dimension of getting your finances under control is to know your weaknesses. The first step to overcoming a problem is to admit that there is a problem. Once you've acknowledged that there is a problem, you can begin to uncover the when, where, how, and why of that problem. Let's explore each of these as they relate to inappropriate spending and purchasing habits.

When does the problem most often occur?

When depressed, happy, lonely, after a long week at work, when children beg, before holidays or major events, whenever there's a big sale.

Where does it occur?

At the mall, at resale shops, at home while viewing mail-order catalogs or cable shopping channels.

How does it occur?

By credit card, by check, by cash.

Why does it occur?

Often our purchasing and spending habits are linked to our self-esteem. How we feel about ourselves when we wear a new dress, new shoes, and so on plays a major part. Many of us are driven by how we'd like others to see us. We protect our false images by buying clothes that we can't afford and living in houses that we can't pay for. For some of us, the pattern was taught to us and set in motion in our childhood. This was definitely the case for my sisters and me.

My maternal grandmother is the type of person who pays her bills before they're due. My mother and father, however, have a history of poor spending habits. This is my mother's account of the beginnings of her spending problems:

My parents experienced the rough years of the depression. During those years, they raised four of their five children. Because my father's job was seasonal, purchasing clothes and other needs from resale shops was a way of life. My first remembrance of the difference between a "brand-new" purchase and a used purchase was in my ninth year at Christmas time.

When I woke up Christmas morning and saw my blue-and-white bike in the middle of our living room, I was so happy and excited. I lost that initial excitement when I took my bike outside and saw my friend's "brand-new" pink-and-white Schwinn bike. When I began working at the age of sixteen, my thoughts were that all of my earnings were to be spent solely on me. I had no concept of budgeting. I felt that everything I wanted, I could buy brand new. This mind-set carried over into my marriage. As a couple, my husband and I never pooled our incomes together and budgeted accordingly. Two years later, when my husband was laid off his job, and I had to take a maternity leave because I was pregnant with our first child, things fell apart. We had purchased all new appliances, living room furniture, and a brand-new car. We lost everything because we had not budgeted or planned ahead. We never learned from that experience. As soon as my husband and I returned to work, we went out and purchased brand-new furniture all over again. The cycle was repeated, and we never budgeted or had a savings account.

This is a prime example of poor money management. It can be passed from one generation to the next. Knowing this has helped me to break patterns set in motion long ago. Once the sources of your problem have been identified, you can begin to set boundaries to help overcome them. Find someone to whom you can be accountable. The next time you're depressed and feel the urge to spend, call your friend and discuss what's bothering you. If you know that taking your credit cards to the mall creates a major stumbling block, leave your credit cards at home. Some of us have such deep-rooted problems with credit cards and bounced checks that it would be best to begin making "cash only" purchases. When the allotted cash is gone, the spending stops.

Be creative. One of my sisters lives out of state. She and I have had a real problem with the amount and length of our long-distance calls. We have resorted to some very interesting measures to help us overcome this weakness. We have tried some of the following: (1) calls to be made only after 6:00 in the evening; (2) calls made only on Saturdays; (3) calls limited to five minutes. Some of our attempts have been more successful than others. In my estimation, we were most successful the time that each of us committed not to call, but to write. Each of us addressed and pre-stamped twenty envelopes to the other one. Then when we thought of something funny or just wanted to say "hello," the envelopes were right there waiting for us. It helped take away the excuses.

Whatever your weaknesses, submit them to the Lord and take an active role in overcoming them. Establishing and maintaining a budget is an important part of combating financial weaknesses.

B-U-D-G-E-T: A SIX-LETTER WORD

Webster's dictionary defines a budget as "a plan or schedule adjusting expenses during a certain period to the estimated or fixed income for that period."

Evaluate

For many, the very mention of the word "budget" evokes thoughts of a confining tool used to squeeze the fun and excitement out of life. A budget should not be viewed this way. It is a tool to be used for you, not against you. The key step in establishing a budget involves deciding where you are, and where you want to go.

I like to picture the budget as a road map to an exotic destination. The fun part is planning what you'll do once you get there. If you have an inaccurate picture, however, of where you are right now, your travel plans may be ruined.

First, you must pinpoint a spot on the map that identifies where you are and label it *you are here*. In my experience, many people think they know the state of their financial affairs, but are shocked when they find out the real deal. To get an accurate assessment, I recommend carrying a small notebook with you for thirty days. Throughout that thirty-day period, record every single purchase that you make in the notebook. When I say *every* purchase, I'm not exaggerating. The twenty-five cents used in the pay phone, the five dollars spent on lunch—all of those things should be recorded. I also recommend getting and keeping receipts for each purchase. These can serve as backup to your notebook. They will also help discipline you to stop after every purchase and make a conscious decision to take note of that purchase. This thirty-day period is not a time to try to change your spending habits. Drastically reducing your purchases during this time just to make it look good on paper will undermine the purpose of this exercise. After the thirty-day observation period is complete, most people are amazed to find out how much money they actually spend every month.

At this point, you will have a pretty good glimpse of your regular monthly expenditures. It will then be necessary to list those expenses that do not occur regularly.

Examples of those expenses are insurance payments, car maintenance costs, holiday gift expenses, and vacations. For instance, if you know that next summer you want to take a cruise and that the cruise will cost $2,400, your task is to find out how you can save $200 per month ($2,400 divided by twelve months) for the next year to take that cruise.

Once you have listed all of your expenses, you also need to list every source of income. Calculate your total annual after-tax income. Then divide that amount by twelve for your monthly income. Note that we only consider our income after taxes as spendable. The government makes sure that it receives its portion off the top. Scripture says that we should give to God from our first fruits, the best, the cream of the crop. "Give to Caesar what is Caesar's, and to God what is God's" (Luke 20:25). As an act of worship, God should be thought of first and receive our best.

Once you have listed both income and expenses, you should have a clearer picture of why your financial situation is as it is. If you are in a debt cycle, you will notice immediately that the expense side of your worksheet is much greater than the income side. When this is the case, bills are often partially paid or left unpaid. Loans and credit are used to substitute for income. At this point, a second or third job is often considered to add to income. That may be necessary. A new job, however, often brings with it corresponding time constraints and pressures. I recommend attempting first to cut expenses as much as possible. It may be difficult to determine which categories should be cut and by how much. I recommend utilizing the budget guideline provided by Christian financial counselor Larry Burkett (see p. 221). His plan is merely a guideline. You may need to adjust categories to meet your needs. It is, however, a helpful starting point.

Establish

When establishing a budget, everyone in the family should participate where possible. Make it a project with a reward for reaching goals. Discuss where to reduce or eliminate categories in order to make your goals and dreams a reality. The process is give and take, back and forth, until your budget is established. Contact your creditors and attempt to make payment plans with each one. Be honest with them, and be realistic about the amount that you can actually pay. I recommend paying off the smallest bills first, when possible. This will help give a sense of accomplishment and aid in encouraging progress toward your goals.

Once an agreement is reached, be faithful. Maintaining your commitment on a consistent basis will work in your behalf if ever you have to approach the creditor again to make additional arrangements. And, more important, keeping your word should be a part of your testimony as a Christian.

Review

Once you have set your goals and your budget has been established, it will be important to do a regular budget review. You need a system of accountability in place. The type of budget system you choose should give you access to immediate feedback on a regular basis. Two very popular budget systems are the ledger system and the envelope system. The ledger system allows you to continue to pay your obligations by check. Clear records are kept in a ledger of how much has been allocated to each budget category and how much of the allocated amount has been spent. The trick is to keep records current, and never to spend more than the amount previously allocated.

Those who use the envelope system actually keep an envelope for each budget category. The amount allocated for each category is recorded on the corresponding envelope. The money (cash) is placed inside the envelope. You would then take that envelope with you whenever purchases in that category are necessary. For example, if you have $100 allocated to your clothing envelope, you would take that envelope with you when you go to purchase clothes, shoes, and other articles of clothing. If after making several purchases, you have only $23 left in the envelope and the blouse you like costs $30, you don't buy the blouse. Thus, you have instant accountability. The trick here is not to begin juggling money between envelopes, which is another version of "robbing Peter to pay Paul." Be committed to your budget for your own well-being. Many other financial systems exist also. You might even create your own. Whatever system you choose should be one that's simple for you to use.

The budget is a powerful tool that can be used to help ease financial pressure and uncertainty. Make it work for you. It should be updated and adjusted to reflect changes in your life. Raises, a new baby, a home purchase, a decrease in insurance costs, etc., are all examples of changes that should be reflected in the budget. It's also good to have a plan in place for unexpected financial gifts. An example of such a plan is as follows:

10%—Tithe
20%—Savings
50%—Debt repayment
20%—Miscellaneous (for example, personal spending money)

So, if you were to receive $100 from "Aunt Martha," instead of heading for the mall to spend it, you would

Tithe $10
Save $20
Pay $50 on bills
Spend $20 on whatever you want

Such a plan will help you to stay focused on your goals.

Warnings

Once you begin working toward debt freedom, keeping your goals a priority can sometimes be a challenge. As you move forward, it's helpful to be aware of potential financial pitfalls. Beware of the following:

"Buy Now/Pay Later" Promotions. Make sure you read the fine print. Even though the principal payment may not be due for six months, the interest charges often begin accumulating at the time of sale.

Erroneous Charges Included in Your Bills. Be careful to check the accuracy of your bills. Itemized long-distance phone bills, credit card statements, and restaurant tabs have been known to include charges for goods and services not received.

Hidden Costs. This is especially important before buying a house. Don't forget to include insurance, repairs, lawn care, taxes, and utilities when calculating what you can really afford.

"Free Trial" Offers. We are often enticed by the "free gifts" sent along with these promotions. These offers often allow you to view the item for

thirty days with "no obligation." The problem is that after the time period is up, people rarely send the item back. Even if they don't want it or need it, they keep it. When it's all said and done, the "free gift" is very expensive.

Prizes and Awards. Many times the postcard reads like this: "You have won a trip to Florida. Call the enclosed phone number within two days to receive your prize." Usually this technique is used to get you to view a costly club or membership. The telephone operator will often ask for a credit card number to "guarantee" your prize. Be careful.

Co-Signing Loan. The person who co-signs a loan is legally as responsible for the loan as the person to whom the loan is made. If you can't afford to pay for the loan, don't sign for it (see Proverbs 6:1–5).

Bankruptcy. Although there are legal provisions for bankruptcy, there are no scriptural ones. Even if we are legally discharged from our financial responsibilities, Scripture admonishes us to pay our debts (Psalm 37:21). If bankruptcy is sought and the root of the problem is not solved, the cycle will repeat itself.

These are just some of the more popular "snares" to be aware of. I'm sure you can think of others. Be wise in evaluating potential expenditures. Pray about everything.

HOPE FOR THE FUTURE

Those of us who are seeking to yield all that we are and have to the Lord can be assured that He will cause all things to work together for our good (Romans 8:28). The process is not always fun, but the results are guaranteed. In spite of our past, God says that He will restore the years that the locusts have eaten (Joel 2:25). We can choose to start anew. He ultimately wants what is best for us. "'For I know the plans I have for you,' declares the Lord, 'plans to prosper you and not to harm you, plans to give you hope and a future'" (Jeremiah 29:11). This moment is the first moment of the rest of our lives. The best is yet to come!

PERCENTAGE GUIDE FAMILY INCOME
(Family of Four)

Gross Income	$15,000	$25,000	$35,000	$45,000	$55,000
1. Taxes[1]	2%	15.5%	19%	21.5%	23.5%
2. Charitable Gifts	10%	10%	10%	10%	10%
NET SPENDABLE	$13,200	$18,625	$24,850	$30,825	$36,575
3. Housing	38%	38%	34%	30%	27%
4. Food	15%	15%	12%	12%	12%
5. Auto	15%	15%	12%	12%	12%
6. Insurance	5%	5%	5%	5%	5%
7. Debts	5%	5%	5%	5%	5%
8. Entertainment/Recreation	4%	5%	6%	6%	7%
9. Clothing	4%	5%	5%	5%	6%
10. Savings	5%	5%	5%	5%	5%
11. Medical/Dental	5%	5%	4%	4%	4%
12. Miscellaneous	4%	5%	5%	7%	7%
13. School/Child Care[2]	10%	8%	6%	5%	5%
14. Investments[3]	—	—	8%	9%	13%
15. Unallocated Surplus Income[4]	—	—	—	—	—

Larry Burkett, *Family Financial Planning Workbook* (Chicago: Moody Press, 1990), 19b.

[1]Guideline percentages for this category include taxes for Social Security, federal tax, and a small estimated amount for state tax. At the $15,000 level of income, the Earned Income Credit drastically reduces the tax burden.

[2]This category is added as a guide only. If you have this expense, the percentage shown must be deducted from other budget categories.

[3]This category is used for long-term investment planning such as college education or retirement.

[4]This category is used when surplus income is received. This would be kept in the checking account to be used within a few weeks; otherwise it should be transferred to an allocated category.

References

Burkett, L. 1990. *Family financial planning workbook*. Chicago: Moody Press.

1984. *The holy Bible: New international version*. Grand Rapids: Zondervan.

1988. *Webster's new twentieth-century dictionary*. Edited by J. L. McKechnie. New York: Simon & Schuster.

1990. *Women's Devotional Bible*. Edited by M. Manikas-Foster and J. E. Syswerda. Grand Rapids: Zondervan.

Victoria Johnson

Examining Difficult Passages in the Bible: Woman to Woman

VICTORIA JOHNSON is a freelance writer and editor and an Instructor at the Moody Bible Institute in Chicago. She was born and raised in Joliet, Illinois, and has a bachelor of science degree in counseling psychology from Ottawa University in Ottawa, Kansas. She and her husband, Curtis, live in Milwaukee, Wisconsin, and have three children: Lydia, Candacee, and Andre. She coordinates women's Bible studies and prayer groups for the community.

Chapter 13

Victoria Johnson

Examining Difficult Passages in the Bible: Woman to Woman

*The Old Testament does not speak disapprovingly of godly
women who took on leadership roles or prophesied. Disapproval
is expressed only when a woman used her influence against
God's will.*

How to have a relationship with God through the person of Jesus
Christ is the primary theme in the Bible. God could have clearly communicated this central idea without specifically mentioning a
woman's name. God, however, chose to delicately lace the pages of
Scripture with the experiences, faces, and names of women.

Several years ago I decided to study women and women's issues in the
Bible. I journeyed through all sixty-six books, pausing to analyze meticu-
lously each passage that specifically concerns women. I asked three simple questions: What is God saying about women? What is God saying to
women? What does this have to do with me, a twentieth-century African-
American woman? My life was spiritually enriched and dramatically
changed as a result of this study. Upon reflection, three important truths
come immediately to mind:

1. God is compassionate and sensitive toward women.
2. He is keenly aware of her psychological and physical makeup.
   (After all, God created women.)
3. He eagerly desires for her to receive instructions, encouragement,
   and reassurance through His Word.

One needs to study the *entire* Bible to hear clearly God's message to women. God's heart and mind are not revealed in one isolated chapter or verse. Certain patterns and themes can be identified when the Bible is examined as a whole book. Particular Scriptures pertaining to women are difficult to understand, and therefore they are commonly misinterpreted and incorrectly applied. Moreover, just as plantation owners used the Bible to justify slavery in America, various denominations, pastors, husbands, and others have manipulated portions of Scripture to justify unfair treatment of women. This chapter will concentrate on expanding our comprehension and appreciation of complex Scriptures relating to women—and, where needed, perhaps help to set the record straight.

I admit that, before personally studying women and women's issues in the Bible, the mere mention of certain biblical phrases or words caused an immediate negative reaction. I would wag my finger in the face of Titus, Peter, and Paul for their "sexist" statements. God, however, gently reminded me: "No prophecy of Scripture is a matter of one's own interpretation, for prophecy was never made by an act of human will, but men moved by the Holy Spirit spoke from God" (2 Peter 1:20–21). As I traveled through God's Word, I realized the ground I walked upon was holy. The Bible is not a scholarly, debatable essay, but God's precious words to be understood and obeyed.

THE BEGINNING: GENESIS 1–3

The book of Genesis is the best place to start moving through the maze of Scripture passages about women. What did God have in mind when He created woman?

Genesis 1 summarizes the seven days of God's activity in the Creation. On the sixth day He created man and woman. He distinguished them from other creatures in the universe. Both the male and female were to mirror God's image, giving the world an idea of what God thinks and feels. The task of populating the world was awarded to this first couple, along with the control and care of "every living thing" (vv. 27–28).

Genesis 2 records the specific details of creation and the precise order of each event. Some biblical feminists (those who strongly believe in the ideas of the feminist movement and use the Bible to back up their beliefs) believe that man was not in a leadership, or headship, position before the Fall. However, both male and female were created on the same day, and the man was given instructions about the forbidden tree before the woman was fashioned. God could have waited until after the creation of woman and issued the warning to both, but God placed the spiritual responsibility squarely on the shoulders of the man.

For the first time since the beginning of creation, God declared something in His perfect universe to be not good: "It is not good for the man to be alone" (Genesis 2:18). God said that life for the man without a woman was uncomfortable, unprofitable, and unpleasant. His creation lacked completeness until He made woman. So God established the purpose for woman before she came into existence. He addressed her as *'ezer kenego,* "a helper fit for him."

The term "helper" (Hebrew: *'ezer*) is also used in reference to God, Jesus Christ, and the Holy Spirit. Surely the persons in the Godhead are not viewed as inferior or slaves. Helpers do not usually obtain their position because of a lack of intelligence or competence. The opposite is true. Helpers comprehend the needs of others, then govern themselves accordingly. In the same way, God designed woman "for the man's sake" (1 Corinthians 11:9). She is to support and use her abilities to assist him.

> God's assignments may sound like job discrimination. Men get to be bosses and women have to be secretaries. We feel a twinge (or maybe a pang) of resentment because we do not know what a sin-free hierarchical arrangement can be like. We know only the domination and arrogance that even the best boss/underling relationship can have. But in Eden it was different—it really was! The man and the woman knew each other as equals, both created in the image of God and thus having a personal relationship with Him. Neither doubted the worth of the other nor of oneself. Each was to perform one's tasks in a different way, the man as the head and the woman as his helper. They operated as truly "one flesh," one person. In one body does the rich rebel against or envy the head? (Foh 1979)

The title "helper" is not a "put-down," but a special calling by God for the woman to fulfill.

In Genesis 2, God demonstrated man's need for a counterpart. God paraded all the living creatures in front of Adam, assigning him the task of naming each one. Can you imagine Adam turning to God with a perplexed, lonely face: "Where's mine? Everybody has a missus but me." God developed in man a yearning and appreciation of the woman before He brought her into the man's life.

God spoke the universe into being. He molded man from the dust of the ground. But God designed the woman from a piece in man's side. "So the LORD God caused a deep sleep to fall upon the man.... He took one of his ribs.... And the LORD God fashioned into a woman the rib which he had taken from the man, and brought her to the man" (Genesis 2:21–22). Matthew Henry (1706), in his commentary, creatively and clearly explains God's intention: "[Woman was] Not made out of his head to top him, not out of his feet to be trampled upon by him, but out of his side to be equal with him, under his arm to be protected, and near his heart to be beloved."

Adam went to sleep with an ache for a woman and woke up with one in his presence. The Scripture page explodes with Adam's pleasure when he saw woman for the first time. "This is now bone of my bones, And flesh of my flesh; She shall be called Woman, Because she was taken out of Man" (Genesis 2:23).

The woman (*isha*) was made from the essence of the man (*ish*). He was given the privilege of naming her, which some Bible scholars believe is another indication of his headship position before the fall.

Chapter 2 concludes with God performing the first marriage ceremony. "For this cause a man shall leave his father and his mother, and shall cleave to his wife; and they shall become one flesh" (Genesis 2:24). God was setting a precedent for future marital relationships. He specifically instructed the man to break ties from parents and stay as close to the wife as humanly possible. God said to the *man*, "For this cause a *man* shall leave his father and his mother." God could have included the woman in these instruction and said, "For this cause *a man and a woman*," but He did not. The weight of the marriage commitment was placed on the husband. Another original pattern, started in the Garden, proceeds down through the pages of God's Word.

Male and Female Distinctions Before the Fall
(Genesis 2)

Man	Woman
Created from the dust (v. 7)	Not yet created
Given spiritual instructions about the tree of knowledge of good and evil (v. 17)	Not yet created when instructions given
Declared by God not good to be alone, and would be given a helper (v. 18)	Given the title "helper," meaning assistant, aide (v. 18)
Allowed to name the animals (v. 19)	Not yet created

Man	Woman
Put to sleep, and rib extracted (v. 21)	Created from Adam's rib (v. 21)
Expresses pleasure in the woman God made. Names her "woman" because she was like him and from his flesh (v. 23)	Named by the man (v. 23)
Instructed to leave his parents and cleave to his wife (v. 24)	Given no instructions
Naked and unashamed (v. 25)	Naked and unashamed (v. 25)

The Scriptures do not record how long this wonderful marital bliss lasted between the first couple before the devastating events related in Genesis 3 took place. In the historical account of the Fall, the serpent addressed the woman with a question that caused her to question and doubt God. The serpent twisted God's words and then lied. The woman bought Satan's entire deception package. Adam made the same purchase: He stood there *with* his wife and listened to Satan, fully aware of what God had commanded. He did not attempt to take charge of the situation. He ignored his spiritual and marital headship obligations. As a result, sin entered the world, and its consequences followed.

> *To the woman He said,*
> *"I will greatly multiply*
> *Your pain in childbirth, . . .*
> *Yet your desire shall be for your husband,*
> *And he shall rule over you."*
> *Then to Adam He said, "Because you have listened to the voice*
> *of your wife, and have eaten from the tree about which I com-*
> *manded you, . . .*
> *Cursed is the ground because of you;*
> *In toil you shall eat of it*
> *All the days of your life. (Genesis 3:16–17)*

P. B. Wilson (1990) does an excellent job of explaining the aftermath of the Garden sin in her book *Liberated Through Submission*.

> Although Adam and Eve committed the same sin, their punishments were totally different. That seems strange until we remember that God

is our Father. In our home, Frank and I do not chastise our children "just to be mean." We do it because we love them.... Our chastisement usually consists of taking things away (TV, telephone privileges or special outings), or giving them things they would rather not have (gardening, cleaning, washing responsibilities).... God chastised Eve in two ways: by giving her something she did not want and by taking away the one thing she most desired. First of all, God allowed Eve pain in childbirth.... The second chastisement was the loss of something that was very important to Eve: Control. She really believed when she ate the fruit that she would become like God. And so God said to Eve, "And thy desire shall be to thy husband and he shall rule over thee." (pp. 56–57)

Wilson further explains that the word "desire" in Genesis 3:16 is the same word found in Genesis 4:7, in which God tells Cain that sin was seeking to master the course of his life. In the same way, when God cursed Eve, He was saying to her, "Okay, Eve. You want to be the boss and make the decisions? When you leave this garden you will always want to control and lead the course of your husband's life. But he will rule over you instead!" (Wilson 1990).

This "curse" describes the beginning of the battle of the sexes. Sin has corrupted the willing submission of the wife and the loving headship of the husband. The relationship is now full of dominating, negative attitudes, manipulation, and struggle.

In spite of Adam and Eve's serious blunders, God continued to use both men and women significantly throughout the Scriptures. Some scholars down through the centuries have tried to say that women were dishonorably discharged and were not enlisted in God's service because of Eve's sin. The Old Testament is often considered "male chauvinistic" and biased when it comes to women. Both statements are untrue, as I seek to show.

WOMEN AND THE OLD TESTAMENT

God viewed women highly in the Old Testament and placed very few limitations on their activities. Women were expected to attend and participate in Jewish feast days, bringing their own sacrifices. They ministered at the door of the tent of meeting, were allowed to take a Nazerite vow, and required to be present at the reading of the Law. God employed Deborah, Huldah, Miriam, and Esther for special tasks. He recognized Abigail, the woman from Tekoah, and others as women of good understanding and wisdom. Also, God gave women free reign in regard to civil affairs. Women pleaded their own cases in court. The daughters of Zelophehad presented their own proposal for the right to inherit land and changed a major Old Testament law.*

The Old Testament does not speak disapprovingly of godly women who took on leadership roles or prophesied. Disapproval is expressed only when a woman used her influence against God's will. Most theologians believe that men wrote all the books of the Bible. Yet the beautiful songs of worship written by Hannah the mother of Samuel and by Mary the mother of Jesus inform us that the reason did not lie in any lack of comprehension of God or capabilities or intelligence. Deborah was a judge ministering outside under a tree, not in the temple. The prophetesses (*nebiy'ah*) mentioned in the Old Testament received messages from God and delivered them to His people.

Some Limitations Explained

It is true that the office of the priest—whose duties included ministering in the temple, sacrificing inside the Holy of Holies, and interceding between God and man—was reserved for men. This follows the precedence established in the garden of Eden, which assigned to the man the main spiritual obligations (Genesis 2:16).

One has to admit that some of the Old Testament statements and laws appear to place women in an inferior position. Several facts, however, must be considered. First, the derogatory things done or said to women were not God's intention or will. For example, it was Lot's idea to offer his two daughters to the homosexuals outside his home, not God's command or desire (Genesis 19).

Second, some limitations were placed on women by God because of His sensitivity to their physical makeup, not as an indication of their inferiority or weakness. Women were considered unclean during their menstrual cycle or after the birth of a child; therefore they were not allowed to participate in various forms of temple activities. This can be perceived in different ways: God is prejudiced against women, or He is considerate of their unique needs. God permitted women to stay close to home, to rest and recover and be near the items that could be needed during this cum-

---

*To find these women's stories, consult a Bible concordance or a Bible dictionary.

bersome time, instead of traveling by camel or by foot hundreds of miles away to worship.

Finally, in several passages in the Old Testament, God reemphasized the headship of man. The father was responsible for the sacrifices during the patriarchal period. According to the law, a woman's time of uncleanness was longer after the birth of a girl than a boy. God was not expressing a lesser value for women, but put man out in front as the leader.

WOMEN AND THE GOSPELS

When Jesus came on the scene, did He abolish the Old Testament distinctions concerning women? Are they now equal in every way with men? Scholars radically disagree on these issues, but all acknowledge that Jesus demonstrated to the world how women are to be perceived, valued, and treated.

> They [women] had never known a man like this Man—There never has been such another. A prophet and teacher who never nagged at them, never flattered or coaxed or patronized; who never made arch jokes about them, never treated them either as "The woman, God help us!" or "The ladies, God bless them!"—who rebuked without querulousness [habitual complaining] and praised without condescension; who took their questions and arguments seriously; who never mapped out their sphere for them, never urged them to be feminine or jeered at them for being female; who had no ax to grind and no uneasy male dignity to defend; who took them as he found them and was completely unself-conscious. There is no act, no sermon, no parable in the whole Gospel that borrows its pungency from female perversity; nobody could possibly guess from the words and deeds of Jesus that there was anything "funny" about a woman's nature. (Sayers 1971, p. 47)

Rabbis did not speak to women in public. God spoke to women numerous times in both the Old and the New Testaments, so this rabbinical injunction was not a mandate from God, but foolishness from men. Jesus not only talked to women, but also called on them to witness for Him and learn from Him. He encouraged women to be an essential part of His ministry.

Jesus, however, selected men to assume the bulk of the spiritual leadership responsibilities in His ministry. He did not choose a woman apostle, nor do we read that any of the women who were a part of His ministry ever publicly taught or preached.

WOMEN AND THE NEW TESTAMENT CHURCH

Women were visible and active in the early church, in the years following Jesus' ascension. They were in the upper room praying when the Holy Spirit came. Both men and women believed in Jesus, were baptized, helped spread the gospel, and were cruelly persecuted because of their Christian beliefs. Lydia was the first convert in Europe. Tabitha is described as being full of good works and charity. Philip's four daughters were prophetesses. Priscilla is called Paul's co-worker, and she explained the gospel more accurately to Apollos than he had heard before. But there are several passages in the New Testament that have perplexed and confused Christians about the role of women in the church. Let us try to unravel some of them.

Galatians 3:28

Women did indeed play an important part in accomplishing God's purposes during the development of the early church. As in the Old Testament, however, women were limited in certain areas. Yet some biblical feminists oppose this idea and ask, "What about Galatians 3:28?" This verse says, "There is neither Jew nor Greek, there is neither slave nor free man, there is neither male nor female; for you are all one in Christ Jesus."

The book of Galatians explains faith, in contrast to law, as the means of salvation. In this verse Paul makes clear the point that all believers are justified by faith and become children of God without respect to nationality, social status, or sex. Men and women have the same relationship to God through Christ. This verse does not erase the headship roles of the man, nor does it set guidelines for leadership in the church; it simply clarifies who can be a member in the body of Christ.

When God established the nation of Israel, He said, "I want you to be a separated, sanctified, unique people, different from the other ungodly nations." He gave them the Law to exemplify His desires, thoughts, and ways. In the same way, the church as the body of Christ is God's representative in the world today. God appointed the apostles to establish guidelines for Christians, distinguishing them from unbelievers in reference to worship, church administration, marriage, and the family unit.

In the first century, cultic practices surrounded the developing early church. God did not want the Christian church or Christian family to reflect any of their ungodly ways. It was common for a temple priestess to be the head intercessor for pagan deities and conduct the idol worship ceremonies. Could this be one of the reasons God placed men in the leadership roles in the Christian church and entreated the women to take a subjective role?

If we examine and combine the facts, we conclude that

1. God's desire is to establish a unique body of people who identify and represent Him in this world.
2. God's original plan is that the weight of the spiritual responsibility is on the man, and the husband is the principal caretaker of the marital relationship.
3. God's appointed consequences of the Fall place the wife in a subjective position.

If we keep these conclusions in mind, the complex Scriptures about women in the New Testament may be easier to understand.

1 Corinthians 14:34–35

To understand 1 Corinthians 14:34–35 we must understand the religion situation in the Greek city of Corinth. As the following chart demonstrates, Paul's exhortations to the new believers in Corinth were directly correlated to the temple activities of a pagan cult centered in that locale.

Temple of Delphi	Christian Church
A person entered the temple and sacrificed an animal to a deity.	*"Therefore concerning the eating of things sacrificed to idols, we know that there is no such thing as an idol in the world, and that there is no God but one"* (1 Corinthians 8:4).
The priestess would deliver the oracle (a message from a deity).	*"Let the women keep silent in the churches; for they are not permitted to speak.... let them ask their own husbands at home; for it is improper for a woman to speak in church"* (1 Corinthians 14:34–35).

Temple of Delphi	Christian Church
The priestess would utter incoherent sounds.	*"... unless you utter by the tongue speech that is clear, how will it be known what is spoken?"* (1 Corinthians 14:9).
The sounds were interpreted but still not clear to the one inquiring and wanting answers. (Zodhiates 1984)	*"What is the outcome then, brethren? When you assemble, each one has a psalm, has a teaching, has a revelation, has a tongue, has an interpretation. Let all things be done for edification* [for the understanding and building up of those who hear]"(1 Corinthians 14:26).

First Corinthians 14:34–35 is not meant to completely silence women during the worship experience. In 1 Corinthians 11:5 Paul gives the women instructions concerning prophesying and praying in worship services. Women were not prohibited from doing these activities. But in 1 Corinthians 14 women were instructed *not to participate in the public interpretation of tongues and prophecy.* Instead, they were to discuss matters with their husbands at home.

This is not to say that women are incompetent in divine interpretation or unable to discern God's Word. We have cited several examples, in both the Old and New Testaments, of women who received messages from God and delivered them to His people. But in 1 Corinthians God sets policies that will make Christian acts of worship dissimilar from the cultic practices of unbelievers.

During my study of women's issues in the Bible I meditated on the word "silence." In Paul's letters the word "silence" is used four times, all in reference to women keeping quiet or witnessing without words (see also 1 Peter 3:1). I was tempted to anger: "God, why did you give women 'motor mouths,' then, tell us to be quiet?" But as I listened to God speaking through these Scriptures, I began to see another unique calling for women.

When people are silent, they are usually listening, organizing their thoughts, or inwardly talking and listening to God. I believe our heavenly Father is not simply saying to women, "Shut up your traps; you talk too much." I hear Him encouraging women through Paul's exhortations to silence: "Be still; be calm while confusion is all around you. Help your husband, your pastor, and the other men in the church by quietly organizing your thoughts. Take time to think things through and make solid, godly statements rather than flippant comments off the top of your head. Speak less with your mouth and increase your private prayer time, talking and listening to Me."

1 Timothy 2

Another distinction of Christianity from the pagan religions is the matter of church administration. "But I do not allow a woman to teach or exercise authority over a man, but to remain quiet" (1 Timothy 2:12).

Once again, the limitation is not placed on women because they are ignorant or weak-minded. If this were true, God would not have used women to teach anyone at anytime. God used Priscilla to teach Apollos. The book of Proverbs instructs both mother and father to teach their children. Nor is this verse saying women should not interpret Scripture. For Priscilla to teach Apollos, she must have used Old Testament prophecy. Paul tells Titus to teach the older women, who will then teach the younger women. (As a young pastor, it was better for Titus to teach the older women, who would minister to the younger women, rather than the young pastor having direct contact with the younger women. It is a wise principle for pastors to follow today.) I am sure that Titus taught these older women the Scriptures. They, in turn, used the Scriptures to teach the younger women.

This verse also states, however, that women are not to usurp authority. The Greek word for authority is *authenteo*. *Auto* means self, alone, or independent; *hentes* means a worker. When the two words are placed together in the context of this verse, it suggests that women are not to operate independently or practice dominance over men. Contrary to the cults in Paul's day, women in the Christian church were to allow the men to be in charge.

In succeeding verses Paul gives other reasons for this policy.

First: "For it was Adam who was first created, and then Eve" (v. 13). God's intention from the beginning was for the man to hold the headship position.

Second: "And it was not Adam who was deceived, but the woman being quite deceived, fell into transgression" (v. 14). At first glance it seems that Eve is the one looking bad here. Scholars have accused women of being incapable of leading and weak because of Eve's beguilement. However, if that were the case, Adam also would be disqualified from leadership because he chose to do what was wrong. Some have concluded that this prohibition is here because women are more susceptible to false teaching and to leaders of anti-Christian groups than are men. Both concepts are totally false.

So what is 1 Timothy 2:14 communicating? I believe it is saying that Eve was tricked by Satan, but Adam sinned with his eyes fully opened. Adam was not deceived, but persuaded by his wife to disobey God. Adam allowed Eve to lead him; she took control and he failed to take charge of the situation. Therefore her punishment was to be placed under the authority of man. Scripture does not say that the consequence of her sin was annulled by Christ's coming and His death on the cross. The other consequences—pain in childbirth and the mandate for man to work by the sweat of his brow—have not been eliminated; therefore we should assume that a submissive position for women is still in effect.

Third: "But women shall be preserved through the bearing of children if they continue in the faith and love and sanctity with self restraint" (v. 15). Various explanations have been offered for this verse, the three that are foremost being the following:

- A Christian woman will be brought safely through childbirth. This is not true, since many godly Christian women have suffered and even died in childbirth.
- Women will be saved through the birth of Christ. The phrase refers to more than one child, thus invalidating that idea.
- Women's greatest achievements are childbirth, devotion to husband, and following a chaste way of life. This explanation is eliminated when the question is raised, What about the single woman?

As I have prayed, read, studied, and talked with others about this verse, the one explanation that seems to line up with the rest of Scripture is this: It primarily shows a woman how to keep out of danger and to stay out of trouble by embracing the God-given responsibilities that pertain to women: childbearing, mothering, and nurturing. These are the areas in which women can be domineering and powerful. But in order to be effective in these matters, one needs an attitude of faith, unconditional love, and self-control. Even a woman who has no children can be nurturing to others. This seems to be a natural part of the feminine sexuality that God created within women.

When I was pregnant with my first child, someone asked me, "Has God given you any special revelations or instructions about this child?" I smiled and replied, "There is enough in the Bible already concerning parenting. I really don't want anything extra." In the same way, when I list all the instructions given specifically to women and mothers in the Bible, there is plenty to keep me busy pleasing God for a lifetime. I don't feel a need to attempt to take on any of the responsibilities God has given to the man. Let him carry the bulk of the spiritual duties, be in charge of the home, and account to God in the end for it all.

1 Corinthians 11

We have looked at God's desires in regard to the worship service and church administration. Now let us examine his desires for the Christian home.

To understand 1 Corinthians 11 it is essential to know what was happening at the time Paul wrote and whom he was addressing. The epistle was written to new believers in Corinth. The Corinthians' Greek tradition dictated that men's heads were uncovered, women's heads were covered. This symbolized a married woman's submission to her husband. A man with no covering on his head showed that he was in charge, in contrast to a slave, whose head would be covered. The woman whose head was covered was communicating "I am a submissive wife and I respect my husband's leadership." The Jewish tradition was just the opposite. During a service in the synagogue, men's heads were covered and women's heads were uncovered.

In the early church, Jews and Gentiles were coming together in Christ and also beginning to worship together. Some Jews believed that the new Greek Christian converts should obey the traditional Jewish laws and customs and cover their heads during worship. The Greeks apparently felt uncomfortable breaking this long-standing tradition that sent a strong message to the public at large. This single issue caused confusion in the church. Therefore the apostles were given divine authority and guidance to help these new churches establish God's instructions. Here in Corinth they wrote to Paul and asked for his divine insight: Should the new Greek converts discard this tradition of head coverings that witnesses publicly of their relationship with one another?

The first thing Paul said in response was, "Christ is the head of every man and the man is the head of a woman and God is the head of Christ" (1 Corinthians 14:3). In other words, submission (yielding to or obeying the authority placed over us) is not exclusively for the married woman. God is the head, meaning the top authority, one who is superior. God gives Christ instructions that He obeys. The man is to listen and follow Christ's instructions, and the wife is to follow her husband's instructions. This does not mean that the wife cannot receive directions directly from the Lord. Nor does it mean that a wife has to obey even when her husband is asking her to do something unbiblical. It is simply explaining that all in the body of Christ are to have an authority over them and see themselves in a submissive position.

The second aspect of Paul's response has specific implications for the marriage relationship.

> *Every man who has something on his head while praying or prophesying, disgraces his head. But every woman who has her head uncovered while praying or prophesying, disgraces her head; for she is one and the same with her whose head is shaved. For if a woman does not cover her head, let her also have her hair cut off; but if it is disgraceful for a woman to have her hair cut off or her head shaved, let them cover her head. For a man ought not to have his head covered.... (1 Corinthians 11:4–7)*

The new Greek converts were asking, shall we break tradition now that we are Christians? Paul responded, No! Stick with your tradition. The Greek women who covered their heads said to the public, "I am a respectable, submissive woman." A Greek man who had nothing on his head communicated, "I am in charge of my family, and I am not a slave."

Paul explained that if the Greek women were to start wearing no covering, they would be like the temple prostitutes of Aphrodite, who wore no head covering and also shaved their heads. Once again Paul was making a distinction between the Christian church and a cultic temple. He did not want Christian women looking or acting like women in a pagan cult.

> *... he [the man] is the image and glory of God; but the woman is the glory of man. For man does not originate from woman, but woman from man; for indeed man was not created for the woman's sake, but woman for the man's sake. (1 Corinthians 11:7–9)*

Paul advised that the Greek man should not have his head covered, because he is the bodily representation of God's order and the recognition goes to him as the head. This is not saying that the woman is not made to reflect the image of God. Genesis states quite clearly that both male and females reflect God's image. But Paul was reiterating that woman was made from the essence of man and for the purpose of being his helper.

The apostle also exhorted the men, "However, in the Lord, neither is woman independent of man, nor is man independent of woman. For as the woman originates from the man, so also the man has his birth through the woman and all things originate from God" (1 Corinthians 11:11–12). Men are not to abuse their authority. Male and female are mutually interdependent of the other. God designed man and woman to work and fit together. In fact, the verse emphasizes that the man would not be in existence if a woman did not bring him forth.

Paul left the final working out of the problem to the Corinthians: "Judge for yourselves" (v. 13). Then he addressed one more point: Is it proper for a woman to pray to God with head uncovered?

Does not even nature itself teach you that if a man has long hair, it is a dishonor to him, but if a woman has long hair it is a glory to her? For her hair is given to her for a covering. But if one is inclined to be contentious, we have no other practice, nor have the churches of God. (1 Corinthians 11:14–16)

Paul said that by nature a woman's hair grows longer than a man's, implying that there should be a noticeable distinction between males and females with regard to length of hair. In cases of cultures where men's and women's hair lengths are similar, there should be some kind of symbol that indicates a difference (for example, earrings or clothing).

I believe the overriding principle here is that traditions are okay if they do not conflict with Scripture. The personal application we can draw for women today is that every culture has a distinctive way to demonstrate respect for those in authority. Whatever that symbol is in our community, church, or home, that ritual should be respected. For example, today some women wear hats to church to demonstrate respect for their pastor. If that is the tradition and what the pastor is requiring, one should do so. But if a person is not at rest with this instruction from the persons in authority, she should find a different church rather than continue under God-appointed authority and behave rebelliously. "Do as much as possible to be at peace with all men" (Romans 14:19).

CONCLUSION

As a child, my favorite Sunday school teacher, Mrs. Estelle Walton, taught me a biblical principle that has stayed with me through my adult life. One Sunday I incorrectly answered a biblical question off the top of my head. She said gently, "Get your own Bible. Now, read the verses for yourself slowly and a little bit more carefully." As we women struggle with these difficult passages, I pass this excellent advice on to you.

References

Foh, S. 1979. *Women and the Word of God.* Phillipsburg, NJ: Presbyterian and Reformed.

Henry, M. 1706. *Matthew Henry commentary.* Reprint. McLean, VA: MacDonald Publishing.

1987. *New American standard Bible.* Iowa Falls, IA: World Bible Publishers.

Sayers, D. 1971. *Are women human.* Downers Grove, IL: Intervarsity Press.

Wilson, P. B. 1990. *Liberated through submission.* Eugene, OR: Harvest House.

Zodhiates, S. 1984. *The Hebrew-Greek key study Bible.* Chattanooga: AMG Publishers.

Patricia J. Larke

Dealing with the "Isms": Racism, Classism, and Sexism

PATRICIA J. LARKE is an Associate Professor at Texas A&M University in College Station, Texas. Born in Daytona, Florida, and raised in Florence, South Carolina, she has a bachelor of science degree and a master of education degree from South Carolina State University. She has a doctorate in education from the University of Missouri, Columbia. Patricia and her husand, Alvin Larke Jr., have two children, Altricia and Aaron. Patricia is a member of St. John AME Church in Brennan, Texas, where she is a Sunday school teacher, Bible study leader, and church trustee.

Chapter 14

Patricia J. Larke

Dealing with the "Isms": Racism, Classism, and Sexism

As society becomes more global, everyone must take the stand that if one woman suffers, then all women suffer. After all, we are each other's keepers.

The "isms" of racism, classism, and sexism have been an integral component of the world since its existence. Women in general, and African-American women most specifically, have a history that documents these practices. The Bible speaks as strongly today as it has in the past that racism, classism, and sexism are a violation of spiritual principles. There are no Scriptures in their wholeness that support behaviors and attitudes that are racist, classist, and sexist. There are, however, many who use parts of the Scripture out of context to support their beliefs and actions.

Historically, the structure of society has promoted more freedom for men than for women. This freedom for men was legitimized by laws and upheld in traditions that have supported and defined the roles of both men and women. For example, when God gave Moses the Ten Commandments (Exodus 20), there is no mention of commands designated exclusively for women or men. These commandments are the foundation of spiritual principles. Although biblical scholars and laypeople may argue about the interpretation of the statement, the fact remains that these codes of conduct do not support behaviors that are racist, classist, or sexist. Within the parameters of the Bible, however, there are many stories that describe the roles and responsibilities of men and women in which women are victims of racist, classist, and sexist behaviors overwhelmingly more often than men.[1]

Biblical literature provides many examples of how the isms have been pervasive in many ways. The Bible discusses how many leaders sought to control women as property; for example, Solomon and his many wives and concubines (1 Kings 11:3) and King Ahasuerus and his ability to select a queen from a group of harems (Esther 2:2–4). Yet Luke records, however, how Jesus allowed women to travel with him (Luke 8:1–3). Such a position conveys the belief that all were equal in God's sight. In fact, Jesus had a special care for women and He demonstrated that boldly throughout His teaching and in His ministry. Of the four Gospels that record the life of Jesus, Luke vividly describes how Jesus treated women with equal respect in a culture that legitimized subservient roles for women (Luke 7:11–17; 7:36–50; 8:1–3; 10:38–42; 13:10–17; 23:27–31).

There are Bible stories that show women as courageous, strong, and God-inspired despite the isms they had to encounter. The list includes Deborah (Judges 4–5), Esther (book of Esther), and Mary Magdalene (Luke 8; Mark:15–16). There are over 400 named and unnamed women in the Bible (Lockyer 1988) who can provide many examples of the way the isms have affected their lives and their biblical strategies for attacking the isms. This chapter will define and discuss the impact of racism, classism, and sexism on African-American women and provide a dozen strategies that will help African-American women to respond spiritually when attacked by the isms.[2]

---

[1]For the brevity of this chapter, I will not expound thoroughly upon the issue of roles and responsibilities of men and women according to books of the Bible. An in-depth study of the Bible will provide pertinent information about the laws and how they were developed and enforced and will provide a historical background of the times and how they will apply to today's life experiences.

[2]The purpose of this chapter is to discuss the isms as related to African-American women. Even so, I must say that these isms are faced by all women. Yet, this is not to diminish the importance of the unique roles that isms play in the lives of African-American women and other historically oppressed women. As the society becomes more global, everyone must take the stand that if one woman suffers, all women suffer. After all, we are each other's keepers.

RACISM, CLASSISM, AND SEXISM DEFINED

The unique history of African-American women reveals that they have been and continue to be victims of the isms of racism, classism, and sexism. Within sociology and multicultural education literature these isms have been defined as triple jeopardy for historically oppressed women (Council on Interracial Books for Children [CIBC] 1985). The isms for African-American women involve more than the mere identification of their color; rather, the isms are manifested in the ways that women have been treated. The treatment is based on a combination of factors that are associated with fear, hatred, bitterness, stereotypes, lack of accurate information, and historical treatment. The evils of these isms have been manifested in how African-American women are treated and perceived in institutions such as churches, schools, government, housing, and hospitals.

African-American women are viewed differently in society from other women. The historical role of abuse for African-American women is different from any other woman because emotional, physical, and sexual abuse was institutionalized since slavery. Such institutionalization makes their experiences unique from any other woman in America. Some may want to argue with that point, but the fact remains that no other group of women has had such a long history of abuse in such a legitimized way. This institutionalized abuse has developed into a mind-set, causing stereotypical behaviors that view African-American women differently and subjugate them to differential treatment in schools, in the workplace, and in society in general.

Racism

Racism has been defined in several ways. For our purposes, racism will be defined as *a system of privilege and penalty based on a person's race*. It consists of two components: (1) the inherent superiority of some people and the inherent inferiority of others, and (2) the acceptance of the way goods and services are distributed in accordance with these judgments (Weinberg 1990). Such a belief system is manifested in three ways: through individuals, within institutions, and by cultures.

An individual demonstrates racism by the attitudes, beliefs, and behaviors displayed to others that imply superiority or inferiority. While many examples could be used to demonstrate this point, I will single out two: colorism, and hair length and texture.

"Colorism," a term coined by Alice Walker in a 1982 essay, is a preferential treatment given by the power structure and within the African-American community because of a light skin complexion (Glanton 1989). Colorism has been used to denote differences in people and has provided a reason for people to demonstrate racist behaviors. For many in the African-American community, a variety of skin colors has been derived from consensual and nonconsensual interracial relationships. As a result of sexual exploitation of female slaves by White Anglo-Saxon males, the children of these relationships usually combine characteristics of both ethnic groups. The dominant ethnic genes decide the child's skin color, hair texture, eye color, and other physical features. (The video *Teaching Children About Prejudice* [1993] provides an easy-to-understand scientific analysis of the complex reasons for varying skin colors.) Often the multiracial child's skin complexion is a lighter hue than many African-Americans and the hair texture is straighter or more wavy. These physical differences cause others to perceive these children as superior or inferior.

Historically, colorism racist behaviors have affected African-Americans in general, and African-American women in particular, in employment decisions (professional, paraprofessional, and nonprofessional jobs), and in the selection of beauty queens.

In the past, the only African-American women who were in advertisements often "passed for White" and if their true identification were exposed, their employers would fire them. As advertising began to employ identifiably African-American women, the ones selected had lighter complexions and shared some of the same facial features (such as eye colors, lips, and nose shape) as women from the dominant culture. Body features (such as breasts, buttocks, and legs) fell into the same category. In fact, it has only been within the last ten years or so that a few African-American women of darker skin tones have been on the covers of leading magazines or in media advertisements for clothing, cars, and perfume.

The general absence of darker complexioned women sent a powerful message to both darker and lighter complexioned African-American women: the lighter the complexion, the more qualified one was to participate in certain types of experiences and to receive supposedly "better" treatment. In addition, the absence of darker complexioned African-American women in the media supported an assumption that if those African-American women wanted to participate in advertising and other media jobs they had to develop other talents such as education, poise, and other job-related skills before they could gain entry into the profession.

Hair length and texture have been the source of racist behaviors for many African-American women. Beauty for many women has been defined in the length and texture of their hair. Again, the standards for beauty have been set by advertising and models (beauty contest winners, artists' subjects). The standards for hair include a length that reaches the shoulder or a length that is about six to eight inches below the shoulder, and a texture that is able to bounce and is wavy and/or curly (natural curls or hot-rolled curls). An overwhelming number of African-American women do not have either the "standard" hair length or the texture. For many years, they have felt the racist implication of this standard in both the larger society and in their respective communities. In many African-American communities, hair is defined as good and bad—nappy or straight, short or long. An underlying perception says that good hair enhances beauty while bad hair diminishes beauty. Good hair is straight and long, implying a superiority, while bad hair is nappy and short, implying an inferiority.

C. J. Walker and others have responded to the racist implications of these feelings about hair with their inventions of beauty supplies that "turned bad hair into good hair" by using instruments such as "hot straightening combs," curlers, and beauty products such as petroleum jelly, shampoos, and scalp treatments. During the sixties, the civil rights movement and the Black Power movement promoted the acceptance of hairstyles such as "Afros" and "Afro Puffs," helping African-American women and others to accept and view complexion and hair length and texture differently.

Today the Afrocentric movement and the African-American historical emphasis are doing much to help African-American women understand the need to embrace the variety of skin complexions as well as hair textures and lengths. This self-pride has caused African-American women to analyze racist behaviors and provide creative ways to highlight their beauty in an array of skin complexions and of hairstyles that enhance the length and texture of their hair.

Institutionalized racism is embedded in laws, customs, and practices that legitimize the treatment of some groups over other groups. For years, African-American women were victims of institutionalized racism. They did not have access to education and employment opportunities due to racism institutionalized in laws, customs, and traditions. Traditionally the role of

African-American women has been that of domestic workers.[3] What is critical, however, in the argument about institutionalized racism in domestic work is when that role is devalued and the people who serve in that role are viewed as inferior. Another critical point in the argument is when people believe the role can be fulfilled by only a select group of people and if African-American women select other professions, they are "out of their place." These critical points explain how racism is manifested and how it causes stress to African-American women who are employed in places that have supervisors or others with an "out of their place" mentality.

Cultural racism validates or invalidates the culture of groups, ranging from art and music to spiritual beliefs, by standards of what is accepted or not accepted by the dominant group. Cultural racism inflicts assimilation in the most subtle way. When African-American women promote a culture that violates the acceptance of traditional ways of doing things, they are ostracized. Some have found it necessary to travel to other countries to be accepted. The limited number of African-American artists, writers, and actresses serve as examples of cultural racism.

African-American women have been instrumental in promoting spiritual beliefs. Although many names of famous females are not common household names, there are names that are associated with the women in African-American families and communities such as Grandma, Big Ma, Mama, aunt, cousin, and others who were the religious sources. This may be due in part to how the behavior of women has been sanctioned by churches. Historically, the role of women in the church and in religion has been one of participant or missionary, not a decision maker or religious leader.

African-American women face racism every day, and it impacts their lives in many ways. They face undue stress in the workplace, they are stigmatized in the media, and they are treated differently in businesses and public places. For example, in the workplace, many African-American women have to prove that they are competent more often than do other

---

[3] I believe that the role of domestic work is very important to the lives of all African-Americans. It was that profession that provided the college tuition, food, shelter, and clothing for many African-Americans to be where we are today. Racism, coupled with sexism, prevented African-American women from participating in other higher-paying jobs. Domestic work is an honorable profession and continues to provide this country its foundation of values. African-American women are instrumental in shaping the values of this country as they raise the children of both African-American and European-American families.

workers. They become the super worker, overachiever, thinking that they have to be "twice as good as the average worker." Each African-American woman carries the burden of over 16 million African-American sisters on her shoulders. In many instances, African-American women find themselves in conflict with their inner selves and very stressed by trying to disprove the American myth about the role of African-American women as domestic workers.

Classism

The economic structure of society categorizes people into socioeconomic classes of high, middle, and low based on income. Classism is defined as *an attitude or institutional practice which subordinates people due to their economic condition.* In the United States, poor people and members of the working class are not accorded the dignity and respect (let alone economic rewards) accorded to wealthy people. People with wealth, educational credentials, property, and business have greater power (CIBC 1985).

People are treated differently based on their social class. The higher the class the more preferential treatment, and the lower the class the less preferential treatment. According to the Bible, there was a difference between how the rich and poor were treated. This treatment has caused much grief and pain and produced a mentality that good comes from the rich and evil comes from the poor. Such a belief has been visible in several ways. For example, a rich person received the status of a first-class citizen while a poor person received the status of a second-class citizen. The foundation of spiritual principles, however, consists of a belief that all are equal and that God is not a respecter of persons (Romans 2:11).

The fact that class is based on income level, which is directly related to job and educational attainment, affects African-American women severely. The 1990 census revealed that the average income for African-American women was below those of other groups. The most startling statistics revealed that about 60 percent of African-American children are born in poverty in single-parent households. Often these statistics are used negatively to portray stereotypes without further explanation as to why these statistics exist.

When looking at classism from a historical perspective, the information grants a deeper insight into the impact of classism on African-American women. A historic role African-American women played in society is that of caregiver. During the days of slavery, there was no pay for services. African-American women, like African-American men, were viewed as property and abused mentally, physically, emotionally, and sexually. Yet, within this inhumane treatment, they sought refuge in biblical sayings and spiritual principles. (For more information read some of the slave narratives such as *Linda Brent—Incidents in the Life of a Slave Girl* and *Six Women's Slave Narratives*. See the Recommended Reading at the end of the chapter.)

After slavery, the majority of jobs available to African-American women were domestic work, with very little pay. Many of these jobs continued through the sixties, except during World War II when many were employed in factories in the lowest paying jobs until the European-American men returned from the war. Even today, African-American women and women in general have lower salaries than men. Since class is related to jobs and educational level, African-American women fall disproportionately into the lower class. Although there are more African-American women going to and graduating from college, overall the percentages are low when compared with other groups.

Often African-American women are stigmatized with the perception of being poor. They are stereotyped as being on welfare, having babies, and not wanting to work. The "welfare queen" syndrome causes many African-American women undue stress and causes people to perceive them negatively. Again, the behaviors of a few are exaggerated to all 16 million African women in America. In reality, women of any ethnic group can be "welfare queens" or system abusers. Therefore, classism causes many African-American women undue pressure to behave in ways that are contradictory to stereotypes or in ways that adhere to others' stereotypical perceptions. Yet, there are many who use biblical principles and stories as a coping mechanism in dealing with the negative implications of classism.

Sexism

Since the creation of Eve from Adam's side, sexism has played a prevalent role in society. The issues of who was made first, Eve's encounter with Satan, and Eve and Adam's sin in the garden have supposedly generated a foundation for the idea that men must be in charge of women. Sexism is defined as *a system of beliefs or attitudes which delegate females to limited roles and/or options because of their sex.* A bias toward males is generally embedded in institutional structures, schools, the job market, the political system, and religious institutions (CIBC 1985).

Although it is true that men and women are biologically and physically different, little evidence has shown that they are intellectually different. The whole debate that men are smarter than women is a value judgment established by traditional roles and responsibilities. Both men and women hold roles as decision makers that require a knowledge base and academic understanding before competent decisions can be made. Again our reference point is the Bible. Men in the Bible were warriors, conquerors, and kings. Women in the Bible frequently were caregivers and queens. Each role requires a knowledge base. If caregivers did not care for their families and others, men could not fight effectively in battle. As in the Bible, each gender is made for a specific purpose, and God is not a respecter of persons (Romans 2:11).

Now, what implications does sexism have for African-American women? When comparing European-American men and women to African-American men and women in relation to standards of American society (job, educational levels, money, power, position, etc.), European-American males rank first, European-American females rank second, African-American males rank third, and African-American females rank fourth.[4] Sexism affects participation rates for African-American women in such areas as employment opportunities, academic discourse, and public office. When combining sexist practices that are based on racist treatment, African-American women are often further limited in these areas.

STRATEGIES FOR RESPONDING TO THE ISMS

For centuries women of African descent have developed strategies to respond to the isms. I present these strategies in a spiritual hierarchy. I believe the first three strategies form a foundation for seeking out other believers who will encourage others in their daily encounters with the isms.

1. Develop a spiritual relationship with God

"Seek ye first the kingdom of God, and his righteousness; and all these things shall be added unto you" (Matthew 6:33 KJV). For non-believers and those at a low level of spiritual growth, the most important thing that you

---

[4]When the data are disaggregated, however, and Asian Americans, Native Americans, and Hispanic Americans are included, the rankings are different.

can do for yourself is to develop a relationship with God. To develop a relationship with God requires commitment, endurance, perseverance, persistence, and time. Set aside time to sit and reflect on God through reading and praying. Begin by assessing your sin and ask God for forgiveness. As Paul states, all have sinned and fallen short in God's sight (Romans 3:23). Many times we think that because we go to church, do good things, say the right things, help others, give money, or have not done the really "bad" sins (murder, stealing, or adultery), we are good and have a relationship with God. Unless you have been born-again in the spirit, your relationship with God is shallow. To be able to fight the isms requires a *godly* relationship with God, not just a *good* relationship with God.

A spiritual relationship requires time and commitment in studying the Word. That time can vary from ten to fifteen minutes to hours daily. The key to developing a relationship is to be consistent and desire to know God. Invest in a study Bible. There are many choices in the local Christian bookstores.

2. Pray often

Praying is an excellent way to deal with the isms. Praying keeps you in close contact with God and this contact allows you to place your concerns about the isms before the Lord. Praying strengthens your relationship with God and provides a means to discuss the isms in a productive way. There is much truth to the statement that prayer works. To enable you to see how prayer works, keep a prayer diary about your daily battles with the isms. Each time there is a conflict, record it in your prayer journal and every time the Lord answers your prayers record the date. People are surprised when they pray for things and go back months or even years later and see how the Lord blessed them with answered prayers. If you don't know how to pray, read Joyce Marie Smith's book *Learning How to Talk with God* or Rosalind Rinker's *Prayer:Conversing with God*. Again, these are only two examples. You will find those books and many more in a Christian bookstore.

3. Participate in daily meditation

Daily meditation can take several forms, including Bible reading/ study, reading biblical books, devotional guides, praying, listening to religious music, or conversing with God. These types of meditation set the tone for the day and provide you with positive thoughts. A specific time that is convenient for you is important. Since I am a morning person, I get up at 4:00 A.M. to do my mediation, and I either go back to bed or begin my day. Some people like to mediate before retiring for the evening and reflect on the thoughts during the night and the next day.

Daily meditations provide us with strategies for dealing with the isms. They assist God's wisdom to help us daily in our lives. Just recently, I found in the *Secret Chamber* (a daily prayer guide) a daily mediation prayer entitled "Why rock all day in the rocking chair of worry and stay up late at night eating the bread of sorry? Trust God." As we think about these kinds of concepts on a regular basis, it will help us deal with the isms and to trust God. Perhaps the isms will not go away, but your attitude will change about how you will address them.

4. Memorize Scriptures that provide support when being attacked by the isms

"Thy word have I hid in mine heart, that I might not sin against thee" (Psalm 119:11 KJV, see also Proverbs 3:3; 7:3). To write the laws upon your heart requires memorization of the Scriptures. There are several techniques that are used to memorize Scriptures: writing them on note cards and placing them in places where you can look at them often; listening to Scriptures on tapes; making songs out of Scriptures; and just reading Scriptures over and over again until they are memorized.

The purpose of learning the Scriptures is to be able to repeat them when you are under attack from the isms. For example, Jesus' summary of the Ten Commandments states, "Love the Lord thy God with all thy heart . . . and thy neighbor as thy self" (Mark 12:30–31 KJV). When you are attacked by others, you are required to love them. This Scripture helps you to do the impossible when you have been denied jobs because of your race or sex. The Scriptures help you to think about godly things during times of despair. The Scriptures allow you to focus on your faith and inner strength to endure racist, sexist, and classist remarks and provide you a godly way of responding. Bible promise books provide a selection of Scriptures for various topics such as anger, discontentment, fear, self-denial, and peace. Many of these topics are pertinent when dealing with the isms.

5. Locate a church and get involved with a fellowship of believers

Being in fellowship with other believers is one of the most important decisions you can make to help you deal with isms. This fellowship provides others who are going through some of the same issues and attacks that you are dealing with regarding the isms. If you are from a family in which church has been an instrumental component of your upbringing and for some reason you have not attended church recently (moved away from home, got too busy, etc.), then make contact with your church again. Look around your workplace and talk about your needs to others who are involved in a church. If you are away from home, locate a church in the telephone book and make an appointment with a minister to discuss how to select a church that is appropriate for you.

It seems that if African-American women want to find a doctor or seek a professional service, they do not have problems finding information. The same attitude of wanting the best doctor or lawyer should be demonstrated when searching for the right church. Do not expect all churches to be the same and without fault. Many people try to find perfect churches, because they believe that churches are without sin. A true believer knows that all have sinned and fallen short in God's sight. Strong churches have committed believers who have programs that focus on the well-being of people at all age levels through Christian education programs and outreach programs. They display an aura of welcome and allow you time to make choices about your commitment.

6. Participate in support groups

Support groups within African-American communities assist others with coping strategies for dealing with the isms. Often these support groups are spiritually based and use biblical literature to provide the coping strategies. Most of the groups are informally organized church groups meeting in church facilities. Many are open to the community and are nondenominational. Participants in these groups have a range of academic levels, yet each member feels comfortable that their experiences are making a contribution to the group. Effective support groups respect the confidentiality of the issues and provide responses to concerns that are biblically based. They employ effective listening strategies, and when the issue is beyond the scope of the group, they recommend professional services or encourage the participant to talk to a minister. These groups help others to see their "isms attacks" from multiple perspectives and provide them with multiple strategies from which to respond to the isms.

7. Develop self-improvement attitudes and behaviors

Living with the effects of the isms can be devastating for the lives of African-American women. The place to begin with self-help is to know that God made all things good. He loves all people and wants them to receive salvation. You can receive forgiveness from God and it does not matter what you have done or what you think. The problem is that you have to begin to think in a positive manner. To begin that spiritual healing requires faith in God that he will heal you. A good place to start is with Joyce Marie Smith's book *Fulfillment*, Hobart Freeman's *Positive Thinking and Confession*, and Susan Taylor's *In the Spirit*. These books focus on self and provide ways to help you think differently through positive self-control.

Jesus promises to send us the Comforter, the Holy Spirit (John 5:26). The Comforter will help you learn how to think positively about yourself. It requires mind control and the belief that you can control your thoughts. These are the times that Scripture memorization can be helpful. These Scriptures will help you think positively. It does not matter how the isms attack. With positive thinking you are able to decipher between yourself as a person and the behavior of another person who has attacked you.

8. Develop strategies of spiritual empowerment

Knowing how and when to apply God's Word is the development of spiritual empowerment. Many people spend time studying the Bible, but during a crisis are unable to apply the principles of spiritual growth to their particular crisis. These principles include faith, trust, understanding of the Word, obedience, acceptance, self-denial, and application. Spiritually empowered Christians know when to act, yield, obey, trust, commit, and wait. They realize that their empowerment is directly related to the spiritual wisdom that comes through their daily study with God and Christian experiences. Christ becomes the center of their life and self takes a lesser role. They believe that through Christ all things are possible. When attacked by the isms they quickly rely on biblical teachings to help them understand and analyze the events from a Christian perspective.

9. Surround your environment with positive sayings and Scriptures

"As he thinketh in his heart, so is he" (Proverbs 23:7 KJV). When you constantly read positive thoughts and understand the thoughts, then you are able to apply those thoughts to the situations that you encounter. These sayings and Scriptures will help you build strategies. For example, I have used the saying from Psalm 94:19: "When doubt fills my mind, when my heart is in turmoil, quiet me and give me renewed hope and cheer." Such Scriptures can provide directions for addressing the isms. When others visit your home or workplace or ride in your car, there is no doubt that they know where you stand as a Christian. In many instances, the Scripture or saying can diffuse many sexist, racist, and classist remarks and help you to react to the attacks in a positive way.

10. Immerse yourself in spiritual and practical readings and activities about how others cope

There are many self-help books in bookstores, public libraries, and college libraries which provide psychological understanding and coping mechanisms for dealing with the isms. Increase your reading time to learn about others who have coped with similar experiences. The Bible is filled with stories about how people have endured the isms. For example, the book of Psalms, 2 Timothy, the Gospels, and Paul's letters offer examples of how King David, Jesus, and Jesus' followers coped with discriminatory practices.

11. Develop a scholarly knowledge base about the isms

Attending adult education or college classes about race and ethnic studies, or workshops or seminars about issues of diversity, can help you develop an academic base for understanding the isms. These workshops, seminars, or courses are often given titles such as "multicultural education," "cultural diversity," or "race and ethnic studies." They provide a historical background of the issues, theories, and constructs that define the issues and strategies that have been used to empower people to attack the isms. If time does not permit you to participate in the aforementioned activities, then participate in a self-study by using books and references from the local library. The appropriate topics are listed in the education and sociology sections of the library.

12. Seek working environments that enhance your life

Sometimes it may be necessary to seek employment environments that have fewer overt and covert ism practices. Every workplace is not conducive to enhancing the employment skills of African-American women. Selecting appropriate work environments that positively enhance you as a professional is a good decision. Every battle that deals with isms in not the battle of every African-American woman. Decisions about jobs and decisions about life experiences should be taken to the Lord in prayer before you make a final decision. Through prayer, the Lord will provide you with the right decision as to when to leave a job or when to take a new job.

CONCLUSION

Across this country and the world, women of African heritage are daily faced with overt and subtle practices of the isms. The practices may occur in the workplace, public places (restaurants, shopping centers, businesses, financial and educational institutions, and even in religious institutions) or wherever they come in contact with people. Additionally, these practices may occur within the confines of their homes, among their families. The history of African-American women is filled with a variety of coping mechanisms that have assisted them in dealing with racist, classist, and sexist practices. Many will agree that the unique way that African-American women dealt with the isms was as much a part of the historical legacy as their inventions, leadership positions, and professional and nonprofessional roles. African-American women continue to make invaluable contributions to this country despite their opposition. As African-American women take their rightful place among the voices of society, they can take comfort in knowing that it has been their relationship with God that provided the strength to endure the isms. This spiritual relationship can only be developed through daily reading of God's Word, spiritual meditation, and continued prayer. These are the foundations that will forever attack the isms.

Recommended Reading

Bell, D. *Faces at the Bottom of the Well: The Permanence of Racism*. New York: Basic Books, 1992.

Berg, M. *The Thorn in the Flesh*. Denver: Alpha and Omega Books, 1981.

Birchett, C., ed. *How I Got Over: Testimonies of African American Reflections on the Books of Job and Psalms Bible Study Applications*. Chicago: Urban Ministries, 1994.

Champion, G., ed. *The Secret Chamber*. Orlando, FL: Department of Worship and Evangelism of the A.M.E. Church, 1995.

Cloninger, C. *Postcards from Heaven: Messages of Hope, Courage, and Comfort from God's Heart to Yours*. Dallas: Word Books, 1992.

Cooper, J. *Family: A Novel*. New York: Doubleday, 1991.

Freeman, H. *Positive Thinking and Confession: The Key to Victorious Living 365 Days a Year*. Warsaw, IN: Faith Publications, n.d.

Gates, H., ed. *Six Women's Slave Narratives*. Schomburg Library of Nineteenth-Century Black Women Writers. New York: Oxford University Press, 1988.

Johnson, D. *Proud Sisters: The Wisdom and Wit of African-American Women*. White Plains, NY: Peter Pauper Press, 1995.

Rinker, R. *Prayer: Conversing with God*. Grand Rapids: Zondervan, 1970.

Smith, J. *Learning How to Talk With God*. Wheaton, IL: Tyndale House, 1976.

_____. *Fulfillment*. Wheaton, IL: Tyndale House, 1972.

Taylor, S. *In the Spirit: The Inspirational Writing of Susan Taylor*. New York: Harper Perennial, 1994.

Teller, W. ed. *Linda Brent—Incidents in the Life of a Slave Girl*. New York: Harvest/HBJ Books, 1973.

Washington, M. *Invented Lives: Narratives of Black Women 1860–1960*. New York: Doubleday, 1987.

Witter, E. *Mahalia Jackson: Born to Sing Gospel Music*. Milford, MI: Mott Media, 1985.

ℛeferences

Champion, G., ed. 1995. *The secret chamber*. Orlando, FL: Department of Worship and Evangelism of the A.M.E. Church.

1985. *Triple jeopardy*. New York: Council on Interracial Books for Children.

Freeman, H. N.d. *Positive thinking and confession: The key to victorious living 365 days a year*. Warsaw, IN: Faith Publications.

Gates, H., ed. 1988. *Six women's slave narratives*. Schomburg Library of Nineteenth-Century Black Women Writers. New York: Oxford University Press.

Glanton, A. D. 1989. "Colorism" still divides the Black community. *Bryan College Station Eagle* (September 1): 3C, 1.

The King James version of the Bible.

Jennings, P. 1993. "Teaching children about prejudice." (Video). New York: ABC Television.

1988. *Life application Bible: The living Bible*. Wheaton, IL: Tyndale House.

Lockyer, H. 1988. *All the women of the Bible*. Grand Rapids: Zondervan, 1988.

Rinker, R. 1970. *Prayer: Conversing with God*. Grand Rapids: Zondervan, 1970.

Smith, J. 1976. *Learning to talk with*. Wheaton, IL: Tyndale House.

Smith, J. 1972. *Fulfillment*. Wheaton, IL: Tyndale House.

Taylor, S. 1994. *In the Spirit: The inspirational writing of Susan Taylor*, edited by W. Teller. New York: Harper Perennial.

Teller, W., ed. 1973. *Linda Brent—Incidents in the life of a slave girl*. New York: Harvest/HBJ Books.

1990. *The Bible promise book: New international version*. Uhrichsville, OH: Barbour & Co.

Weinberg, M. 1990. *Racism in the United States: A comprehensive classified bibliography*. New York: Greenwood Press.